D0546212

Playing for Dollars

Labor Relations and the Sports Business

PAUL D. STAUDOHAR

ILR Press

AN IMPRINT OF
CORNELL UNIVERSITY PRESS
ITHACA AND LONDON

UNIVERSITY OF CENTRAL
LANCASHIRE LIBRARY
SHAROE GREEN SITE

1 F 130

Copyright © 1986, 1989, 1996 by Cornell University

All rights reserved. Except for brief quotations in a review, this book, or
parts thereof, must not be reproduced in any form without permission in
writing from the publisher. For information, address Cornell University
Press, Sage House, 512 East State Street, Ithaca, New York 14850.

First edition, titled *The Sports Industry and Collective Bargaining,*
published 1986 by ILR Press.
Second edition published 1989.
Third edition, titled *Playing for Dollars: Labor Relations and the Sports Business,*
published 1996 by Cornell University Press.

Library of Congress Cataloging-in-Publication Data

Staudohar, Paul D.
　　Playing for dollars : labor relations and the sports business /
　Paul D. Staudohar.
　　　　p. cm.
　　Rev. ed. of: The sports industry and collective bargaining.　2nd
　ed. c1989.
　　　Includes bibliography references and indexes.
　　ISBN 0-8014-3280-4 (alk. paper). — ISBN 0-8014-8342-5 (pbk. :
　alk. paper)
　　　1. Sports—Collective bargaining—United States.　2. Professional
　sports—United States.　I. Staudohar, Paul D.　Sports industry and
　collective bargaining.　II. Title.
　GV716.S72　1996
　331.89´041796—dc20　　　　　　　　　　　　　95-49456

Printed in the United States of America

⊗ The paper in this book meets the minimum requirements
of the American National Standard for Information Sciences—
Permanence of Paper for Printed Library Materials, ANSI Z39.48-1984.

344·099 STA NL

UNIVERSITY OF CENTRAL
LANCASHIRE LIBRARY
SHAROE GREEN SITE

1310.

①

P128.

Playing
for
Dollars

This book is due for return on or before the last date shown below.

11. JAN. 1999

-8. FEB. 1999

26. MAR. 1999

13. MAR. 2000

Don Gresswell Ltd., London, N.21 Cat. No. 1207   DG 02242/71

In memory of my grandmother, Katerina

CONTENTS

PREFACE

Followers of professional sports in the print and broadcast media are aware of the increasing influence of collective bargaining. Players in the major sports leagues are well organized for negotiation with management. Unionization has accompanied the growth of the sports industry, as players strive for greater shares of gate receipts and television revenues.

This book is written for the sports fan who wants to know more about labor relations. It uses an interdisciplinary approach to examine employment in the four major professional sports—baseball, football, basketball, and hockey—and to explain the dynamics of key issues such as free agency, salaries, drug abuse, and strikes. No single approach is appropriate for understanding these issues, because each has legal, economic, and psychological implications.

Earl Warren, the late chief justice of the U.S. Supreme Court, used to say that he always read the sports pages of the newspaper first because he liked to read about man's accomplishments rather than his failures. Although games were lost as often as won, players were regarded as winners. But this is no longer always true. Today, the sports pages record generous evidence of the failure of human character. Unsavory topics such as greed, deceit, and cocaine keep cropping up. In a sense, the socioculture of professional sports mirrors life itself.

To the frustration of many sports fans, collective bargaining disputes resulted in long strikes in baseball in 1981 and 1994–95 and in football in 1982 and 1987, and a lengthy lockout in hockey in 1994–95. Like any newly unionized industry, sports is going through a period of acrimonious confrontation between labor and management. As collective bargaining evolves, conflict should diminish, with the parties settling down to explore ways to enhance their mutual welfare. Although signs of maturity are appearing, the adversary relationship remains prevalent.

Although this is a relatively short book, there is a long list of people who deserve thanks for their generous contributions. Since little has been written on the topic in the literature, library resources were limited. Nanette Sand and Clara Stern, librarians at the Institute of Industrial Relations at the University of California, Berkeley, were helpful in locating much of what was available. Other primary sources of information were the league and players' association offices in the respective sports and newspaper accounts. Representatives from the leagues and players' associations provided original data and helped verify materials from other published sources. In baseball, these persons were Marvin J. Miller, John J. Gaherin, Kenneth Moffett, Peter Gold, Sue Carr, Donald M. Fehr, and Pamela Pitts. Information on football was received from Pete Rozelle, Edward Garvey, Frank Woschitz, Jack Donlan, Bob Epstein, Jay Benoit, George R. Berman, Don Weiss, Terry Bledsoe, Mark Levin, David Meggyesy, and M. J. Duberstein. In basketball, thanks are due Lawrence O'Brien, Lawrence Fleisher, Russell Granik, Gary B. Bettman, John Kosner, John Neves, Jeffrey Mishkin, and Alice Alves; and in hockey, Clarence S. Campbell, John A. Ziegler, Jr., R. Alan Eagleson, S. G. Simpson, Gary Meagher, Carole Robertson, Michael Griffin, John Halligan, Roger Gottlieb, Suzanne Greenwald, Dolores Antonacci, Karen Levine, Steve McAllister, and Ian C. Pulver.

I would also like to express my appreciation to Colonel Edward M. Smith, United States Air Force; Margaret Magnus, editor, *Personnel Journal;* Bart Wright, sports writer, *Tacoma News-Tribune;* Christ P. Zivalich of Central Michigan University; and the late Edwin C. Pendleton of the University of Hawaii. Special thanks are due the all-star team at Cornell: Frances G. Benson, Holly M. Bailey, Erica Fox, Andrea Fleck Clardy, Kay Scheuer, and Kim Vivier.

PAUL D. STAUDOHAR

Hayward, California

Playing
for
Dollars

Introduction 1

Some people begrudge professional athletes their high salaries, yet few players feel they are overpaid. It seems unfair that Wayne Gretzky, a hockey player for the Los Angeles Kings, should have a yearly salary (over $7 million) that far exceeds that of the president of the United States ($200,000). Although the astronomical salaries of so many professional athletes are a recent phenomenon, they are not without precedent. Much of the country was shocked in 1931 when baseball star Babe Ruth was offered $80,000 to play for the Yankees, while President Herbert Hoover was paid only $75,000. When Ruth was asked if he deserved to make more than the president, he is said to have replied, "Why not? I had a better year than he did."[1]

Contests in skill, strength, and speed have occupied an important place in every culture throughout the ages. But the meaning of the term *sport* and the effect that sport has on society are different things.[2] The characteristics of sport can be thought of as neutral or isolated qualities, devoid of implication for society. When one runs, jumps, or throws as pure sport it is an internalized response to a human desire for physical and psychological exercise. Viewed apart from social meaning, sport involves play for the body and spirit—for health and happiness. Play provides a sense of creativity and eases tension. When sport is organized into games for competition, these events satisfy such needs as achievement, affiliation, and self-esteem.

Social meanings are assigned to sport by the culture. Sports that reflect high social status, such as sailboat racing, polo, and horse racing, do not have any inherent status apart from that conferred by society. Certain sports become popular because society places a high value on them. As a sport becomes institutionalized, it takes on its own meanings and values, which reflect on the society.[3] For example, American culture awards great social significance to baseball, the national pastime. That sport—from Little League to major leagues—provides play, entertainment, rules, and competition that in turn shape our culture.

American culture has a particular fascination with winning, which explains some of the attention given to competitive sports and the boom in these sports at the professional level. Yet other sports that do not emphasize winning, such as backpacking, jogging, and fishing, are also widely practiced. Much of the cultural identification with competitive sports is by spectators, who derive vicarious satisfaction from watching highly skilled athletes engage in bold and often violent competition. Few professional athletes themselves, however, identify strongly with the play element in sport. They are motivated by winning, maximization of economic reward, fear of injury or loss of skill, and achievement of personal goals. Nearly all suffer fatigue, not euphoria, from a lengthy season. They have little sense of play for the joy of it.

Professional players have become bureaucratized. They pursue their playing careers as businesses. Many players are even legally incorporated. Most of their time is spent on nonplay endeavors. Players deal with agents, who represent them in salary negotiations and commercial endorsements, and they are active in affairs of the players' associations, which attend to much of the business with the teams. The teams and the leagues they comprise are also bureaucratized. Authority for important functions at the league level is centralized in the offices of commissioners, presidents, and other governing bodies. Although team owners employ these representatives to act on their behalf, thus retaining some control over decision making, there is a system of offices that define what role each office holder is to play, and within each team there is a hierarchy of offices and positions with specific division of work and responsibility.

Professional players, teams, and leagues have a symbiotic relationship with the print and broadcast media, which are themselves compartmentalized into specialized units. Games receive extensive coverage in newspapers and magazines and are broadcast on radio and television. Income from consumers, who pay for the use of these services, and from advertisers, who sell their wares through the media, provides impetus to the commercialization of sports. Cities take pride in their teams, and numerous satellite industries that derive substantial revenues from sports have sprung up.

The big business that the professional sports complex represents has a profound influence on cultural values, norms, and behavior in the United States. Are the effects of it positive or negative? They are both.[4] Sport for youth is generally positive, although more observers are expressing qualms about the excessive organization and competition found in youth leagues today. Team games and exercises stimulate health, comradeship, self-control, and perhaps even intelligence. Sport teaches youngsters the importance of discipline, cooperation, and how to handle winning and losing gracefully. It also provides entertainment for millions of spectators of all ages. Fans look forward to the beginning of seasonal play and enjoy following their favorite teams in competition.

Excessive emphasis on certain aspects of sport can produce negative results, however. The heavy significance attached to winning creates feelings of inferiority when one loses and detracts from the joy of sport. Evidence is mounting that violence in sport promotes aggressive behavior in society, and violence by spectators at sporting events has increased dramatically in recent years. The drug abuse issue has tainted certain professional sports and has called into question the value of players as role models. Televised sports mesmerize viewers who sit for hours in their fantasy world of jock power, to the neglect of active participation in sports that promote good health. Youngsters who aspire to professional athletic careers, which can be achieved only by a tiny proportion, may neglect their education and other important aspects of normal living. Organized sport may also foster an elitism and militaristic behavior that are unhealthy in people of any age.

Spectator sport provides an outlet for viewing the vitality of youth, speed, and strength. The levels of skill displayed fascinate people. Men identify more directly than do women with spectator sport because of their childhood experiences and the macho nature of physical contact games. For men there is an additional attraction in the fantasy that because they are male they could be called on to be there on field or court, asked to contribute their playing or coaching skills. Viewing sport thus provides the raw material for dreams. Nevertheless, women too feel vicarious satisfaction of a desire to win, and more women are becoming active in competitive sports. In a way, competition is life in microcosm. If only the strong survive in Spencerian competition for determining the fittest, one must do his or her part to ensure identification with winning. No one wants to be known as a loser. Of course, teams lose half the time, but losses, especially on television, can be rationalized; they are quickly forgotten. But victories are savored and remembered.

Labor relations did not play a dominant role in professional sports until the early 1970s. Although player conflicts over work practices came early in the development of professional sports, they were characterized by infrequent and transitory confrontations with team owners. In the decades before unions and collective bargaining became ingrained in the sports industry, professional athletes were treated like privileged peons. They had adulation from the public and generally made larger incomes from playing games than they would have made in outside pursuits, but hardly any made big money. Players viewed themselves as knights on a noble mission to provide entertainment and have fun in the process. They were not engaged in the contests for power with management that coal miners and steelworkers were. Sport was more avocation and pastime than career and business.

A few players thought they suffered injustice by being locked into servile relationships with tight-fisted owners who controlled their present and future. But this injustice was endured for the good of the sport to which these players dedicated their lives. In any event, players had no real alternative. They could be sold, traded, and released like any other business asset. Power was exclusively in the hands of the owners, who dictated contract terms knowing that they were the sole parties the players could deal with.

By the early 1970s, growing fan interest in the games, heightened by network television, had transformed professional sports into lucrative business enterprises. Leagues expanded to take advantage of population explosions in the cities of the West and South. Wealthy business moguls bid for sports franchises as tax havens and ego builders. Entirely new leagues sprang up to compete with established organizations and lure away players at attractive salaries. As sports became more like traditional businesses, players increasingly turned to agents to represent them in individual salary negotiations. More important, players' associations, formerly weak or nonexistent, became a countervailing power to the owners' exclusive interests. Professional sports entered a new era, featuring collective bargaining, court actions, and strikes.

Industrial Relations Models

The sports industry is a part of the larger industry providing services to entertain the American public, and labor relations in the industry comprise key components that are applicable to the industrial relations systems in any free society. This is shown by John Dunlop's classic model explaining an industrial relations system as a response to a universal labor problem, the construction of a set of acceptable rules by which the participants in productive work are related to one another.[5] An industrial relations system is designed to resolve important questions affecting work: How is work to be organized? Who is going to perform it? What standards of discipline apply at the workplace? How will the economic rewards from work be distributed among the participants? The answers to these questions are determined by rules, established by what Dunlop calls the "actors"—management, workers, and government. Management is a hierarchy of decision makers who issue instructions. Workers are also viewed as a hierarchy, which is formalized if they are represented by unions or informal if they are not. Government comprises specialized agencies that may either substantially regulate management and workers or be relatively weak and overridden by them on important issues.

Regardless of the relative power of Dunlop's three actors, they interact in an environment determined by the larger society. The principal features of this environment are technology, market constraints, and societal power. Although the actors determine the rules, the content of the rules is influenced by environmental constraints, and the actors' strategies are based in large part on changes in the environment.[6] Technology has far-reaching effects on production hardware, skills, and techniques, which in turn determine the size of the work force, its concentration in a narrow area or diffusion, and the stability of the work group. Market or budgetary constraints affect the size of the enterprises, competitive position of organizations and industries, economic expansion, and the ratio of labor costs to total costs, and these factors may force management to seek greater control over work rules. The distribution of societal power determines the actors' prestige, position, and access to ultimate authority within the larger society. Frequently, the economic power within an industrial relations system comes into conflict with the political power in a society. Workers and management seek to channel conflict into the political or economic arena in which their control is perceived to be greater.

The vast network of industrial relations rules governs three basic subjects: (1) compensation, (2) duties and performance of workers, and (3) rights of workers in the workplace. There is considerable variation in these rules among industries and individual enterprises. Whatever their specific content, however, the detailed and technical nature of the rules tends to create a distinct group of experts or professionals for the design and administration of rules. It is not uncommon for problems of communication or conflict to arise between the experts and the rest of the hierarchy, and it is necessary to control these tensions when they occur.

Underlying the industrial relations system is a set of beliefs held by the actors, a body of common ideas that define the role of each actor and the relationships among them. A stable system implies congruence among beliefs. If views are incompatible—managers perceive workers paternalistically or workers view managers as having no useful purpose—the actors have difficulty reconciling their roles, and relationships tend to be volatile. Conflicting ideologies present a formidable challenge to the operation of industrial relations systems, as the actors search for a compatible set of ideas that recognize the needs of each.

The Entertainment Industry

Although there are many differences between sports and the other sectors of the entertainment industry, there are important similarities. The entertainment industry is a diverse amalgam of subgroups, primarily film production and distribution, radio and television broadcasting, live performing arts, and professional sports. Some observers exclude sports from the entertainment industry, focusing instead on its more traditional components, which have a long history of unionization and collective bargaining. But with the emergence of formalized union-management relations in sports, geographic expansion of the business, and heavy exposure of sporting events on television, professional sport is clearly within the ambit of the organized entertainment industry in its industrial relations structure and its share of the total income of the entertainment industry. Although sport competes with some segments of the entertainment industry for consumer spending, it also has a close relationship with television in presentation of live events. The televising of sporting events has increased such that a large proportion of the revenues of professional sports franchises comes from this source.

As David Tajgman observes, the demand for television programming depends on the size of the television distribution system.[7] He notes that technological developments, such as cable and pay television and direct satellite broadcasting, are expanding broadcast time and the demand for programming. This has caused organizational and revenue distribution problems for management and unions in the entertainment industry as a whole. Sport is affected because expanded broadcast of amateur and professional events has brought a mixed blessing of greater exposure to the public but decreased attention to individual events as a result of oversaturation of the market. The extent of influence that television has on sports has also changed. Schedules, locations, and times of games are readily shifted to adapt to the needs of television. Ownership of sports franchises has moved toward vertical integration; that is, sports entrepreneurs more often have ownership interests in other parts of the entertainment industry—especially in the broadcast media—so that these elements can be combined for greater income potential.

There are some interesting similarities between the labor force of the entertainment industry and that of its sports component. Management is highly dependent on the work force—live entertainment cannot go on without it. In general, workers are well educated and know how to use their economic power to greatest advantage. Both are subject to the "star system," in which exceptionally talented people dominate the worker hierarchy. Whether actors, rock musicians, or athletic superstars, these elite persons command vastly disproportionate influence on their professions and derive substantial incomes from

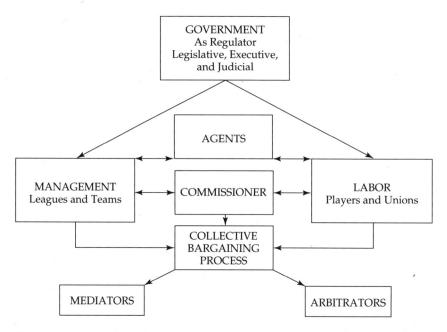

Figure 1.1 Model of Labor Relations in the Sports Industry

outside sources. Although exceptionally talented performers will always be able to derive exceptional incomes, one of the important reasons that unions have arisen in sports and other segments of the entertainment industry is the need to further the economic interests of workers farther down in the hierarchy— marginal players, equipment operators, and stagehands—whose talents are more easily replaced. Along with the older unions, which have long had a strong voice in the determination of institutional roles, sports unions are increasingly getting more control over the rule-making process. In seeking greater influence over membership destiny, the sports unions are following the lead of their antecedents in the entertainment industry, unions such as the Screen Actors Guild, National Association of Broadcast Engineers and Technicians, and American Federation of Television and Radio Artists.

Sports Industry Model

A simple model illustrating the key elements of labor relations in the sports industry is shown in Figure 1.1. Underlying this model is the proposition that industrial relations includes the institutions, theories, and processes for resolving contending money and power claims in the employment relationship.[8] The three principal participants in the industrial relations function are government, management, and labor, and government's role is primarily that of regulator of the other two institutions.

The federal government performs the regulatory function under its legislative, executive, and judicial branches. Labor relations in sports are formalized under a system of union representation and collective bargaining, and therefore the National Labor Relations Act of 1935 provides a basic legal framework that carries with it a half-century of experience in other areas of American commerce. Hundreds of decisions by the National Labor Relations Board and federal courts, which interpret and apply the law to collective bargaining, right to strike, and antitrust policy, have substantial effects on the sports industry.

Management, operating through league structures and team ownership, provides for the planning, supervision, and control of corporate enterprise decisions. The leagues have the responsibility for such functions as negotiating collective bargaining agreements, setting rules for drafting of players, determining policies for the enforcement of management rights, and negotiating national television agreements. Owners of clubs give up much of their authority to the league offices but retain decision-making authority in areas such as negotiating individual player contracts, movement of players to other teams (subject to negotiated agreement with the union), hiring coaches and front office personnel, and entering into local television contracts.

Labor refers to the players and their unions. The principal objective of the sports union is to promote its effectiveness in collective bargaining. In achieving its objectives, the union (1) engages in organizing its membership for solidarity, (2) negotiates contracts applicable to all players, (3) uses pressure tactics such as strikes and picketing, if necessary, (4) enforces the terms of the negotiated agreement through the grievance procedure, and (5) serves an internal governmental function in conducting meetings, voting on contracts negotiated, and providing other means of communication to members. Since nearly all players at the major league level pay substantial dues to their unions, these organizations constitute a formidable presence in collective bargaining.

As shown in Figure 1.1, two other participants interact with management and labor in sports: the commissioner and agents. The role of the commissioner varies among sports. Theoretically, the commissioner is supposed to serve both management and labor and be a public spokesperson. As a practical matter, in that they are selected, paid, and retained at the discretion of management, commissioners tend to line up more on the side of management on contentious issues. Nonetheless, commissioners serve as a kind of buffer between the two sides in areas of dispute and seek to represent the interests of both in areas of mutual benefit.

In contrast, agents are clearly a thorn in the side of management. As the representatives of players in individual salary contract negotiations, agents have added a powerful impetus to raising average salaries to dizzying heights. Some agents also represent players in managing their assets and in outside commercial ventures such as television commercials. Management resents the intrusion of agents in matters of their control over players, and some impartial observers view agents as a destructive force in sports. But their success in enhancing the economic welfare of their clients is undeniable, and agents will retain their influential role unless the players' unions take over the individual contract negotiating function. A possible compromise, which is currently being done in football and basketball, is the screening of agents to help avoid players being taken advantage of by unscrupulous agents.

The figure does not depict a role for agents in the collective bargaining process. They are involved only in the limited sense of handling individual salary negotiations, which may include incentives and bonuses but not for all players as a group. In contrast, minimum player salaries, meal money, playoff play, pensions, and other compensation issues are negotiated by the unions for all players.

There are two additional participants shown in Figure 1.1 who may become involved in the collective bargaining process: mediators and arbitrators. These are neutrals who assist in the resolution of disputes, either negotiation impasses or grievances. Until recently, many of the battles between management and labor in sports have been fought in the courts. As labor relations in sports evolves and becomes more mature, third-party neutrals are taking on a more varied and important role than in the past.

Collective Bargaining

National Labor Relations Act

Workers involved in interstate commerce, which includes professional team sports, are covered by the National Labor Relations Act (NLRA), as amended.[9] Section 7 of this law provides three basic rights that form the heart of labor relations policy in the United States: (1) the right to self-organization, to form, join, or assist labor organizations; (2) the right to bargain collectively through representatives of their own choosing; and (3) the right to engage in "concerted activities" for employees' mutual aid or protection. In short, workers are permitted to unionize, bargain collectively, and use pressure tactics (e.g., strike and picket) to achieve their legitimate objectives. Administration is carried out by the National Labor Relations Board (NLRB) and the federal courts.

The NLRB enforces the law by policing unfair labor practices committed by either labor or management. For example, the employer and union are forbidden from interfering with employees' rights under section 7, and allegations of such violations are handled by the NLRB. Also administered by the NLRB is a machinery for determining appropriate units or groups of employees qualified to vote in a union representation election and for conducting such elections by secret ballot vote. Finally, the NLRB reviews questions concerning what issues are subject to negotiation under the law. The NLRB is not currently active in the administration of unit determination and elections in the major sports, although it may become so if a new league is formed. Units include active players, and elections involving players have resulted in the choice of an exclusive bargaining agency. Most of the NLRB's current work in sports involves unfair labor practices and scope of bargaining.

On unfair labor practices, two common allegations in sports are that the employer has disciplined or discharged players for engaging in union activities and that the employer has refused to bargain in "good faith." Good faith bargaining requires that the parties communicate through proposals and counterproposals and that they make every reasonable effort to reach agreement. In certain cases, employers must furnish basic information about finances and budgets in order to comply with good faith dictates. There has been recurring conflict over this issue in sports, since owners are reluctant to disclose financial data to unions.

The scope of bargaining is defined in the NLRA as including wages, hours, and working conditions. Wages include pay, fringe benefits, and bonus payments; hours refer to time spent on the job; and working conditions are factors influencing the work environment, such as work rules, safety, and seniority. These topics are considered by the NLRB to be mandatory subjects for bargaining that must be negotiated in good faith. So-called permissive subjects for bargaining are those on which management is not obligated to negotiate but may do so if it wishes. This includes management rights or prerogatives that the employer has an exclusive right to determine. Illegal subjects are those the law prohibits from being negotiated. From time to time, the NLRB has been asked to rule in a sports industry case on whether a subject, such as wage scales or use of artificial turf, is negotiable.

The Structure of Bargaining

The characteristics of bargaining units are generally the same throughout the team sports. All active league players are in the unit, and nearly all players are members of their respective unions. Clubs join together in bargaining with unions, so that the negotiated contract in each sport applies to all teams uniformly. The formal bargaining structure influences the diversity of individual and organizational interests that must be accommodated during the negotiation of an agreement. Conflict is inherent in nearly all negotiating situations, both between the parties and within the union or team management.

For most private industry and public employment, bargaining is limited to a single union dealing with a single firm or government employer. In several industries, however, contracts are negotiated on a national basis, applying to employees throughout the country. Because of the weakening of some firms in major American industries, the traditional style of pattern bargaining—in which agreements reached with a target firm have a substantial influence on agreements reached by the same union with other firms in the industry—is becoming less important. In the United States about one-sixth of all collective bargaining agreements are negotiated by associations of private employers.[10] Multiemployer bargaining is found in the lumber, coal, construction, longshoring, railroad, trucking, hotel, and retail grocery industries. It is also found in professional sports, in which individual teams band together through the league format to negotiate a contract with the players' union that applies equally to all teams. The agreements reached in professional sports are not industry-wide, however, because each of the sports has a separate contract with unions. Another feature that makes sports unique is the multilateral nature of bargaining. The clubs bargain as a group with unions over certain aspects of wages, hours, and working conditions, but the most important issue—individual salary—is negotiated between the club and player. The significance of this distinctive element of the structure of sports bargaining will be evident in several examples offered in later chapters to illustrate the dynamics of the process. Unions have been actively involved in clearing the way for greater labor market freedom for players to negotiate individual contracts, but their role is indirect in that they are not responsible for reaching agreement on individual salaries.

Jack Barbash calls bargaining a "love-hate," "cooperation-conflict" relationship.[11] The parties realize their common interest in maximizing the income that finances their respective shares. But conflict arises over division of the economic pie. Most American managers and union leaders, and particularly in professional sports, view negotiations as a contest in which the "smart player" wins. Negotiation *strategy* is the overall plan of how to proceed at the bargaining table—at one pole is taking the "hard line," while at the other end is cooperating. *Tactics* are the specific methods that a party uses to implement its strategy, for example, adopting unrealistic positions, trading off issues, or such pressure tactics as strikes and lockouts. The adversarial strategy thus sets the tone for the labor-management relationship and the kinds of tactics that are employed.

Tactically, both sides usually adopt extreme positions. The union has its "shopping list," in which it asks for gains on many issues far beyond what it thinks realistically possible. Management typically offers very little at the outset. Both parties recognize the need to bluff and make dire threats with no real intention of carrying them out. Although the union is ordinarily the moving party in making demands at the outset of negotiations, an effective position for management is making high, hard demands of its own at the outset. Underlying this tactic is the adage that the best defense is a good offense. In recent years, throughout American industry and increasingly in professional sports, management has been trying to get unions to accept give-backs that reduce benefits gained under the previous contract. This tactic has been generally successful in much of U.S. industry, but did not produce significant retrenchment in sports until 1995, when concessions occurred in hockey as a result of a lengthy lockout. Negotiators are keenly aware that they must ultimately secure the approval of their principals for whatever they tentatively agree on. Rejections create serious problems for both parties, who must then return to the bargaining table for further efforts at shaping acceptable compromise.

Contents of Agreements

Typical collective bargaining agreements contain many pages of legalistic language spelling out the formal relationship between the parties. Key areas of these agreements include:

1. Specification of contract length. The duration is usually from one to five years, with three years most common. There may be provision for reopening the contract during its life for renegotiation of certain issues.
2. Compensation, which includes wages, pensions, and other fringe benefits. In sports, there are several areas of individual compensation that are not covered in the negotiated agreement. Unions in sports negotiate the minimum standards, but supplements to the minimum are covered in the individual bargaining process.
3. Rules for the utilization of labor, such as length of the workday, work practices, overtime, and health and safety. In sports, the big issue is free agency for players, which allows them to move liberally among teams to command greater individual bargaining power.
4. Individual job rights in such areas as seniority and discipline. Concern in sports has centered on discipline for aberrant behavior such as violence, gambling, and drug abuse.

5. Rights of union and management in the bargaining relationship, such as a management rights clause and provision for union security (e.g., union shop, dues checkoff). The prevailing practice in sports is for negotiation of an agency shop. This requires players who elect not to join the union to pay a service fee to the union (usually the equivalent of union dues) for its bargaining, legal, and grievance handling services.
6. Methods for enforcing, interpreting, and administering the agreement terms on a day-to-day basis: for example, grievance procedures, grievance arbitration, and no-strike clauses.

The provisions of a collective bargaining agreement are applied to situations that arise in the employment relationship. Management and union representatives may differ in the meaning they attach to a particular contract clause. The typical pattern is for management to act on its interpretation. Then, if the union objects to management's action, a grievance will be filed and may later be decided by an arbitrator. These actions and reactions give vitality to the language of the agreement throughout its duration.

UNIVERSITY OF CENTRAL
LANCASHIRE LIBRARY
SHAROE GREEN SITE

16130

Baseball   2

There is a lively debate among sports historians as to when baseball began and who invented it. Ball games, including the British game of rounders, were played with bats, balls, pitchers, and four bases in the early nineteenth century in New York and New England. The individual who first codified the rules of baseball, roughly as they are today, was Alexander Joy Cartwright. Much of the credit for invention of the game, however, is given to Abner Doubleday, who later became a U.S. Army major general in the Civil War. According to legend, Doubleday handed down the rules and laid out the first baseball diamond at Cooperstown, New York, in 1839. But this was several years after Cartwright's rules and the real beginnings of the game.

Baseball is the oldest major professional sport in America. In the sport's pioneering era, it was the players rather than the owners who were the main force behind the game's growth and development.[1] In 1858 the National Association of Base Ball Players (NABBP) was formed. It was not a labor union in the modern sense but more an organization of teams that took control of the game. Run by the players, the NABBP emphasized their financial interests, insisting on their right to sell themselves on the open market to the highest bidder. It was not unusual for players to jump contracts, freely moving from one team to another, in what famed sportswriter Harry Chadwick called "revolving."

When the National League was formed in 1876 by William A. Hulbert, a Chicago businessman, control was wrested from the players and placed in the hands of the club owners. A regular schedule of games was devised, and in 1880 the reserve clause was established in player contracts to allow a team unilaterally to reserve a player's services for the following year. The reserve clause was later expanded to allow for the trading and selling of players to other clubs. As a result, not only was the practice of revolving eliminated, but players were denied freedom of contract and movement. It was the reserve clause more than anything that led to formation of the early baseball unions.

In 1885 John Montgomery Ward established the Brotherhood of Professional Base Ball Players. Ward, later elected to the Hall of Fame, was a star pitcher and infielder for the New York Giants and had a law degree from Columbia University. The Brotherhood, with chapters in all the National League cities, attacked the reserve clause and sought free agency for players who had been with their clubs for a certain number of seasons, depending on negotiations with each club. When Ward's attempts to meet with the owners on free agency and other grievances were rebuffed, the so-called Brotherhood Revolt of 1890 was called by about two hundred major league players. The outcome was the formation of the Players League, consisting of the best players in the game. This rival league lasted for only a single season, however, collapsing in the face of verbal and financial assaults from National League club owner Albert G. Spalding, a former star player and sporting goods entrepreneur who was later elected to the Hall of Fame.

The players tried their hand at organization a second time in 1900 under the banner of the Players Protective Association (PPA). Motivation for forming the union was a reduction of teams in the National League, which caused sixty players to lose their jobs. The PPA was headed by veteran players, including two future Hall of Famers, pitcher Clark Griffith and infielder Hughey Jennings. Griffith, along with Ban Johnson and Charles Comiskey, was instrumental in the establishment of the American League by becoming its dominant player in 1901. Jennings earned a law degree at Cornell University and later coached the Cornell baseball team and the Detroit Tigers. Another former player turned lawyer, Harry Taylor, became the chief strategist of the PPA. In meetings with National League owners he urged modification of the reserve clause and reforms on sale and trading of players and farming them out to the minor leagues. The PPA lasted until 1903, but by failing to protect its members from jumping from the National League to the American League, the organization lost its credibility as a bargaining agency.

Next in the line of early baseball unions was the Baseball Players Fraternity (BPF). Creation of this group was triggered by an incident in 1912 involving legendary Detroit star Ty Cobb. In a game at New York, Cobb leaped into the stands to beat up a persistent heckler. He was suspended for ten days by American League president Ban Johnson. Cobb's suspension prompted a one-day strike by Detroit players, the first ever in baseball. This incident fanned union sentiment among players, and a few months later the BPF was established by David Fultz, another former player turned New York lawyer. The BPF viewed itself as a professional association rather than a labor union and eschewed the strike weapon as well as the idea of forming a rival league. Pushing for higher salaries for all players, including minor leaguers who were members, the BPF was eventually recognized by major league owners. Meanwhile, in 1914, the Federal League formed as a third major league, and the interleague warfare that resulted was beneficial to the BPF. The Federal League folded, however, after just two seasons. Its owners lost a landmark antitrust suit against the major leagues on the issue of the reserve clause. This case, decided by the U.S. Supreme Court in 1922, is discussed later in this chapter. The collapse of the Federal League and the inability of the BPF to achieve gains for players led to a decline in membership and ultimate dissolution in 1917.

It was not until 1946 that major league baseball players reorganized into the American Baseball Guild (ABG). Sparking its formation were the low salaries of players, which caused several of them to jump for higher pay to the Mexican League. One of these players, Danny Gardella of the New York Giants, was suspended from the majors for five years and blacklisted for violating the reserve clause. Gardella sued Commissioner Albert B. Chandler and major league baseball for a conspiracy to deny him his livelihood. The litigation was eventually settled by the parties. In response to the Mexican League incident, Robert Murphy, a lawyer and former NLRB examiner, chartered the ABG and urged reform, including a minimum salary, salary arbitration, modification of the reserve clause, and a pension plan. A minimum salary of $5,000 was agreed to by the owners, who also funded a pension plan out of revenues from sale of national television and radio rights. Like its predecessors, however, the ABG was dominated by the owners and did little to advance the interests of players.

Baseball is the first sport in which a union broke through to achieve significant gains for players. As such, it has had a great influence on the collective bargaining models that have emerged in football, basketball, and hockey. Until recently, however, the union representing players in major league baseball was relatively weak compared to the owners. Monopolistic control by owners over salaries and the labor market gave the union little room to maneuver. But arbitration and court decisions in the mid-1970s dramatically shifted the balance of power toward the players. These changes are still stimulating player salaries, so that in addition to the power structure, the economics of baseball have been radically altered.

Economics of Baseball

In the business of baseball, as in other professional sports, the product is the game itself, presented by players as entertainment. This entertainment is consumed by the public through live viewing or, more commonly, through the print media, radio, and television. Economic rewards to clubs and players alike are directly related to success at the box office and with television contracts. But in baseball myriad other factors additionally motivate economic behavior.[2]

Until recently, baseball was considered the most popular sport in America. According to a Harris Poll in 1993, however, the proportion of people citing baseball as their favorite sport was 18 percent, down from 23 percent in 1985 and lower than the 24 percent who cited professional football as their favorite.[3] The strike in 1994–95 hurt attendance and turned off many fans. Still, baseball remains the American pastime. In 1995, 35 percent of Americans claimed to be fans.[4] Far more people attend major league games than other sports. The minor leagues have enjoyed a resurgence in recent years. There is more baseball-licensed merchandise sold than in other sports, about $2.4 billion in 1993, although the 1994–95 strike hurt sales.

League rules divide gate receipts with 80 percent to the home team and 20 percent to the visiting team in the American League, and about 95–5 in the National League. Teams share equally in revenue from sale of national broadcasting rights but get to keep most if not all of their revenues from local broadcasts. Although a typical team has $50–60 million in annual revenue, several teams each year are at about the break-even point or are losing money. Player salary escalation as a result of free agency and salary arbitration has raised costs significantly, and teams in small markets find it especially difficult to maintain profitability. Player salaries account for about 58 percent of revenue, which is not that high a percentage compared with other service industries. But major league teams have the additional expense of maintaining minor league farm systems for development of young players, unlike football and basketball, which get most of their players directly from college. Baseball has a draft system for young players, who are eligible for selection at age eighteen.

While it is clear that baseball franchises are not as profitable as they were before free agency, reports that the baseball business is in deplorable shape are somewhat exaggerated. Tax advantages to clubs, such as depreciation of players, can turn what appears to be a loss into a profit, and reports of player salaries can be deceptive, since some of the payments to players are deferred and do not involve immediate out-of-pocket costs to clubs. A detailed picture of the economics of baseball is difficult to draw because clubs do not reveal their books and accounting practices to the public.

Monopoly Control

Baseball leagues constitute a cartel, or self-regulating monopoly. This monopoly control is the cornerstone on which the industry is based and influences its economic rewards. The leagues are subject to some control from the outside by the government; however, this regulation is far less burdensome than it is for other monopolistic industries, such as public utilities. Internal control in baseball is affected by the players' union, and the contest for economic power in the industry is between management and labor. Yet the union has only nominal, if any, influence on the arrangements between owners on matters of mutual interest, such as scheduling games, advertising, promotion of the game, rules, expansion of teams, and drafting of players. This level of control is consistent with the management rights or prerogatives that employers have in industries outside sport. The important difference is that, because of an antitrust exemption that the industry enjoys, baseball owners can engage in noncompetitive arrangements to collude, fix prices, and restrain trade.

When artificial barriers are erected, the normal checks and balances of the market and free enterprise systems are not allowed to operate. The operation of the baseball cartel cuts two ways. Suppose, for example, that players had complete freedom to move in the labor market. This would probably escalate salaries to far higher levels than they are now and could do serious damage to the continuity of teams that spark fan loyalty. At the same time, the restraint of trade that owners carry out through the league cartel has the potential for public harm in that people wind up paying a higher price for the entertainment.[5] The saving grace for baseball is that ticket prices are still a relative bargain because of high stadium capacities and the relatively large number of games played by teams.

Table 2.1 shows the average cost for a family of four attending a major league game in 1994 at each of the ballparks. Even for a New York Yankee game, the most expensive to attend, baseball entertainment is relatively affordable compared with football, basketball, and hockey. Moreover, many games are televised free for viewers. Therefore, because baseball entertainment is available to the public in relative abundance and at low prices, government regulators have been wary of interfering with the operation of the industry.

Tax Advantages

A primary attraction to ownership of a professional team in baseball, and in other sports, is that it is a low-tax operation. Businesses in general are allowed to depreciate their assets under rules of Internal Revenue Code. If a tractor, building, or computer is purchased, it can be depreciated or deducted from revenues with the rationale that it gets used up or wears out. As a deducted cost of doing business, depreciation reduces taxes. Only sports businesses are allowed to depreciate their human assets. Player contracts are purchased by owners, in transactions separate from the purchase of the franchise, and then players are

Table 2.1. Fan Cost Index of Major League Baseball Teams, 1994

Team	1994 Fan Cost Index[a]	TEAM	1994 Fan Cost Index[a]
New York Yankees	$115.25	Pittsburgh Pirates	$93.40
Toronto Blue Jays	113.53	Florida Marlins	92.18
Atlanta Braves	112.98	St. Louis Cardinals	91.72
Chicago Cubs	108.97	New York Mets	91.06
Chicago White Sox	106.13	Philadelphia Phillies	91.00
Baltimore Orioles	104.96	Los Angeles Dodgers	90.73
Cleveland Indians	103.75	Minnesota Twins	90.61
Detroit Tigers	103.45	California Angels	90.24
Boston Red Sox	102.55	Houston Astros	89.26
San Francisco Giants	100.80	Milwaukee Brewers	87.53
Oakland Athletics	100.47	San Diego Padres	83.34
Texas Rangers	99.26	Montreal Expos	82.89
Kansas City Royals	98.79	Colorado Rockies	82.08
Seattle Mariners	95.42	Cincinnati Reds	79.31

[a]The Fan Cost Index consists of four average-priced tickets, two small beers, four small sodas, four hot dogs, parking for one car, two game programs, and two twill baseball caps.
Source: Team Marketing Report, Chicago, reported in *Wall Street Journal,* 5 April 1994, p. B1.

written off as depreciable assets in three to seven years. The franchise, or right of ownership, itself is a nondepreciable asset. It therefore makes sense to assign a low value to the franchise for tax purposes and a high value to the players' contracts so that depreciation can be maximized. Despite some tightening of depreciation rules in sports in recent years, allowing no more than 50 percent of the acquisition price of a club to be written off in player depreciation, ownership of teams remains a lucrative tax haven.

Another tax advantage available to many baseball owners is the free or low rent of stadium facilities. Communities eager to lure or retain major league franchises are willing to give tax breaks that are in effect underwritten by the citizens. This taxpayer subsidization is not unjustified, because teams generate substantial revenues from parking, food and beverage services, and souvenir stands. The games attract tourists who patronize local business establishments. Moreover, the image of a community is enhanced by having a major league baseball team.

Television

Apart from attendance, the other big source of revenue to baseball is national and local television. For many years NBC was the exclusive network covering baseball nationally, first on radio and then on television beginning in 1947.

Major league baseball's national television agreements with NBC and ABC for the six-year period from 1984 through 1989 provided a total revenue package of $1.125 billion. This revenue, shared equally by the owners, raised the amount received by nearly four times over the old national television agreement.

Although the next television agreement continued to increase revenues significantly, the proportionate rise was not as great. Indeed, some observers predicted that the network agreement might show a drop in revenues, because ratings were down and television was saturated with sports programming. But CBS, trailing the other major networks in overall ratings, sought to boost its image by agreeing to pay $1.1 billion in 1988 for four years starting in 1990. The package included rights to the World Series, League Championship Series, All-Star game, and twelve regular-season games. Shortly after the CBS deal, baseball reached its first national cable contract for games on the Entertainment and Sports Programming Network (ESPN). The package with ESPN was for four years, totaling $400 million, and provided for 175 games per season, beginning in 1990.

The CBS and ESPN contracts turned out to be disastrous for the networks. For one thing, the CBS deal was controversial in that the twelve regular-season telecasts were a reduction from the thirty-two games a year on NBC and eight on ABC. Even though ESPN televised many more games to cable viewers, about half of America's homes, which did not receive ESPN, had to rely entirely on the paucity of games on CBS. This controversy caused CBS to increase its games from twelve to sixteen, but many fans were still disappointed with the coverage. More important, both CBS and ESPN lost huge amounts of money on the deals. Low ratings caused CBS to lose about $500 million and ESPN about $150 million. This was the first time that networks lost such large amounts on sports programming.

As a result of the low ratings and losses, in 1993 the national television rights contracts were drastically restructured in the form of a joint venture. Baseball returned to NBC and ABC for what was ostensibly a six-year agreement, but with no up-front guarantee of revenues from the networks. Instead, major league baseball was responsible for selling all the advertising time on its game broadcasts known as the Baseball Network. Baseball received 85 percent of the first $140 million of commercial airtime sold, split the next $30 million with the networks, and got to keep 80 percent of additional revenue. A separate entity was created by baseball and the networks to handle the production and advertising. The ESPN agreement was also reduced, to $255 million over six years, less than half of the rights fees under the old agreement, and the number of weekly games was reduced from six to three.

Because of the new deals baseball's revenues from television were cut by at least half (see Table 2.2). More than any other factor, this revenue shortfall is

Table 2.2. National Television Rights Fees

Year	Television Rights Fees	Amount per Team
1980	$47.5 million	$ 1.8 million
1984	187.5 million	7.2 million
1990	365.0 million	14.0 million
1995[a]	190.0 million	6.8 million

[a] Estimate.
Note: Data in this table and the others for which no credit is given were compiled by the author from various sources.

what led to the owners' tough stance in the 1994–95 negotiations and precipitated the strike. Ironically, it was the strike and declines in television revenue that led, in turn, to the dissolution of the NBC–ABC–baseball agreement. Under the terms of the agreement it could be voided by any party if the venture did not produce a minimum of $330 million in revenue over the first two years. Revenue fell well short of this amount because of the strike and refunds that had to be made to advertisers for cancellation of the 1994 postseason play. When baseball stubbornly refused to restructure the agreement, the networks angrily pulled the plug, effective at the end of the 1995 season. The collapse of the partnership underscored the need for baseball to hire a commissioner, who could not only have helped achieve compromise on continuing the television venture but might have been able to avoid or shorten the strike itself.

Following the 1995 season, baseball negotiated a five-year television contract with the Fox network and NBC. This package, valued at $1.7 billion, is considerably better than the one it replaced and is a straight rights deal that removes baseball from the business of selling advertising on television. Fox's package includes a weekly regular season game, three World Series, two All-Star games, and half of the League Championship Series games annually. NBC gets two World Series, three All-Star games, and half of the LCS.

Local television agreements are also negotiated by clubs. These agreements provide additional revenues depending on the size of the market. The Atlanta Braves' games are broadcast throughout the nation by owner Ted Turner's cable television network. In 1985, at the urging of Commissioner Ueberroth, Turner agreed to pay nearly $30 million to major league baseball over five years in return for no restriction on the number of games that he could telecast. Although several local television contracts are with local or regional stations and provide free entertainment to viewers, the trend is toward cable television, which charges a fee for its service. Local television creates large disparities in potential revenue to clubs, with New York, Los Angeles, and Chicago able to generate far greater amounts than clubs in Minnesota, Seattle, and Pittsburgh. This causes teams with extensive market areas to be able to attract higher quality players with bigger salaries. As pay television expands, the gap between rich and poor markets will widen. For instance, in 1989 the Madison Square Garden Network agreed to pay $500 million to the New York Yankees for exclusive local cable rights. This is about $42 million a year for the Yankees compared to the $1.5 million or so that the Seattle Mariners get annually for their local contracts.

A possible solution to the rich-get-richer problem of local market disparity is to share these television revenues the way teams do under the national contracts. Teams in rich markets, however, have little incentive to divide this wealth. Prevention of excessive dominance by the rich teams at the expense of the poor ones may eventually find its solution in revenue sharing.

Structure of Employment

Professional baseball is covered by the National Labor Relations Act. While the National Labor Relations Board has the statutory power to decline jurisdiction if the influence of an industry on commerce does not warrant it, it has ruled that baseball is subject to its jurisdiction.[6] The antitrust laws have not been found to extend to baseball, however, because of a 1922 U.S. Supreme Court decision.[7] The Court, in an opinion written by Justice Oliver Wendell Holmes, ruled that playing exhibition games was not within interstate commerce. This exemption from the antitrust laws is unique to baseball. It does not apply to football, basketball, or hockey.

The absence of antitrust law regulation enabled owners to maintain full control over the market through their exclusive rights to bargain with players allocated to them. If a player sought to challenge the reserve clause, the courts, citing the 1922 decision, would find for the club. For instance, in a case involving player Curt Flood, the Supreme Court refused to go against a half century of precedent by overruling the 1922 case, despite Flood's claim that the reserve clause was illegal and severely reduced players' salaries.[8] The Court based its decision on its recognition and acceptance of baseball's unique characteristics and needs. The antitrust exemption continues to apply formally to baseball, but it has come under closer scrutiny in recent years. For example, the joint Senate-House Committee on Professional Sports in 1977 stated that there is no justification for baseball's immunity from the antitrust laws and recommended that Congress remove the exemption. In 1988 a Senate task force threatened to repeal the antitrust exemption for baseball, arguing that the commissioner was not doing enough to encourage expansion to new cities. In 1994, in response to the baseball strike, the Baseball Fans and Communities Protection Act was introduced in Congress to apply the antitrust laws to baseball.

Congress has not taken action on baseball's antitrust immunity, mostly because the players' union has been able to achieve greater leverage with management than in the past. The exemption for baseball is thus a less onerous burden for today's players.

Management

It is customary to think of management as individual owners because of their visibility in the media, which portray such flamboyant owners as Ted Turner of the Atlanta Braves and George Steinbrenner of the New York Yankees as modern captains of industry with unquestioned control over operations. Although owners do exercise substantial domination over the internal management and finances of their teams, much of the labor relations is conducted through the league, where authority is shared. Baseball owners and their outside interests are shown in Table 2.3.

The National and American Leagues of Professional Baseball Clubs are jointly responsible for two of the most important functions affecting industrial relations: collective bargaining and selection of the commissioner of baseball. Owners of the twenty-eight teams have equal votes in these determinations, but they are subordinate to the will of the leagues under consensus management. In effect, the league is a cooperative pool or cartel. If its power is unchecked by a union or by government regulation, it can exercise exclusive control over labor markets. As a result, players can be paid far less than they would be worth under competitive circumstances. In response to this monopoly power, players have unionized and government has exercised a sharper oversight in its regulation of baseball.

Collective bargaining for the leagues is conducted by the Player Relations Committee (PRC), which is selected by the owners. The director of this committee is the chief negotiator. The 1973 and 1976 basic agreements in baseball were negotiated by John J. Gaherin. He was replaced by Raymond Grebey, who handled the negotiations of 1980 and 1981. Grebey resigned in 1983 under pressure from the owners and was replaced by Lee MacPhail. Grebey's abrasive style in negotiations had not been successful, so the owners chose a more moderate representative. In his former position as president of the American League, MacPhail had considerable experience at the bargaining table as a member of the management team, and his relations with the union were generally good. His capable leadership helped limit the duration of the 1985 players' strike. Barry Rona, general counsel of the PRC, succeeded McPhail. Then Charles O'Connor replaced Rona in 1989 and was chief negotiator during the 1990 lockout. In 1991 the owners picked Richard Ravitch, former negotiator for New

Table 2.3. Ownership of Major League Baseball Franchises

	Principal Owners	What They Do
American League		
Baltimore Orioles	Peter Angelos and others	Angelos is an attorney
Boston Red Sox	Jean R. Yawkey Trust John Harrington, trustee	Management of the trust
California Angels	Gene Autry	Retired movie cowboy and former TV station owner
Chicago White Sox	Jerry M. Reinsdorf Edward M. Einhorn	Reinsdorf runs Balcor/American Express Realty; Einhorn is an ex-TV executive
Cleveland Indians	Richard Jacobs	Real estate development of shopping malls
Detroit Tigers	Michael Ilitch	President of Little Caesar's Enterprises, Inc.
Kansas City Royals	Ewing Kauffman Trust	The late owner ran Marion Labs
Milwaukee Brewers	Allan H. Selig and others	Selig is a Chevrolet dealer
Minnesota Twins	Carl R. Pohlad	Banking
New York Yankees	George M. Steinbrenner III	CEO of American Shipbuilding Co.
Oakland Athletics	Ken Hofmann Steve Schott	Real estate developers
Seattle Mariners	Hiroshi Yamauchi	President of Nintendo, Inc.
Texas Rangers	Edward Rose George Bush	Investments
Toronto Blue Jays	John Labatt Ltd.	Labatt is a beer and food conglomerate
National League		
Atlanta Braves	Ted Turner	Owns a TV broadcasting station and cable services
Chicago Cubs	Tribune Co.	Newspapers, TV and radio stations
Cincinnati Reds	Marge Schott	Chevrolet and Buick dealer
Colorado Rockies	Partnership led by Jerry McMorris	McMorris is in the trucking business. Another partner is Coors Brewing Co.
Florida Marlins	H. Wayne Huizenga	Blockbuster Video
Houston Astros	Drayton McLane, Jr.	McLane Co., wholesaler to convenience stores
Los Angeles Dodgers	Peter O'Malley	His major business is the Dodgers
Montreal Expos	Claude R. Brochu and others	Various businesses
New York Mets	Nelson Doubleday	Former president and CEO, Doubleday & Co.
Philadelphia Phillies	Bill Giles and others	Investments
Pittsburgh Pirates	Various Pittsburgh investors	ALCOA, Carnegie-Mellon University, and others
St. Louis Cardinals	Anheuser-Busch Co.	Brewers and bakeries
San Diego Padres	John Moores	Computer software
San Francisco Giants	Peter A. Magowan	Safeway Stores, Inc.

York's Metropolitan Transit Authority and Urban Development Corporation, to deal with the union. Ravitch resigned during the strike in 1994, giving way to a tag-team of owner negotiators led by John Harrington of the Boston Red Sox and Jerry McMorris of the Colorado Rockies, with behind-the-scenes influence from Jerry Reinsdorf of the Chicago White Sox and Bud Selig of the Milwaukee Brewers.

The Commissioner

Baseball's first commissioner was Kenesaw Mountain Landis, a dominating figure and former federal court judge, who was hired in 1921 to restore sanctity to and banish from baseball the "Black Sox" players who fixed the 1919 World Series. His successors, Albert ("Happy") Chandler, Ford Frick, and General William D. Eckert, were uninspiring leaders who seemed unable to act decisively. In 1969 the owners elevated the National League's attorney, Bowie Kuhn, to the job of commissioner. Kuhn's tenure was controversial among the owners, but he brought an enlightened and spirited leadership to the position. He overturned player trades by Charles O. Finley, owner of the Oakland A's, in the "interests of baseball"; fined San Diego Padre owner Ray Kroc $100,000 for tampering; and banned retired player Willie Mays from participation as an official in baseball because of his business relations with an Atlantic City casino. Over the years Kuhn had to slap the hands of numerous owners, which built up animosity and resistance to his continuing as commissioner. Yet he presided over unprecedented prosperity for the game. His apparent indecisiveness over the 1981 baseball strike was the result of his job description, not his leadership ability.[9]

Kuhn needed approval of three-fourths of the owners in each league to win another term in office. A disgruntled minority of the owners finally managed to force him out, but he was retained in a lame duck capacity through the 1984 season when his successor, Peter Ueberroth, who achieved national prominence as head of the Los Angeles Olympic Organizing Committee, took over.

Before taking the job of baseball commissioner, Ueberroth, in consultation with Kuhn, who really designed the changes to be proposed to management, was able to get the owners to accept a considerable strengthening of the position. The most important change, and one which had a significant effect on industrial relations, is that the commissioner was formally recognized as baseball's chief executive officer and all departments reported directly to him. This allowed the commissioner to exercise a more decisive role in the collective bargaining process. The commissioner does not actually participate in the negotiations but acts more like the president of a company, with power to determine, ratify, and reject arrangements that are made by management representatives at the bargaining table.

Another important change in the rules affecting the operation of the commissioner's office is that he needs approval of only a majority vote of the twenty-eight teams for reelection, with a minimum of five votes from each league. Had such a rule existed before, Kuhn would have been able to remain in office. Also, the commissioner is empowered to fine teams a maximum of $250,000. This strengthening of the office gave Ueberroth greater freedom to act than any commissioner since Judge Landis.

Similar to Kuhn's experience, however, Ueberroth's leadership ruffled the feathers of owners, who seemed to expect a less bipartisan stance on controversial issues involving the players. Although Ueberroth's decisions appeared in nearly all cases to have been in the interests of baseball, he frequently alienated the party on the short end of important rulings. The owners, for example, resented Ueberroth's order to disclose their financial statements during the 1985 negotiations. Eddie Chiles, owner of the Texas Rangers, bridled when Ueberroth fined the Rangers $250,000 for prematurely calling up pitcher Steve Howe, a previous drug abuser. Many players and their union were vexed over the commissioner's tough stance on drugs in general and for bypassing the union in attempting to put a drug-testing program into effect. Perhaps wary of a negative reelection vote from the owners, Ueberroth resigned when his term expired in 1989.

Ueberroth's successor was the redoubtable Angelo Bartlett "Bart" Giamatti. Literally a "Renaissance Man," he earned his Ph.D. in comparative literature at Yale University, achieved renown on the Yale faculty as a scholar of the Italian Renaissance, and became president of Yale in 1978. Giamatti, who served as president of the National League from 1986 to 1989, is especially remembered for two things, his poetically articulated love of the game and the Pete Rose affair. It was his distasteful job as commissioner to have to preside over accusations against legendary player Pete Rose for betting on baseball and ultimately to banish him from the game. The strain of this incident may have taken its toll, as Giamatti died of a heart attack only nine days after the Rose decision.

Giamatti's replacement was Francis T. "Fay" Vincent, his longtime friend and deputy commissioner. A Yale Law School graduate, Vincent was formerly the chief executive officer of Columbia Pictures and a partner in the New York office of the Washington, D.C., law firm of Caplin and Drysdale. It was fortuitous that such an experienced executive and fan of the game was available to step into Giamatti's shoes. Vincent was an able commissioner, perhaps too much for his own good. His bugbear was George Steinbrenner, owner of the New York Yankees. Steinbrenner conducted an investigation of the charitable foundation of former Yankee outfielder Dave Winfield and paid $40,000 to a former gambler,

Howard Spira, to gather dirt on Winfield. Vincent found that the payment violated baseball's rules, causing Steinbrenner to resign rather than face suspension.

Whereas Commissioner Ueberroth was highly successful and perhaps also a bit lucky in turning baseball from a money-losing industry into a highly profitable one, it was Vincent's misfortune to preside over the game when a longer-term decline was setting in. Although Vincent was helpful in ending the 1990 lockout, he gained the owners' resentment for doing so. He became a scapegoat for declining attendance and television ratings and alienated American League owners by ruling that they had to contribute 55 percent of the players in the 1992 expansion draft for two additional National League teams while getting only 22 percent of the revenues from expansion. Vincent also incurred the wrath of the Chicago Cubs when he realigned the National League teams following the expansion. With too many enemies among the owners he resigned under pressure in 1992. Since then, the position of commissioner has been vacant, and in 1994 the owners reduced the power of the commissioner to act in the best interests of the game on various business and labor relations matters. The commissioners of baseball and their terms of office are shown in Table 2.4.

Labor

The Major League Baseball Players Association (MLBPA) was formed in 1952. Like its predecessor, the American Baseball Guild, the association was initially dominated by the team owners. Negotiated agreements were reached on a limited number of issues such as pensions and insurance. But in 1966, Marvin Miller was hired as the MLBPA executive director. Miller took a more traditional trade union stance with the club owners, and in 1968 he negotiated an agreement on a broad range of issues.[10]

Table 2.4. Baseball's Commissioners

Term of Office	Commissioner
1920–44	Kenesaw Landis
1945–51	Happy Chandler
1951–65	Ford Frick
1965–68	William Eckert
1969–84	Bowie Kuhn
1984–89	Peter Ueberroth
1989	Bart Giamatti
1989–92	Fay Vincent
1992–95[a]	Vacant

[a]Technically, the position of commissioner was vacant during this time, although the job of "acting commissioner" was carried out by Bud Selig, owner of the Milwaukee Brewers.

Then, in the 1970 agreement, the MLBPA negotiated a significant break-through, a provision for a tripartite grievance arbitration panel with a permanent impartial chairman. This replaced a system under which disputes over the interpretation of the collective bargaining agreement were finally ruled on by the commissioner of baseball.

The more forceful posture of the players' union became apparent in 1972 when the season was delayed ten days as a result of a strike. In the ensuing 1973 agreement, another key change was negotiated by the union. This was a clause providing for determination of players' salaries by neutral arbitrators, if the player and club were unable to come to terms.

When the 1973 collective bargaining agreement expired on December 31, 1975, the parties were unable to come to terms on a replacement until July 1976 (the agreement was made retroactive to January 1). The new contract, in effect through the end of 1979, continued grievance and salary arbitration. An important new provision revised the reserve clause, which previously tied a player to a particular team. Players were thus permitted, under certain conditions, to become free agents, selling their services to the highest bidder.

These accomplishments by the MLBPA established the modern era in labor relations, which has affected all professional team sports. Especially important are the use of grievance arbitration for contract interpretation disputes, salary arbitration, and rules regulating free agency. Each of these collective bargaining agreement provisions was the brainchild of Marvin Miller.[11] A former assistant to the president of the United Steelworkers of America, Miller was known as a creative thinker and had experience as a negotiator before he became executive director of the MLBPA. He took a weak, owner-dominated union and fused its membership into a united front. He not only excelled in winning unprecedented gains at the bargaining table, but managed to preserve those gains from later attack by management. Reggie Jackson and Tom Seaver are among the prominent players who assisted Miller as team representatives during the years in which important breakthroughs were made in collective bargaining.

In 1982 the aging Miller announced his intention to retire as MLBPA executive director. He was replaced by Kenneth Moffett, who as acting director of the Federal Mediation and Conciliation Service had played a peacemaker role during the baseball strike of 1981. The choice seemed a good one, particularly in light of the changing of the guard on the management side. Miller and Ray Grebey were old antagonists. With them guiding the bargaining, future strike possibilities loomed large. Fresh leadership would help the parties move toward a more cooperative relationship that would help ensure labor peace.

About a year after his appointment, however, Moffett was fired by the MLBPA's executive board, ostensibly for his lack of militancy toward management. The MLBPA denied that Miller had anything to do with the decision to fire Moffett. But Moffett believed that Miller orchestrated his ouster. Whatever the case, one matter that created controversy within the union was Moffett's stand on drug abuse. He was a key member of a joint labor-management committee that was drafting guidelines for handling players who commit drug violations. Donald Fehr, the union's general counsel, and Mark Bellanger, Moffett's assistant, opposed Moffett's view that the union should participate in disciplining players for drug abuse. Fehr and Bellanger did not want the union to have a disciplinary role because they preferred to work out problems through the grievance procedure. Their position was consistent with the adage "managements acts, and the union reacts," which describes traditional labor relations. Whether a more proactive role by the MLBPA was a wise solution to a problem that affects both players and management was uncertain at the time, especially since the magnitude of the drug problem had not come to full light. There had been little joint problem solving in baseball, however, and traditional models had not worked out successfully, so it might well have been beneficial to adopt a more cooperative approach.

When Moffett was fired, Miller resumed leadership of the union on an interim basis. His eventual replacement was Donald Fehr, with whom Miller had worked closely for several years. A law school graduate of the University of Missouri, Kansas City, Fehr joined the Kansas City law firm of Jolley, Moran, Walsh, Hager and Gordon, which represents the union. He successfully handled the landmark Andy Messersmith free agency case, which led to his becoming general counsel for the MLBPA in 1977. Fehr has the same astute but often acerbic approach to negotiations as Miller, and the two have kept in close contact. Although Miller continues to influence union policy, his legendary work pace was slowed by a heart attack in 1985. Fehr has proved to be an able successor to Miller, leading the union at the bargaining table and in legal and business matters. Among his major accomplishments are winning the collusion cases against the owners and negotiating agreements with baseball-card companies that raised revenues for the union from $2 million in 1981 to $70 million in 1992.[12] He was roundly criticized, however, for his role in the long shutdown of baseball in 1994–95.

Strike of 1981

The strike is the players' ultimate weapon for achieving negotiation objectives. Because of the multiemployer bargaining structure in baseball, a strike affects all teams in the league. Once playing dates are lost they are difficult, if not impossible, to make up later. A shutdown in the games affects numerous other businesses that derive their revenues in whole or in part from baseball. Television loses a major attraction; concession stands close; and airlines, hotels, restaurants, and bars lose their baseball fan clientele. Before 1981 there had been brief strikes in baseball, but none had a significant effect on regular-season play. Players struck in 1972 over a pension dispute, but the strike resulted in the cancellation of only eighty-six games. In 1976 the owners shut down training camps for seventeen days as a result of an impasse in bargaining over free agency.

Negotiations that ultimately led to the 1981 strike began the previous year with an attempt to reach a new collective bargaining agreement. Under the old agreement the players had solidified their rights to achieve free agency, and the owners were trying to regain greater control over player mobility. The crux of the dispute was compensation for clubs that lost free agents. The owners reasoned that if they could require teams that signed free agents to compensate teams that lost them by replacement with a good player, this would put a crimp on free agency and moderate salary escalation.

A strike appeared imminent before the start of the 1980 season but was headed off when the parties agreed to separate free agency compensation from other bargaining issues. A committee with management and union representatives was created to study free agency. Although an agreement was reached on the other issues, the study committee was unable to resolve the free agency issue. When the owners indicated their intention to put their own compensation plan for free agents into effect, the players announced their intention to strike on May 29, 1981. Meanwhile, the NLRB intervened when the union filed an unfair labor practice charge maintaining that the owners' refusal to disclose financial data was a refusal to bargain in good faith. But when the NLRB went to U.S. District Court to try to get an injunction to postpone the strike for another year, the court refused to grant it.

Because of the legal wrangling to avert the strike, its commencement was delayed until June 12. The owners sought to minimize the effect by purchasing $50 million in strike insurance from Lloyd's of London and by creating a $15 million strike fund from owner contributions in the previous two years. The players had no previously planned insulation from the financial impact of the strike. They relied on player solidarity within the union to make the strike successful. The owners hoped that as the strike went on and the players realized how much they were losing in forgone salaries, they would start warring among themselves. But the players stuck together.

A notable feature of the bargaining that went on during the strike was the acrimonious relationship between union leader Marvin Miller and the owners' chief negotiator, Ray Grebey. They exchanged sharp verbal attacks in the media regularly, which only served to make compromise difficult and prolong the strike. Mediation was attempted by Kenneth Moffett of the Federal Mediation and Conciliation Service, but he made little progress in bringing the hostile negotiators to common ground. What finally created pressure to end the strike was fear that the entire baseball season would be lost.

The strike resulted in the cancellation of 713 games. The strike ended after fifty days when both sides made substantial compromises. Free agency compensation rules were tightened, but the players retained the right to move to other clubs without much market restraint. In effect, the players won the strike, because their salaries continued to increase rapidly.

Attendance and television ratings flagged after the strike, as many fans lost interest in the truncated season. But fears that the strike would do permanent damage to fan interest proved unfounded. With a fresh start in the new season of 1982, attendance reached record levels and the strike faded into history. It is clear that owners, players, and fans all suffered from the strike, and its occurrence became a moderating force against another strike, especially a long one, for a few years anyway.

Player Salaries

Salary Trends

The MLBPA negotiates minimum player salaries and the maximum amount that salaries can be reduced from one year to the next (no more than 20 percent of the previous year or in excess of 30 percent of the salary two years previous). Otherwise, salaries are negotiated by the individual players, often through agents, and team management. The player seeks a salary that is more than adequate to provide sufficient income in his productive years in the game. To most players and their agents, this means the maximum amount obtainable. Although many former players get high-paying jobs in a second career because of their earlier sports affiliation, they try to offset in present salaries the future negative effects on income caused by loss of experience in the nonsport job market.

As shown in Table 2.5, average salaries in baseball have increased dramatically, especially since 1976. The leveling off of salaries in 1987 is largely due to collusion by owners in not signing free agents. This collusion, which was struck down in arbitration, is discussed later in the chapter. The rising salaries in baseball, which reached an average of $1.2 million in 1994, do not appear to reflect qualitative differences in the players. Expansion of the major leagues has brought in a far larger number of players than would have qualified in earlier times. Along with economic factors such as tax advantages to owners, rising

Table 2.5 Major League Baseball Salaries, 1970–94

Year	Average Salary	Percent Change
1970	$ 29,303	—
1971	31,543	7.6
1972	34,092	8.1
1973	36,566	7.3
1974	40,839	11.7
1975	44,676	9.4
1976	51,501	15.3
1977	76,066	47.7
1978	99,876	31.3
1979	113,558	13.7
1980	143,756	26.6
1981	185,651	29.1
1982	241,497	30.1
1983	289,194	19.8
1984	329,408	14.1
1985	371,157	12.7
1986	412,520	11.1
1987	412,454	—
1988	438,729	6.4
1989	497,254	13.3
1990	597,537	20.2
1991	851,492	42.5
1992	1,028,667	20.8
1993	1,116,353	8.5
1994[a]	1,200,000	7.5

[a]The actual average salary was less for this year than
shows in the table because players went on strike on August
12, 1994, causing forfeiture of pay for the remainder of the
season.
Source: Major League Baseball Players Association.

attendance, and lucrative television contracts for the clubs, collective bargaining has been a crucial factor in the salary increases. The opportunity to achieve free agency status, won by the union, has been especially important. Also contributing to the salary increases is the availability of arbitration for determining individual player salaries.

In addition to such circumstances as overall wealth of the team owner, access to free agency, and salary arbitration, several performance factors are important in determining an individual player's salary. One is hitting or pitching performance, measured by various comparative statistical categories. Another is the weight of the player's contribution to team performance, which is more difficult to measure accurately. Number of years in the major leagues carries weight as a seniority and fan recognition factor. Also, acknowledged star or superstar players, whose charisma or clutch performances stand out, command higher salaries.[13] Agents compile computerized information on the players they represent, as well as on comparable players, for use in salary negotiations and arbitrations with owners.

There is a strong correlation between pay and performance, and there is a positive correlation between high salaries and winning teams. A common occurrence is that teams in low-population areas, such as Minnesota, sell, trade, or lose by free agency their good players to high-population areas such as New York. The player is simply worth more to the richer teams than to the poorer ones because of demographics and local television revenues. Contrary to this pattern, however, the New York Yankees, one of the highest paying teams, did not make the playoffs from 1983 to 1993. The Detroit Tigers, Kansas City Royals, Minnesota Twins, Oakland Athletics, and Cincinnati Reds, who won the World Series in 1984, 1985, 1987, 1989, and 1990, respectively, have generally avoided the free agency market and concentrated instead on developing young players in a strong farm system.

Deferred Compensation

Multimillion dollar contracts signed by baseball players have become commonplace in baseball. A large and growing number of players are reaping huge rewards for playing the game. These financial bonanzas are not always what they appear to be on the surface, however, because most of these contracts provide for some form of deferred compensation. Before 1976, multiyear contracts were very rare in baseball. With the signings of free agents under the new rules, teams tried to lock players into longer terms. Instead of receiving all the compensation up front or within a short period, payments may be spread out for ten, twenty, or more years.[14] Players ordinarily receive a guaranteed salary for the period of time that they play. The deferred payments usually start after the player retires from the game. Annual salaries involve direct out-of-pocket costs to the club, but if payments are deferred, the cost to the club is reduced significantly.

Suppose, for example, that a player signs a "ten million dollar" contract providing one million dollars a year spread over ten years. If the team invests the ten million dollars at a 10 percent return, the player would still receive ten million dollars, but the actual cost to the team is reduced dramatically by deferring payments to the player and securing returns from investing the balance of the ten million dollars.

Teams with strong financial positions may opt for high-return investments to fund amounts due players under deferred contracts. Less financially capable teams may use their available funds to keep afloat; therefore they too prefer deferred payments. Aside from helping their cash flow, these teams are in effect mortgaging the future in hope that operating revenues in years to come will cover their contractual debts. Of course, the risk involved for the player who signs a deferred compensation contract without guarantee is that the corporation or person who owns the team will go bankrupt.

The benefits of deferred compensation are not one-sided. Not only do the teams gain, but so can the players. Deferred compensation is taxable in the year it is paid rather than the year it is committed. Assuming a maximum tax bracket for individuals of 50 percent, it may not be in the interest of a player to sign a contract that provides large amounts of income taxed at the maximum rate over a short period. By extending the payments under the contract, the player can receive money after his retirement from baseball, when he would probably be in a lower tax bracket. Also, many professional athletes have trouble hanging on to their money, so deferred payments represent a type of forced savings.

Aside from the potential inability of a team to make long-term payments because of insolvency, another risk for the player is inflation. If deferred payments are not protected against inflation, future compensation may be paid in far cheaper dollars. For this reason, more players are insisting on cost-of-living clauses in their contracts.

Free Agency

Under the reserve clause in baseball, when a player signs a contract he becomes the property of the club. If he is traded or put on waivers, the acquiring club obtains exclusive rights to him. Even if he retires and later decides to return to the game, he is bound to the last club with which he had a contract. Before its modification, the reserve clause was a disincentive for owners to pay high salaries to players. Nearly all contracts were for a single year, which gave players hardly any job or pay security. Bound to a single team, the player had no real alternative but to sign a contract for another year with that team, accepting what the owner was willing to pay. Once players signed a contract with a reserve clause, team owners had monopsony control—there was only one buyer of the player's services.

As a result of grievance arbitration cases in 1974 and 1975, and of negotiated agreements between the MLBPA and owners that followed in 1976 and 1981, the rules obligating a player to remain with a team were altered significantly, and free agency came into being for the first time in any professional sport.

A weakness in the enforcement of a player contract was initially exploited by pitcher Jim Hunter of the Oakland A's. Hunter had agreed with club owner Charles O. Finley that half his 1974 salary would be set aside in an insurance trust. In 1970 the MLBPA had negotiated a provision for grievance arbitration in the collective bargaining agreement with the leagues, so that when the dispute arose between Hunter and Finley over payments into the insurance trust, the matter was brought to arbitration. The chairman of the arbitration panel, Peter Seitz, ruled that Finley had not met the conditions of the agreement and declared Hunter a free agent. Although this decision did not deal directly with the reserve clause, it showed that arbitration gave added protection to players whose contracts were not properly followed. Hunter subsequently signed a five-year contract with the New York Yankees, and the Seitz decision was upheld in court.

In 1975 another ruling by arbitrator Seitz made a direct assault on the reserve clause. The case involved two pitchers, Andy Messersmith of the Los Angeles Dodgers and Dave McNally of the Baltimore Orioles. These players contended that since they had played with their clubs for one year without a contract, their employment status could not be further extended unilaterally by the clubs. Seitz agreed, declaring the players free agents. The owners promptly fired Seitz and appealed his decision to the federal courts, contending that he had exceeded his authority as an arbitrator by nullifying the reserve system. But the arbitration decision was upheld.

Because the reserve clause was overturned, the team owners were eager to regain at least some limitation on the players' right to become free agents. Thus, the owners sought and won a provision in the 1976 collective bargaining agreement with the MLBPA that players must have had at least six years of major league service before they could become free agents, and that the clubs would draft free agents in reverse order of team standings. Still, the bargaining power of the players remained far greater than it had been under the earlier reserve clause and before free agency.

At the start of the 1976 season, approximately one hundred fifty players were unsigned. Many were seeking to become free agents at the end of the season, so that they could sign a contract with the highest bidder. Contrary to predictions, however, most of these players signed contracts during the season. By the end of the 1976 season, twenty-four out of the six hundred players in the major leagues had become free agents. This led to a much-publicized financial bonanza for some players, who profited from a bidding war among clubs for their services. In 1977, three players received multi-year contracts for more than $2 million each. Most observers thought that the salaries in the second reentry draft would be moderated, yet several of the thirty-five free agents drafted in the 1978 season were able to get contracts that greatly exceeded the previous levels.

In the first and second reentry drafts, the two teams spending the most money for free agents were the New York Yankees and California Angels, both located in heavily populated areas. In a fifteen-month period, the Yankees spent an estimated $9 million for four free agents. The Yankees were the major league champions in 1977, but the Angels had a mediocre year, largely because of injuries sustained by key free agent draftees.

As a result of the fifty-day baseball strike of 1981 and subsequent collective bargaining agreement, management and the players negotiated changes in the rules for compensation of teams that lose free agents. They were changed again as a result of the 1985 players' strike. Before these changes, the only compensation required for signing a free agent under the 1976 agreement was giving up a choice in the amateur draft. Under the 1982 rules, free agents were ranked as either A or B players, depending on performance. Players rated in the top 20 percent at their position were rated A. Players in the top 21 to 30 percent were rated B. If a player had gone through the reentry draft before or had twelve years of major league service, he was exempt from the rankings.

If a team signed an A-rated free agent, it was required to compensate the team that lost the free agent with a roster player chosen from a pool of unprotected players (only twenty-four players could be protected by each team). In addition, the team that lost a free agent got an extra choice in the amateur draft. When a B-rated free agent was signed, the team that lost the player got two extra choices in the draft of amateur players. Up to five clubs were allowed to exempt themselves from contributing to the compensation pool by agreeing not to draft any A-rated players for three years. The number of free agents who were classified as A or B was not large. This was because only the top 30 percent of the players were classified, and most of these did not opt for free agency in a given year.

The 1982 free agency rules were complex and, in some cases, inequitable. They had little effect in restraining player movement. Perhaps most important, the owners continued to face rapidly escalating salaries. Therefore, in 1985 the rules for free agency were gain changed at the bargaining table. Compensation for teams that lose free agents was eliminated. The reentry draft, in existence since free agency began in 1976, was abolished. Thus, under the new rules, any team is able to sign a free agent without having to select negotiating rights; however, if a free agent's former team wants to retain negotiating rights to him, it must agree to go to salary arbitration with him if he chooses.

The thrust of the new rules is that they lift virtually all impediments to a six-year veteran player's becoming a free agent except the need to fulfill the terms of an existing contract. When that contract expires, the player is free to test the market with other clubs interested in signing him, without the constraint that compensation to his old club entailed. Wide-open free agency in baseball has caused a rapid increase in the number of "lifetime" contracts for outstanding players. These contracts will keep these players with their clubs for the remainder of their careers, unless the clubs decide to trade them.

The players have been the chief beneficiaries from free agency. As indicated in Table 2.5, salaries started to boom after 1976, when the opportunity for free agency affected a large number of players. They have used their new bargaining muscle to help increase salaries by more than twenty-three-fold since then. Individual players have also been able to force other changes in how the game is run. Multiyear contracts, providing greater financial and job security, have become commonplace.[16] Players also have gained more control over their financial destinies by winning contract clauses stating that they can be traded only to certain teams in large cities and thus providing for fatter future contracts. There is also some evidence that free agency has reduced salary discrimination based on race.[16]

Is free agency good or bad for the fans? Some fans argue that players are disloyal to their teams and that, with players more able to move about, there is no longer team continuity. Typically, however, it is about as common for a free agent to re-sign with his team as to move to another club. Many fans take a great deal of interest in the publicity surrounding free agent signings. Although fans become attached to players, what they really want is winning players, with whom they find immediate allegiance. Also, there is a long history in baseball of outstanding players moving from team to team. In fact, the advent of free agency has not caused more movement between teams. Leonard Koppett points out that from 1951 through 1977, under the old reserve system, an average of 4.7 players per club changed teams, mostly through trades; from 1978 through 1992, the average number of switches was 4.6.[17] This suggests that today's players are at least as loyal to their teams as the teams of yesteryear were to their players. Still, while free agent players may remain with their clubs, it is questionable whether their loyalty is to the team or to the dollars they get for staying.

Collusion

In 1987 arbitrator Tom Roberts made the most important decision since the *Messersmith* case. Although Roberts's decision on free agency does not have direct application to other sports, it establishes a significant precedent that should influence determination of subsequent cases on the same basic issue. How did all this happen, and why is it important?

Table 2.5 indicates the speed with which baseball salaries rose in the late 1970s and early 1980s; the increases were double-digit each year. These labor costs were of great concern to owners, who had themselves to blame for spending millions of dollars signing free agents. To slow the salary escalation, something had to be done to reduce substantially the opportunity for players to sell their services to the highest bidder. If there was no bidding for free agents, players would have to take what their old club would offer, which would be far less than on the open market.

At the end of the 1985 season, sixty-two players became free agents. Under the rules of the collective bargaining agreement, clubs that want to retain their free agent players must file for salary arbitration by December 7. The player must reply by December 19. If the player agrees to arbitrate, he will remain with his old club at whatever salary is determined by the arbitrator. The next important date is January 8, because if the player remains unsigned at that time, the club loses the right to sign the player until May 1. Meanwhile, the player can sign with other clubs as a free agent.

What happened in 1985 was that nearly all the free agents (fifty-seven out of sixty-two) wound up signing with their old clubs. Although some interest was expressed in free agents by other clubs, the offers were relatively low. Among the top free agents—pitchers Donnie Moore and Joe Niekro, catcher Carlton Fisk, and outfielder Kirk Gibson—none received significant offers from other clubs. In response to what appeared to be a collusive arrangement among the owners, the MLBPA filed a grievance.

The union was fortunate in having contract language to point to on its allegation of collusion. Paragraph H of article XVIII of the Basic Agreement is entitled "Individual Nature of Rights" and reads,

> The utilization or non-utilization of rights under this Article XVII is an individual matter to be determined solely by each Player and each Club for his or its own benefit. Players shall not act in concert with other Players and Clubs shall not act in concert with other Clubs.[18]

Ironically, this language was originally proposed by the clubs during negotiations in 1976, because the clubs were wary of free agent players joining together to sell their services in a package deal. When the MLBPA insisted that the clubs be subject to the same constraint, and the clubs agreed, the language was incorporated into the collective bargaining agreement.

In seeking to justify its allegation of conspiracy, the MLBPA argued that no club would turn its back on a free agent unless other clubs did the same. The union cited meetings at which Commissioner Ueberroth lectured the owners on the fiscal foolishness of signing high-priced free agents. Reference was also made to reports of the owners' Player Relations Committee to the effect that the high salaries paid to free agents often led to poor performance. The owners denied a conspiracy, however, and argued that the slowdown in free agent signings was nothing more than a predictable evolution toward a more rational marketplace. Moreover, argued the owners, each club made independent decisions on signing free agents.

Arbitrator Roberts determined that the clubs had colluded to avoid signing free agents. He placed particular emphasis on the fact that several clubs that had expressed interest in 1985 free agents had abruptly changed their position after a series of league meetings that emphasized fiscal responsibility and the need for more self-discipline.[19] In effect, the owners were the victims of their own profligacy in the past. Had it not been for this prior generosity in signing free agents, the owners' sudden turn away from the market would not have seemed so unusual. As it was, the contrast was what made the MLBPA's case so strong.

Roberts's decision is important because it reopened the free agency market and created pressure for higher salaries. Kirk Gibson of the Detroit Tigers was declared a free agent by Roberts's decision and a few days later signed a three-year $4.5 million contract with the Los Angeles Dodgers. Gibson thus became the first free agent in three years to sign with a new team for more money than his old team offered. Roberts's decision is also important because of its influence on grievances decided by other arbitrators on free agent collusion during the 1986 and 1987 seasons.

With the Roberts decision as a precedent, it was not surprising that the arbitrator in the second and third collusion cases found the same result. Both cases were decided by arbitrator George Nicolau. An interesting issue in the third arbitration concerned the owners' establishment of an "information bank" under the auspices of the Player Relations Committee, to exchange information on offers to free agents. The owners argued that they had a right to share information on free agents, just as their agent representatives do. Nicolau disagreed, however, finding that by its very nature the information bank was intended to affect free agent salaries and therefore intruded on the free agency process. The key to all three arbitration cases was interpretation of the collusion language in the collective bargaining agreement and the application of that language to the actions of owners in light of the chill on the signing of free agents that resulted from the owners' collusion.

Altogether, the owners wound up having to pay $280 million for the collusion violations. The original arbitration awards totaled $113 million, but the figure was swollen by interest costs and lost-salary compensation for 1989 and 1990, following the collusion period. The filing deadline for claims by individual players was May 20, 1991. Some 3,173 claims were filed by 843 current and former players, and the total claims were for $1.3 billion. Many of the claims, however, were disallowed by the arbitrators. Some players therefore received nothing, while other players were awarded as much as $2 million. Following the collusion decisions, average player salaries resumed their rapid climb for several years, as shown in Table 2.5, but in 1993 the rate of increase again began to moderate. The owners have had to sign more free agents to avoid further charges of collusion, but they have not returned to the free agent frenzy of the pre-1985 period.

Salary Arbitration

In the 1973 collective bargaining agreement a key provision affecting player salaries was introduced—salary arbitration. Salary arbitration was first used for the 1974 season and has been continued in subsequent agreements. Under this arrangement, if the team owner and player do not reach agreement on salary, the dispute is submitted to an impartial arbitrator for final decision. Although salary arbitration is also used in professional hockey, a distinguishing feature of baseball arbitration is that the arbitrator is required to choose either the player's demand or the ballclub's offer, with no compromise between the two positions. For example, if the player asks for $1.4 million and the team owner offers $1.2 million, the arbitrator must choose one figure or the other, not something in between.

To be eligible for salary arbitration, the player must have a total of two years plus of major league experience (until 1987, only two years' experience was required). Submission to arbitration is made between January 15 and 25, and hearings are held from February 1 to 20, with one day of hearing scheduled for each case. Each party is limited to one hour for initial presentation and a half-hour for rebuttal and summation. Arbitration decisions are due within twenty-four hours of the close of hearing. Instead of the customary written opinion, arbitrators are allowed only to write in the salary figure they choose on the duplicate copies of the Uniform Player's Contract provided them and to mail the copies to the appropriate league office. Arbitration provides only one-year contracts.

The criteria for the arbitrator's decision are (1) the player's contribution during the past season, including overall performance, special qualities of leadership, and public appeal; (2) length and consistency of career contribution; (3) past compensation; (4) comparative baseball salaries; (5) existence of any physical or mental defects; and (6) recent performance of the club.

The arbitration clause provides that the arbitrator shall not consider the financial position of the player or club, press comments or testimonials, offers made before arbitration, costs of representation, or salaries in other sports or occupations. The player and club divide equally the cost of the arbitration hearing.

Arbitration decisions in baseball are summarized in Table 2.6. No cases were decided in 1976, because negotiations for a new contract were not concluded until after the season began, or in 1977, because all the players whose contracts expired before the season began were eligible for free agency. The table shows that

Table 2.6. Arbitration in Major League Baseball, 1974–94

Year	Arbitration Awards	For the Player	For the Club
1974	29	13	16
1975	16	6	10
1978[a]	9	2	7
1979	14	8	6
1980	26	15	11
1981	21	11	10
1982	22	8	14
1983	30	13	17
1984	10	4	6
1985	13	6	7
1986	35	15	20
1987	26	10	16
1988	18	7	11
1989	12	7	5
1990	24	14	10
1991	17	6	11
1992	20	9	11
1993	18	6	12
1994	16	6	10
Total	376	166	210

[a]No cases were heard in 1976 and 1977.
Sources: Data for 1974–83 from Major League Baseball Player Relations Committee; 1984–94 data from various issues of *Sporting News*.

the owners have won more cases than the players over the years (210 versus 166). But even in situations where players lose in arbitration, they nearly always wind up getting a far greater salary than they were paid in the previous year.

An interesting area for inquiry is the effect that the arbitration process has on negotiations. In theory, the final-offer feature is designed to stimulate negotiations. Under the conventional method of arbitration in wage determination cases, the arbitrator is empowered to compromise between the positions of the parties. That is, if the union wants a 10 percent increase and the employer offers 6 percent, the arbitrator can choose something in between the two positions, say 7 or 8 percent. This method can reduce the parties' incentive to compromise in negotiations because they anticipate that the arbitrator may wind up splitting the difference. Thus, the more realistic of the parties may wind up losing to the side that budged the least. This is known as the chilling effect, since the possibility of compromise by the arbitrator between the positions of the parties reduces their desire to move toward accommodation.

In contrast, final-offer arbitration would seem to encourage the parties to compromise in negotiations because the arbitrator is confined to selecting one or the other position. If either side gets too far out of line, the other's position will be adopted by the arbitrator. Because of an incentive to be as realistic as possible, i.e., wanting to win in arbitration, the parties may reach a common ground through negotiation and eliminate the need for arbitration altogether.

Evidence from the experience with final-offer arbitration in public employment labor disputes tends to support the theory that it reduces the chilling effect and thus preserves negotiations.[20] What does the experience in baseball indicate? A study by James Dworkin found that, considering the large number of salaries that are negotiated between players and clubs each year, the number of arbitration decisions is comparatively small,[21] so that if there is a chilling effect in baseball arbitration, it is minor. More recently, a study by John Fizel determined that the relative spread between the club's salary offer and the player's salary offer has stayed fairly constant over the years.[22] On the other hand, the filing rate for arbitration has increased significantly. Fizel found that in the first five years of salary arbitration the filing rate was 15 percent, in the middle years it was 51 percent, and in the last five years 83 percent.[23] Thus, while the number of arbitration decisions and spread between offers remain small, more players are using the threat of arbitration to force a favorable outcome in negotiations.

Salary arbitration has increased player bargaining power by giving players an alternative in situations in which they would otherwise have to settle for what the team is willing to pay them. Free agency's upward pull on salaries has caused the awards in arbitration to rise; higher arbitration settlements, in turn, reflect on what free agents are able to command in the market. The spiraling effects of free agency and salary arbitration account for most of the escalation of player salaries in recent years.

1985 Negotiations

The Basic Agreement between the leagues and players' association expired on December 31, 1984. Negotiations began in mid-November with hopes that a new contract could be reached before spring training in April 1985. The predominant issue in the talks was distribution of the six-year $1.125 billion television package that began in 1984. Approximately one-third of the monies under the previous television contract had gone into the players' pension fund. In 1983, for example, the contribution amounted to $15.5 million. Under the new television contract, annual revenues increased fourfold, so that if the one-third practice was continued, the contribution to the pension fund would rise to about $60 million a year. The owners believed that the pension fund was already quite generous, and they were counting on retaining a larger proportion of the television monies to ensure profitability of club operations.

While the distribution of television revenues was by far the number-one issue, several other points of contention arose. One was the free agency compensation rule, which caused the 1981 strike. The union was dissatisfied with the operation of this rule, despite substantial amounts received by some free agents, and the owners wanted to increase the compensation required for teams that lose free agents. The union vowed to fight any retrenchment in players' free agency rights. Another issue was salary arbitration, which the union wanted to change to allow players to use the procedure after one year of service instead of the existing eligibility of two years. The owners wanted to increase the eligibility requirement for salary arbitration to three years. The union sought an increase in minimum salaries. An issue pushed by the owners was expansion of the maximum number of playoff games from five to seven games (the same number as the World Series), which the union countered with demands for a share of revenues resulting from the expanded number of games.

The high hopes for an early settlement were dashed by several events that intruded on negotiations. First, the parties delayed getting their demands on the table, a problem that has plagued baseball and other sports. The parties played a cat-and-mouse game of waiting for the other side to make its move. Another problem was that shortly after negotiations began, Houston Astros owner John McMullen commented publicly that union leaders had too much control over the players. This is the kind of ill-considered remark, characteristic of some sports owners, that accomplishes nothing except to antagonize the union. The baseball owners later had to recant collectively by stating that McMullen's views did not reflect those of management in general. Then there was the flap over an attempt by the Los Angeles Dodgers to provide for mandatory drug testing in the contracts of some of its players. Although this dispute blew over quickly when the union forced withdrawal of the provision from the player contracts, it caused another delay in negotiations.

A more troublesome interruption occurred in February when the owners requested a moratorium on talks in order to review a "serious financial situation." This was a familiar story, with the owners pleading poverty in response to union demands. Despite requests by the union in the past, the owners had persistently refused to open their books. Although the legality of such refusals had not been fully tested for baseball, it was well known from NLRB precedent that the National Labor Relations Act requires management to show proof of financial problems if it claims inability to pay. Supposedly, twenty-two of the twenty-six teams in the major leagues were losing money, but which teams and how much was unknown to the union. Probably in recognition of the need for compliance with the law, Commissioner Ueberroth urged the owners to open their books to the MLBPA. When the owners provided team financial data to the union, a dispute arose over interpretation of the data. Both the owners and the union hired outside consultants to review the data. The reports of the consultants— Roger Noll, a Stanford University economics professor acting for the union, and George Sorter, a New York University accounting professor acting for the owners—were inconclusive. Sorter found the losses to be $27 million rather than the $43 million originally claimed by the owners. Noll did not provide an overall assessment, but found with few exceptions that the teams were profitable, averaging $1 to $2 million per team. It did appear, however, that the financial problems of the owners were likely to worsen in the future unless some kind of limit was placed on expenditures. This limit was proposed by the owners in the form of a salary cap, which would limit high-paying clubs from signing free agents. But this proposal was later dropped by the owners when Commissioner Ueberroth indicated his opposition to the idea.

As negotiations dragged on with limited progress, the players voted against striking the All-Star game in July, but overwhelmingly supported the MLBPA executive board's recommendation to strike on August 6, 1985. There was speculation that Ueberroth might force the owners into a settlement by invoking a clause in baseball's charter to act in the "best interests of the game." The commissioner, however, prudently stayed on the sidelines while encouraging the parties to work hard to achieve a settlement. As the strike deadline approached, negotiations intensified. These discussions centered on two issues: the owner's contribution to the players' benefit plan, which covers pensions and health insurance, and the length of time required for salary arbitration eligibility.

Although no one really wanted a strike, the players walked out on August 6. The parties, however, had been close to agreement at the time, and after just two days, the strike was settled with little cost to the public image of the sport. Most of the games lost were made up later, and the strike had no significant impact on the continuity of the season.

In the end, both sides gave in to get a five-year compromise agreement that was to expire in 1989. The players gained mostly from the increased contribution of monies to their benefit plan, with the owners agreeing to contribute $196 million over six years. While the players' share of national television revenue dropped from the previous 33 percent to 18 percent, they more than doubled the dollar contributions. A ten-year player would receive a pension of about $90,000 annually at age sixty-two. The owners prevailed on their key salary arbitration demand, so that players had to wait three years instead of the previously required two years before being able to arbitrate their salaries. Minimum salaries were increased from $40,000 to $60,000, with cost-of-living increases for future years.

Another important feature of the agreement was that a $20 million fund was established from network television revenues to aid disadvantaged clubs in smaller cities that were losing the most money. Graduated payments are now made to the players' benefit plan, since clubs no longer contribute equally. The amounts paid by clubs are based on attendance and television market size.

At the very least, Commissioner Ueberroth was instrumental in acting as a catalyst to settling the strike quickly, by prodding the negotiators to keep talking. Perhaps the real hero was Lee MacPhail, whose calm and kindly persuasiveness helped placate the owners he represented. Although it is unfortunate that the strike occurred, all the principals deserve credit for keeping the negotiations gentlemanly and avoiding the stridency and acrimony of the past. Regrettably, this civility did not continue.

The Lockout of 1990

The thirty-two day lockout of baseball players from spring training camps by team owners in 1990 caused a renewed sense of frustration among fans. Once again, the great American pastime was shut down by a labor dispute.[24]The principal issues on the bargaining table during the 1990 negotiations are summarized below. The three major positions of the owners were especially controversial because they proposed a radical restructuring of the Basic Agreement. Perhaps their most palatable demand from the players' standpoint was for revenue sharing. Because each side would gain from increases in revenue, there would be mutual incentive to expand the size of the pie. Revenue sharing would also promote financial stability on the downside. That is, should income decrease, say as a result of a serious economic recession, salaries would moderate along with revenues so that clubs would not be caught in a financial squeeze. A related advantage, more to the benefit of the owners than of the players, would be cost certainty, allowing for more accurate planning of budgets and league expansion.

Owners' Proposals

Players would be guaranteed 48 percent of revenue from ticket sales and national and local radio and television contracts, which would make up about 82 percent of owners' total revenue.

A pay-for-performance system, in which players with zero to six years experience would be paid on the basis of seniority and performance based on statistical formulas. Each team would pay 1/26th of the total, and multiyear contracts would not be allowed.

A salary cap limiting the total amount of salary any team could pay to players. Players with six years or more experience would still be free agents, but they could not be signed by a particular team if doing so would put that team over the salary limit.

Players' Proposals

Eligibility for salary arbitration restored to players with only two years of major league experience.

A raise in minimum salary from the current $68,000 to $125,000.

Continuation of the current formula fixing owners' contributions to the benefit plan (pensions and health insurance) at about one-third of television revenues from the All-Star game, league playoffs, and the World Series. This would work out to about $83 million a year for the owners' contribution.

Triple damages for collusion, and language protecting the players' union from future collusion by the team owners.

An increase in roster size to twenty-five players from the current twenty-four.

Implications of the Proposals

The owners' proposal on pay-for-performance was tantamount to establishment of a wage scale for players in the first six years. It would have had the effect of eliminating salary arbitration. Apart from the seniority factor, salaries would be determined by statistical formulas based on performance in the player's previous two seasons. Players would be separated into four categories for statistical purposes: (1) starting pitchers; (2) relief pitchers; (3) outfielders, third basemen, first basemen, and designated hitters; and (4) catchers, second basemen, and shortstops. While a creative idea, this proposal had virtually no chance of acceptance by the players. There are too many variables involved in performance. For example, pitchers in small ballparks like Boston's Fenway Park would be at a great disadvantage compared with those in larger parks like Busch Stadium in St. Louis. Also, no account was taken in the formulas of defensive performance or intangibles like character and sacrifice for the benefit of the team, nor was there a precise indication of how salaries would be computed.

The salary cap was proposed to protect teams in smaller markets, such as Milwaukee and Minnesota, from having their free agent players bought up by prosperous teams in New York and Los Angeles. Teams in large cities would be unable to control the market for star players because the salary cap would limit the number of highly paid players they could sign. Teams spend considerable amounts of money in developing young players. A salary cap would discourage free agency and enable a team to retain more of its quality players, thus yielding a greater return on investment.

In 1985 the owners contended that their financial considerations necessitated an increase in the length of time required for eligibility for salary arbitration from two years to three years. The players' union agreed to this change, making players wait the extra year. But the owners' profits subsequently soared to high levels. With the recent increases in television coverage guaranteeing future revenues, the players wanted the eligibility requirement moved back to two years. This issue became a major stumbling block for the negotiators.

The initial negotiating session was held on November 29, 1989, shortly before the Basic Agreement was scheduled to expire at the end of the year. Little progress was made in the early talks. This is typical of negotiations in professional sports. It seems that a strike deadline or start of the regular season must be impending before negotiators become serious about their task. By mid-February 1990, with spring training two weeks away, Commissioner Vincent began to sit in on negotiations. Realizing a threat to the opening of training camps, because of a possible lockout by the owners, Vincent made several proposals to get the talks moving.

It was not an easy decision for Vincent to become involved. As commissioner of baseball, he is hired and paid by the owners, but he is also responsible for acting in the "best interests" of the game. Failing to try to prevent a lockout or strike would not fulfill that responsibility. While the top management official usually stays in the background during labor-management talks and allows the negotiator to make the deal, there was some precedent for involvement by the commissioner. Commissioner Kuhn had ordered camps to open in 1976 (and was later criticized for not doing more to end the 1981 strike). Commissioner Peter Ueberroth's mediation was helpful in holding the 1985 strike to only two days.

Three of Commissioner Vincent's proposals became the focus of attention: (1) minimum salaries of $75,000, $125,000, and $200,000 for players in their first three years, with a 75 percent cap on increases in salary arbitration; (2) a two-year study commission on revenue sharing, and reopener of the four-year Basic Agreement after two years; and (3) no increase in the players' benefit plan. Vincent helped narrow the issues in dispute. Shortly after hearing his proposals, the owners dropped their demands for revenue sharing, pay-for-performance, and salary cap. Given the groundbreaking nature of these demands, especially in light of baseball's success under the old system, they would have eventually been discarded. Vincent's proposals accelerated this process while allowing the owners to save face.

Meanwhile, on February 15, a lockout occurred when the owners refused to open training camps. Why did the owners resort to this tactic? Although lockouts account for only about 5 to 8 percent of all work stoppages, their frequency is rising. The owners used the lockout mainly as an offensive weapon, to pressure the players into an early settlement. Certain kinds of lockouts may not be legal, such as those calculated to "bust" a union. But, in 1965, the U.S. Supreme Court had held that a company did not violate the Taft-Hartley Act when, after reaching impasse in negotiations, it shut down its plant to put pressure on a union that was threatening to strike during the company's busiest season.[25] Although this case is the leading precedent on the subject of lockouts, its applicability to the baseball lockout was clouded by uncertainty over whether impasse had been reached and the fact that the players' union had not threatened to strike.

Were the owners to start the season after reaching impasse and without an agreement, they would have been able at some later time, perhaps at the end of the season, to impose employment terms unilaterally on the players.

Therefore, the players would almost certainly have had to strike to achieve an agreement before the 1990 season ended. Such a strike—say, in August—would hurt the owners because they derive most of their income from television contracts late in the season, based on revenues from the league playoffs and World Series. Thus, by locking out the players to precipitate an agreement, the owners were defending themselves against a strike later on.

Now that the principal bargaining demands of the owners were off the table, it seemed logical to assume that an agreement would quickly follow. The owners were enjoying unprecedented success with five consecutive years of record attendance and a generous new television deal. Player salaries were averaging $600,000. Why kill the golden goose? With the owners' retreat, however, the union realized that power had shifted dramatically in its favor. At this point, perhaps too greedily, the union made a stand on reducing eligibility for salary arbitration from three years to two years.

In effect, the players got some of what they wanted on salary arbitration and the owners did not give up that much on the benefit fund increase. Key features of the 1990 Basic Agreement follow:

- *Salary arbitration*—Eligibility for the top 17 percent of players with two to three years of major league service.
- *Benefit fund*—Increased owners' contribution to $55 million annually.
- *Minimum salary*—Raised from $68,000 to $100,000.

- *Roster size*—Increased from twenty-four to twenty-five in 1991.
- *Collusion*—Language prohibiting collusion and providing for triple damages.
- *Reopener*—Either side may reopen the four-year contract on major economic issues after three years.

Because agreement was not reached until March 19, the requisite three weeks of spring training delayed the start of the season from April 2 to April 9. This would have cut the full season of 162 games to 158. However, Commissioner Vincent was able to work out an agreement with CBS to push back the start of postseason play so that the postponed games could be made up. Avoidance of a shortened season preserved the sanctity of individual and team performances, which is especially important to baseball purists.

1994–95 Strike

The mother of all sports strikes lasted 232 days, ruining one season and cutting into another. In the end, everything had happened yet nothing really changed. Despite all the monetary losses by both sides, all the maneuvering, all the damage to the game, the collective bargaining agreement remained as is. The agreement will, of course, eventually be changed. But, to the surprise of many, the 1995 season began with the status quo. How did it get back to square one?

The four-year negotiated agreement following the 1990 lockout allowed for a reopener by either side after three years. The first shot in the war was fired when the owners voted in December 1992 to reopen contract negotiations. By this time the owners could see the writing on the wall for the upcoming television contract renewals. CBS and ESPN had lost a bundle of money, and a shortfall in new revenue from television was imminent. The other concern to the owners was that they had overcommitted on salaries. The crunch from high costs in the face of lower anticipated national television revenues would be particularly hard on small-market teams, because they did not have the offsetting local television revenues. A fix was necessary, and revenue sharing, with big-market teams channeling part of their revenues to their less fortunate brethren, looked like at least part of the answer. But the owners also wanted to do something to control labor costs, and they wanted the players to help them do it. Predictably, negotiations went nowhere, but at least the 1993 season was played without interruption.

Early in 1994 the owners agreed to revenue sharing among themselves but made this agreement contingent on the players' acceptance of a salary cap.

Details of the owners' bargaining position became clear in midyear, eighteen months after negotiations were reopened, when the owners proposed a fifty-fifty split of total revenues with the players, with no team to have a payroll of more than 110 percent of the average and no team less than 84 percent of the average. Players with fewer than four years of service would receive an escalating scale of minimum salaries. The owners also proposed elimination of salary arbitration but offered to liberalize free agency by allowing players to become free agents after four years instead of the current six. There was no way the players would accept the proposal, since it was so late in coming and put forth such radical changes. The union's main counterpoint was that the owners should share revenues among themselves without linking it to a plan that would cap salaries and cost the players an estimated $1.7 billion over seven years.

The owners, however, were more committed than ever. Their negotiator, Richard Ravitch, claimed that nineteen of the twenty-eight clubs were losing money. Still, no serious negotiations took place, just posturing in the media. Inevitably, then, on August 12, 1994, the players struck. The strike came at a propitious time for the players, who had secured most of their pay for the season, but was costly to the owners, who faced a huge loss for cancellation of post-season play. Fans, caught in the middle, were especially disappointed because the 1994 season was one of the most interesting in years with tight races and several players chasing individual performance records. Unfortunately, despite attempts by federal mediators to broker a settlement, the strike carried through the end of the season, causing cancellation of the World Series for the first time in ninety years.

After more fruitless negotiations, the owners proposed a payroll or luxury tax which would penalize teams that spent more than a certain amount on salaries. For every $500,000 that a club spent on salaries above the average payroll of the twenty-eight teams, the club would be taxed 1 percent of its total payroll. This proposal, although not technically a salary cap because it allowed free spending, would restrain spending on payrolls. The tax revenues would then be shared with small-market teams with lower payrolls. Another change in negotiations was that President Bill Clinton got the parties to accept William J. Usery, Jr., as a mediator. Usery, former head of the Federal Mediation and Conciliation Service and secretary of labor, is the top labor troubleshooter in the nation. In recent years he has worked some of the biggest disputes, involving Eastern Airlines and its unions, and Pittston Coal and the United Mine Workers.

Early in 1995 President Clinton urged the parties to put aside their differences. Instead, however, the owners decided to try to break the strike by hiring replacement players, similar to what occurred during the 1987 strike in football. The union tentatively accepted the owners' revenue-sharing formula and made its own luxury tax proposal of a 25 percent tax on team payrolls of

$54 million or more. The owners, however, wanted a 50 percent tax on only $40.7 million in payroll. President Clinton tried to turn up the pressure by bringing owner and player representatives to the White House. He also established a deadline for settlement of February 7, and when it was not met he asked Usury to offer recommendations for ending the strike, which the president would then present to Congress for acceptance. Congress, however, was not inclined to take action. Both Senate majority leader Robert Dole and Speaker of the House Newt Gingrich indicated that the strike was a private labor dispute of the sort that Congress should not intercede in. On the other hand, various legislators were more positive about repealing baseball's antitrust exemption as a way to stimulate negotiations.

Meanwhile, legal action was developing that would end the strike. The MLBPA filed unfair labor practice charges with the NLRB on several grounds. When the NLRB indicated that it was prepared to issue a complaint against the owners on the salary cap proposal, the owners withdrew the cap from the bargaining table. Later, the general counsel of the NLRB, Fred Feinstein, indicated he would ask the five-member NLRB to seek a court injunction forcing owners to restore salary arbitration and an open market for free agent players, which the owners allegedly illegally blocked. Union leader Fehr said he would recommend that the players end the strike if the injunction was issued. But then the possibility of a lockout would arise, as the owners might want to keep the pressure on to break the union's resolve and get it to agree on the owners' terms.

The NLRB voted three to two to seek an injunction, and U.S. District Court judge Sonia Sotomayor ruled in New York that she would issue the injunction because failure to do so would irreparably harm players. Judge Sotomayor reasoned that the restrictions imposed by the owners on the free agency system should not have been unilaterally imposed until there was a good faith impasse reached at the bargaining table. In effect, the court ruling restored the provisions of the collective bargaining agreement. When the union announced its intention to end the strike, the owners decided not to continue the stoppage by imposing a lockout. The negotiations continued, however, and the possibility of a future work stoppage over the disputed issues loomed large.

In the end the owners and players lost heavily and a severe blow was dealt to the game in that many fans were disaffected by the long strike, which far exceeded prior interruptions in any sport. On the bright side, the 1995 season began on April 25 with real major league players, not replacements, although only 144 of the regular-season 162 games were played. Another piece of good news that came out during the strike was that baseball added two new teams for the 1998 season—the Arizona Diamondbacks and the Tampa Bay Devil Rays—expanding the sport to thirty teams. Each team was charged an expansion fee of $130 million, up 42 percent from the last expansion fee in 1990.

Umpires' Strikes

Officials in professional team sports are well organized into associations that negotiate with management over a variety of work-related issues. Only in football have officials maintained a relatively quiescent role in dealings with the leagues that employ them. Basketball and hockey referees have gone on strike, and baseball umpires struck in 1970, 1979, and 1991. In each of the umpires' strikes play was disrupted, and after the settlements a residue of bitterness remained, especially against fellow umpires (mostly from the minor leagues) who acted as scabs by crossing picket lines to officiate games. For several years the sixty-man Major League Umpires Association has been represented by a Philadelphia lawyer named Richie Phillips. In the 1984 negotiations with the association, the management bargainers were league presidents Charles Feeney (National League) and Bobby Brown (American League), and at issue was the amount of postseason pay for umpires and how it would be distributed. At the time, umpires received $10,000 for the playoff games and $15,000 for World Series games for a total cost to the leagues of $210,000. Only umpires who worked these events were paid. The umpires asked not only for a sizable increase in pay but also that the monies go into a pool that would be in part distributed to umpires who did not officiate postseason games. They argued that favoritism influenced the merit system selection of umpires for postseason play and that a pool system would provide a more equitable arrangement.

At the outset of the playoffs, just after Ueberroth became commissioner, the umpires went on strike. Bowie Kuhn had forsworn involvement in negotiations when he was commissioner, and Ueberroth initially indicated his intention to do the same. The job description of the commissioner was changed, however, when Ueberroth took office and allowed him to take a more active role in labor relations. Moreover, pressure began to build as playoff games were officiated by minor league umpires. When Phillips asked Ueberroth to intercede in the strike, he was initially reluctant to encroach on the authority of Feeney and Brown, who had greater familiarity with the issues in dispute. Later, when all the negotiators agreed to request Ueberroth to arbitrate the impasse, he acted quickly to bring the parties together for a hearing. This arbitration resolved the issues, and the umpires returned to work for the fifth and final game of the National League playoffs (the American League playoffs lasted just three games, all of which were umpired by minor league officials).

In his arbitration decision, Ueberroth gave the umpires only slightly less than what they wanted. A pool was created for sharing revenues among umpires not working postseason games. Despite what appears to be a one-sided decision in favor of the umpires. Ueberroth was lauded by nearly all observers from both sides, who regarded his ability to resolve the dispute as evidence of strong leadership. One critic was Donald Fehr, director of the players' association, who questioned the commissioner's neutrality in a labor dispute. Fehr was probably apprehensive about the commissioner's role in the forthcoming owner-player negotiations.

Another strike was threatened by umpires in 1985 over the issue of extra pay for the expanded best-of-seven playoffs. The strike was averted when the parties chose former president Richard M. Nixon, a longtime baseball fan, to arbitrate the dispute. Nixon's decision, his first as an arbitrator, granted a 40 percent salary increase to umpires, which was the same as the percentage increase in the number of games in the league championship series. Although strike talk was again in the air in 1987, the umpires' union agreed to a four-year contract that increased salaries by 25 percent.

Umpires struck briefly in 1991, affecting spring training and opening day of the regular season. The dispute was essentially over salaries and benefits and the postseason merit system. The latter issue became important because under the rotation system in effect from 1987 through 1990, an umpire was guaranteed at least one playoff assignment every four years and one World Series assignment every fifteen years. This rotation system increased the union's autonomy while decreasing the authority of the leagues and the performance level of the umpires. The outcome of the strike was that the leagues made significant concessions on money issues but regained the right to select umpires for the playoffs and World Series on the basis of merit.

In 1995 umpire negotiations again resulted in a work stoppage. This time, however, the owners turned the tables by imposing a preemptory lockout to head off a possible umpires' strike later in the season. The lockout lasted for 120 days, and replacement umpires were used for spring training and for nine days into the regular season. In the five-year agreement ending the lockout, salaries were increased by 25 percent to 37.5 percent. Rookie umpires were guaranteed $100,000 (up from $75,000) and thirty-year veterans can make as much as $282,500 (up from $206,000). Despite the missed games, umpires were paid full salaries for the 1995 season.

Minorities in Baseball

In 1987 Al Campanis appeared on the ABC television program *Nightline*, hosted by Ted Koppel. Campanis, then the Los Angeles Dodgers' vice-president for player personnel, was talking about Jackie Robinson, whom Campanis helped bring into baseball as the first black player in 1947. Unfortunately,

Campanis got sidetracked and instead of praising blacks, which he meant to do, responded to a question on the dearth of black managers by saying,

> I truly believe that they may not have some of the necessities to be, let's say, a field manager, or perhaps a general manger. . . . Well, I don't say all of them, but they certainly are short. How many quarterbacks do you have—how many pitchers do you have—that are black?"[26]

These remarks, totally out of character for Campanis, who was well known for his unbiased action over the years, sparked a national controversy. This prompted Commissioner Ueberroth to establish an affirmative action program for baseball. For assistance he hired Harry Edwards, a black activist and sociology professor at the University of California, Berkeley. Edwards created a pool of black and Hispanic former players to qualify for positions at all levels of baseball. Commissioner Vincent was also committed to minority hiring.

Since then, baseball has made some progress. Compared to the approximately 30 percent of the players that are black (including black Latino players), front-office hiring of minorities has increased to about 25 percent. There are also more black managers, coaches, and other baseball staff, and the last two presidents of the National League have been black. The racist remarks of owner Marge Schott of the Cincinnati Reds in 1992, unfortunately, were symptomatic of a larger problem in society toward minorities. She apologized for her remarks, which included the phrase "dumb lazy nigger," and was fined $25,000 and suspended for one year.

Substance Abuse

Alcoholism has long been a major problem in society and at the workplace. Widespread drug problems are of more recent origin. "Drug abuse," as that term is ordinarily used, refers to the nonmedical consumption of psychoactive substances, such as amphetamines, barbiturates, cocaine, marijuana, LSD, and heroin. The most common effect of drug and alcohol abuse on the job is increased absenteeism; other effects are decline in productivity, decreased motivation to do a good job, and increased employee accidents.[27] Drug abuse has been increasingly recognized as a serious problem affecting workers, and numerous programs for rehabilitation exist in American industry.

Alcoholism has always existed as a problem for baseball players and for other professional athletes. Healthy, strong, and in the bloom of youth, many athletes drink to relax from the tensions of the games or for bonhomie with their teammates. Between games and during the off-season, players have long periods of free time. Alcohol abuse is not viewed with as much social disapprobation as drug abuse. It is for this reason that baseball players who acknowledge their alcoholism problems and undertake rehabilitation receive sympathy and even respect from the public.

Drug abuse presents more complex issues because of the diversity of psychoactive substances and the reasons for which they are used. Amphetamines are commonly found in sports locker rooms. When used for getting up for a game, they spark no great protest from the public or club owners. But if used outside the game for social recreation, amphetamines prompt a different response. The public makes similar distinctions between softer drugs such as marijuana and harder ones such as cocaine.

Americans are socialized to rely on the quick fix of drugs. They are exposed to a barrage of television commercials advertising drugs to get rid of headaches, relax, stimulate the bowels, and get to sleep. The message is that life and work are difficult, but drugs can help us get by. Players' careers are short and risky. They experience intense pressure to perform at high levels and win. Some players use drugs to help their performance, to make them feel good, or simply to go along with the crowd.

Before 1983 there were some isolated incidents involving drugs in baseball. Ferguson Jenkins of the Texas Rangers was suspended indefinitely by Commissioner Kuhn in 1980 when cocaine, hashish, and marijuana were found in his luggage at the Toronto airport. He appealed the suspension through the MLBPA, and after a grievance hearing arbitrator Raymond Goetz ordered the suspension lifted with back pay after two weeks. Jenkins eventually was given an "absolute discharge" by a Canadian judge, who found him guilty but did not convict him. His record was cleared when he completed a drug-diversion program and agreed to work with youth groups. In 1982 Allan Wiggins of the San Diego Padres was suspended by his team for one month for possession of cocaine. When Lonnie Smith of the St. Louis Cardinals informed the team that he had a cocaine problem, he underwent treatment without discipline and returned to duty.

In 1983 two incidents brought the cocaine problem in baseball into sharper focus: arrests of four Kansas City Royals players and the suspension of Steve Howe of the Los Angeles Dodgers. In the Kansas City case, the Federal Bureau of Investigation obtained permission to tap the telephone line of a suspected drug dealer and obtained information that eventually led to the arrest and conviction of four Royals players: Willie Wilson, Willie Aikens, and Jerry Martin (for attempting to possess cocaine), and Vida Blue (for possession of cocaine). After plea bargaining, the players pleaded guilty to reduced charges with misdemeanor status, and they were sentenced to ninety days in a federal penitentiary. In the Los Angeles case, Howe was not charged with a crime involving drugs but underwent several periods of rehabilitation for cocaine use. The Dodgers fined him $54,000 and suspended him indefinitely.

On December 15, 1983, Commissioner Kuhn suspended Wilson, Aikens, Martin, and Howe for one year each, although the three Royals' suspensions were subject to petition for reinstatement on May 15, 1984. After a year Howe's suspension was reviewed by the commissioner, at which time it was lifted. The penalties imposed on the players by the commissioner were the toughest for drug violations yet handed out and indicated that future abuse would be dealt with severely.

There were other incidents involving player use of drugs in the 1980s, notably the so-called Pittsburgh hearings in 1985, when twenty-one players were implicated in drug use and eleven players were suspended by Commissioner Ueberroth. After various attempts to devise a workable drug control program, by 1990 baseball had settled on a system similar to the pioneering program in basketball. Baseball has a three-strike program. The first strike is initial detection of drug use, which leads to medical treatment. Violation of the aftercare program constitutes a second strike, for which the player is typically suspended for sixty days. A subsequent relapse, or third strike, results in banishment. Unlike the program in basketball, baseball has no rule about when a player can apply for reinstatement. Also, the punishment of players is more likely to result in review by an arbitrator, which may cause punishment to be rescinded or reduced. Thus far in the 1990s violations have dropped and only about one or two players per year have been punished.[28]

One of the biggest difficulties in any drug control program is getting people to acknowledge their dependency and come forward for help. Some players simply do not want help, and some feel that getting caught is something that happens to the other guy. Because drug abuse affects the integrity of the game's public image and spectator identification with players as role models, baseball tries to keep its house clean. But accompanying the punitive side of the program is the recognition that while drug abuse is a crime it is also an illness that requires medical treatment.

Football 3

Until recently, professional football was plagued with sharp conflict between labor and management. Long and bitter strikes in 1982 and 1987 punctuated the seemingly endless wrangling. Although the players' union won the odd skirmish, the owners held the whip hand and controlled the game. But all this changed in 1993 when the parties reached a new seven-year collective bargaining agreement. Since then, relative tranquility has prevailed, with league expansion, rising incomes for all, and a cementing of pro football's popularity as the nation's premier spectator sport. Owners and players—for the present at least—are starting to view themselves as partners rather than adversaries.

The game of football was derived from rugby, which began around 1840 in England. Football started in the United States in the 1870s with games between colleges. In 1876 the Intercollegiate Football Association was organized. Although the game played was essentially the same as rugby, over the years the association's rules changed the game into the football we know today. In 1920 the first major professional football league was formed, with famous college player Jim Thorpe as president.[1] Known as the American Professional Football Association, its teams were poorly managed, and salaries were minimal. The twelve-team league folded after a year, but was reorganized in 1921. The following year its name was changed to the National Football League (NFL). Little success was achieved by the NFL in attracting public attention until the Chicago Bears signed Harold ("Red") Grange in 1925. Grange, a star halfback at the University of Illinois, was known as the Galloping Ghost, and his play with the Bears brought large crowds to watch professional football for the first time.

Gradually the NFL became well established. Early rival leagues were unable to keep going for long. They were the American Football League, which lasted only one year in 1926; another American Football League (1936–37); and the All-America Football Conference (1946–49). When the All-America Football Conference folded, three of its teams—Cleveland, Baltimore, and San Francisco—became a part of the NFL. The NFL began drafting college players in 1936, which helped provide a steady stream of high-quality talent. Following Elmer Layden as NFL commissioner (1941–46), Bert Bell provided strong leadership from 1946 to 1959 that helped the league to prosper. It was not until the 1960s, however, that the professional game began to reach big-time status as a result of widespread television exposure.

Economics of Football

The economics of football are influenced by two principal factors: sources of revenue and costs of operations.[2] The determinants of revenues include the number of teams and games played; the size of stadiums, luxury boxes, and parking and concession arrangements; marketability to broadcast media; tax laws; and ticket prices and ticket sales. Cost determinants involve primarily compensation to players, scouts, and front office staff; arrangements for stadium rentals; and equipment, travel, and publicity expenses. Unlike baseball, football does not sustain the cost of maintaining a farm system of minor league teams, because nearly all professional football players are recruited from colleges.

Compared with other major team sports, however, football has certain disadvantages. With forty-six players per team, rosters are far larger than for other sports. There are about seventeen hundred and fifty players in the NFL, compared with about six hundred and fifty in baseball's major leagues. With sixteen regular-season games, plus four preseason games and playoffs, football has a significantly smaller number of playing dates.

Football revenues are enhanced considerably, however, by large stadiums, which are usually sold out, at least among NFL teams. The cost of the average ticket has risen steadily from about $10.50 in 1981 to $17.00 in 1984 to $24.00 in 1990 to about $33.00 in 1995. Gate receipts are divided, with 60 percent going to the home team and 40 percent to the visiting team for regular-season NFL games and 50 percent each for preseason games.

Another important source of revenue is NFL Properties. This subsidiary was started in 1963 to protect the league's logos and trademarks. It has three divisions—retail licensing, marketing and promotion, and publishing. The fastest growing part of the business is retail licensing of NFL apparel and novelty items. Altogether, the revenues from ticket sales and NFL Properties make up about one-third of the total income to the league. The remaining two-thirds comes from broadcasting, mostly television.

Television Revenues

Most important to the economic viability of football is its unique adaptability to television. Popularity of the sport is unprecedented. Although some declines began to appear in television ratings for NFL games in 1983 and 1984, largely as a result of oversaturation from the United States Football League (USFL), ratings began to increase again in 1985. Viewing the games on television has become an American institution, and millions of viewers are glued to their sets on Sundays and on Monday nights. The money paid by advertisers for commercials on these games is a cornucopia for the television networks, which have provided the NFL with bountiful contracts for broadcast rights.

Under the NFL contracts with CBS, NBC, and ABC that expired in 1981, each of the twenty-eight teams in the league received about $5.8 million. In 1982 a new five-year agreement was reached in which the networks paid the teams an average of $14.2 million a season. When the television agreements expired in 1987, negotiations for new contracts were especially difficult. During the last two years of the old agreement advertisers were less willing to pay large fees, which caused the networks to lose money. As a result, the networks were looking to get a new deal that would restore profitability.

Another interesting side to the negotiations was the emergence of cable television. In the past, the NFL game was presented exclusively by networks that did not charge viewers extra for games. But entering the scene as active bidders for broadcast rights in 1987 were several cable companies, including ESPN, a twenty-four-hour sports network that is 80 percent owned by ABC and its parent, Capital Cities, Inc. Although NBC and CBS won the bidding for Sunday afternoon broadcasts, and ABC retained its Monday Night Football rights, ESPN agreed to pay $50 million per year for eight regular-season Sunday night games, four exhibition games, and the Pro Bowl. Altogether, the new three-year contract paid the NFL $1.43 billion, about 3 percent per year less than was paid in the final year of the old contract.

In 1990 the NFL again reached agreements with NBC, CBS, ABC, and ESPN, and added a new cable partner, Turner Broadcasting. The contract called for a total of $3.65 billion, with $32.6 million per team, nearly double what each club was making under the prior contract. Two changes were made to sweeten the package for television. One was to increase the number of playoff teams from ten to twelve, thus creating two additional playoff games. The other was

Table 3.1. The NFL's Television Contract History

Years	Total	Annual TV Income per Team	Average Player Salary
1960–61	$600,000[a]	$ 45,000	$ 15,000
1962–63	$4.65 million[b]	$330,000	$ 20,000
1964–65	$28.2 million[b]	$1 million	$ 21,000
1966–69	$75.2 million[b]	1.6 million	$ 22,000
1970–73	$185 million[c]	$1.8 million	$ 23,000
1974–77	$269 million	$2.6 million	$ 30,000
1978–81	$646 million	$5.8 million	$ 60,000
1982–86	$2.1 billion	$13.6 million	$100,000
1987–89	$1.428 billion[d]	$16.7 million	$211,000
1990–93	$3.65 billion[e]	$32.6 million	$355,000
1994–97	$4.4 billion	$39.2 million	$700,000

[a]Fee paid to the league for the NFL Championship Game, aired by NBC.
[b]CBS is the only network broadcasting NFL games.
[c]With NFL and AFL merger, CBS broadcasts NFC games, NBC broadcasts AFC games. ABC begins Monday Night Football telecasts.
[d]ESPN begins broadcasting preseason and Sunday night games in eight weeks of season.
[e]TNT begins broadcasting Sunday night games in first eight weeks of season.
Sources: Sports Illustrated, 27 December 1993, p. 19: *Wall Street Journal,* 24 December 1993, p. A4; and author's estimate of average player salary for 1994–97.

to extend the season—for the 1991 and 1992 seasons there were sixteen games over seventeen weeks, and in 1993 and 1994 there were sixteen games over eighteen weeks.

For the 1994–97 seasons the television contracts continued to increase revenues, but not as much as in the prior contract. Total revenues rose to about $4.4 billion, with each team getting $39.2 million a year. (The revenues from all the NFL television contracts over the years are shown in Table 3.1.) The big change in the 1994–97 television deal is that CBS was outbid by Rupert Murdoch's Fox Network after having televised NFL games for thirty-eight years. Fox, only six years in existence at the time, is a "fourth network" of marginal independent television stations. Apart from bidding more than CBS, part of Fox's attraction to the NFL is potential international exposure for the league through Murdoch's extensive global broadcasting and publishing interests.

These television contracts seem a glorious example of the success of free enterprise in a capitalist economy, yet, ironically, they point up the economic influence of the NFL as a cartel and its sharing of television monies equally among teams. It is interesting to speculate whether cable television, now that it has its foot in the door, will be able to increase its share in later negotiations with the NFL. The National Basketball Association and the National Hockey League have increased their television revenues from cable in recent years, so perhaps the NFL will follow this trend. Receiving too big a share from cable, however, would raise antitrust questions for the NFL. The league currently has an exemption from antitrust law, granted by Congress in 1961, insofar as broadcast income is concerned. Should the NFL decide to remove a sizable share of its games from free public television, it is possible that Congress would revoke the income-pooling exemption. This would cause competition among teams for television revenues and diminish the hegemony of the league.

Tax Advantages

As in other professional sports, an important factor in maintaining the structure and economic success of professional football is that franchises allow for lucrative tax arrangements. Before the Tax Reform Act of 1976, owners were allowed to depreciate 95 percent of the cost of the players over five years. This allowed owners, many of whom were involved in other business enterprises, to show a loss on the team operation while pocketing large sums from ownership of the sports franchise.

The 1976 law allowed owners purchasing a team to allocate only 50 percent of the cost of the franchise to player costs, to be depreciated over five years. Under the Tax Reform Act of 1986, deductions for equipment and facilities expenditures by professional teams were reduced by requiring that such expenditures be depreciated over a longer period. The 1976 law allowed nonmanaging partners in money-losing sports franchises to use their losses to offset income from other sources. Under the 1986 changes, however, deductions on "passive" investments were abolished, so such losses ordinarily are not deductible.

Despite a tightening up of the tax laws, ownership of a football team still presents rewarding financial opportunities. Owners who make money on team operations pay relatively little in taxes, and what may appear to be a money-losing situation may actually be profitable when tax breaks are figured in. Indeed, except for such unusual situations as a players' strike, it is hard not to make money from team ownership. Perhaps the best illustration of long-term profitability in football is the sale prices of franchises in recent years. In 1960 the Dallas Cowboys were purchased by Clint Murchison for $600,000 and sold in 1984 for $75 million. Also in 1984, the Denver Broncos, which had been purchased for about $33.5 million in 1981, were sold for $70 million. In 1985 the Philadelphia Eagles were sold for $65 million, and the New Orleans Saints for $64 million. In 1988 the New England Patriots sold for $82 million, and the Seattle Seahawks for $80 million. In 1989 the Dallas Cowboys were sold for $130 million, and in 1994 the New England Patriots sold for $158 million and the Philadelphia Eagles for $185 million.

Structure of Employment

NFL and Rival Leagues

During the 1960s, under the direction of the new commissioner, Alvin ("Pete") Rozelle, who was formerly general manager of the Los Angeles Rams, NFL attendance soared to 90 percent of stadium capacities, and millions of persons found a new way to spend their Sundays, watching the games on television. The 1960s were not entirely placid for the NFL, however. In 1963 Commissioner Rozelle suspended Paul Hornung of the Green Bay Packers and Alex Karras of the Detroit Lions for betting on league games and associating with gamblers. Five other players were fined for betting. The suspension of Hornung and Karras was lifted after eleven months. Another, more important, problem for the NFL was the formation of a rival league.

The NFL's domination was challenged in 1960 when the American Football League (AFL) began play. It was formed the year before by Texas oilman Lamar Hunt, who became its first president. Cities with the first AFL franchises were Buffalo, Boston, Houston, Dallas, Los Angeles, Oakland, Denver, and New York. Although a measure of credibility and financial support for the fledgling league was provided when a major television network, ABC, agreed to televise selected games, the AFL had to struggle for public recognition in the early years. Clubs had a few big-name players and inadequate television coverage. The league nearly folded when the New York Titans fell heavily into debt and approached bankruptcy. Although located in the nation's biggest product market, the Titans had few followers and were poorly managed. Coming to the rescue was a five-member syndicate headed by entertainment agent David ("Sonny") Werblin. It purchased the sinking Titans in 1963, hired Weeb Ewbank, a successful coach for the Baltimore Colts in the NFL, and changed the name of the team to the New York Jets.

The turning point for the AFL came in 1964, when Werblin negotiated a five-year television contract with CBS for $36 million, with each team guaranteed $900,000 per year. This additional income allowed the AFL to bid for talented players with the NFL. Werblin and Oakland Raiders' owner Al Davis, who later became president of the AFL, touted the star system idea, a strategy in which the new league would try to sign exceptional players out of college, especially quarterbacks. In a bidding war with the NFL, Werblin signed quarterback Joe Namath from the University of Alabama for an unprecedented $427,000 over four years. Other young stars out of college signed large contracts: John Hadl from the University of Kansas, Lance Alworth from San Diego State, Fred Biletnikoff from Florida State, and Mike Garrett, winner of the Heisman trophy at the University of Southern California. The AFL was clearly in business as a formidable rival to the NFL and was costing teams in the older league millions of dollars in competition for players.

To end escalating competition, the NFL and AFL agreed to merge in 1966, thus establishing a common draft of players. AFL clubs agreed to pay NFL clubs a total of $18 million in principal and interest over the next twenty years. The leagues played separate schedules until 1970, when their television contracts expired. In 1967 the first Super Bowl game was played between the NFL and AFL champions. The merged league originally consisted of twenty-six teams (by 1976 the number had grown to twenty-eight teams with the addition of NFL franchises in Seattle and Tampa Bay). Pete Rozelle remained commissioner of the unified league.

In 1974 another rival league began direct competition with the NFL. The World Football League (WFL) was created by Gary Davidson, who earlier had established competitive leagues in professional basketball and hockey. NFL players welcomed the twelve-team operation because it would give them opportunities to jump to a new league for higher salaries and cause upward pressure on all football salaries. The WFL gained some credibility when its Toronto franchise signed three players from the NFL's Miami Dolphins. These players—Larry Csonka, Paul Warfield, and Jim Kiick—received contracts with a total value of about $3 million.

In 1975, however, the WFL folded in the middle of its second season of play, leaving about 380 players without jobs. Some of these players were acquired by NFL teams. Several factors contributed to the demise of the WFL. Although most of its franchises were located in non-NFL cities, attendance was poor. Few big-name players signed with the league, which worked against its efforts to establish public visibility. Without adequate television exposure, ownership lacked financial resiliency, and franchises shifted to other cities or went bankrupt. Perhaps most important, the rival league played its games at the same time as the NFL and was viewed by the public as an inferior alternative.

A new and more formidable rival to the NFL, the United States Football League (USFL), began play in 1983 with twelve teams, each playing a twenty-game season from March through June and a championship game in early July. Realizing the importance of television, the USFL chose as its commissioner Chet Simmons, former president of NBC Sports and chief executive officer of ESPN.

The USFL avoided at least three of the problems that plagued the WFL. First, it was not in direct competition with the NFL because games were played in the spring and early summer rather than the traditional fall season. Second, the owners of the USFL possessed strong financial staying power since they were among the richest people in America. Third, the USFL lined up a two-year television contract with ABC and another contract with ESPN. These contracts, negotiated before the USFL began play, provided greater national television exposure than the WFL had. Also, the USFL was in larger cities than the WFL and had more high-quality stadiums in which to play.

Although the USFL was mostly stocked with players who were marginal in the NFL, the new league utilized the philosophy of the old AFL by creating a star system. By holding its draft of college players before the NFL's, the USFL was able to sign some of the finest college talent in its first year of operation: Kelvin Bryant from North Carolina, Anthony Carter from Michigan, Trumaine Johnson from Grambling, and 1983 Heisman trophy winner Herschel Walker from Georgia. The deep pockets of USFL owners, such as Donald Trump of the New Jersey Generals and J. William Oldenburg of the Los Angeles Express, were evident in the tremendous salaries offered to lure top college players and NFL veterans to their teams. In its second year of operation, the USFL expanded to eighteen teams and continued rapidly signing such attractive college players as Heisman trophy winner Mike Rozier from Nebraska and Steve Young from Brigham Young, as well as NFL stars such as Joe Cribbs and Doug Williams. The pace slowed in 1985, but Heisman winner Doug Flutie from Boston College signed with New Jersey.

In the 1985 season, there was a significant restructuring of the USFL. Beset with low television ratings and losses estimated at $80 million in the previous year, the league reduced the number of teams from eighteen to fourteen. It also announced plans to shift from a spring to a fall schedule in 1986. These changes sounded a death knell for the USFL because they pointed up the franchises' decreasing ability to operate successfully and placed the USFL in direct competition with the NFL. The older league had high-quality play and a dominance of television exposure that made it difficult for the USFL to retain fans. Because the NFL dominated television on Sundays and Monday nights and the networks are legally barred from presenting professional games on Friday nights or Saturdays during the college football season, the USFL narrowed its scheduling opportunities for presenting games. It also ran into problems with use of stadium facilities, some of which had to be shared with NFL teams. At the end of the 1985 season, several star players in the USFL signed with NFL teams. In 1986 the USFL folded after losing antitrust litigation against the NFL.

In 1989 a significant change in NFL leadership occurred when Pete Rozelle decided to retire as commissioner. After several months of reviewing candidates, the owners chose Paul Tagliabue the new commissioner. A former captain of the Georgetown University basketball team, Tagliabue had served for the past twenty years as an NFL attorney for the Washington, D.C., law firm of Covington and Burling. During this time he worked closely with Rozelle and earned the respect of virtually all the owners, even though a crucial antitrust case involving the move of the Raiders from Oakland to Los Angeles was decided against the league. Since becoming commissioner, Tagliabue has proven himself an able executive and has taken a more active role in labor relations than Rozelle did. Among Tagliabue's most important accomplishments as commissioner are the 1990 and 1994 television agreements, the 1993 collective bargaining agreement, league expansion, and drug and alcohol abuse programs.

NFLPA

The idea of a union of football players was conceived in 1954 by two Cleveland Browns players, Abe Gibron and Dante Lavelli, who suggested it to Creighton Miller, a former Browns player who was then serving as the team's attorney. Two years later the National Football League Players Association (NFLPA) was formally organized at a meeting before the 1956 NFL championship game. Miller became legal counsel for the new union. The NFLPA initially signed up members from all NFL teams. At first the owners would not deal with the new union. Then a decision by the U.S. Supreme Court in 1957 finding football to be subject to the antitrust laws prompted the union to threaten the owners with a $4.2 million antitrust suit. Using this threat, Miller was able to get the owners to agree to a $5,000 minimum salary, $50 for each exhibition game played, and an injury clause that continued a player's salary and provided medical and hospital care. In 1959 the union achieved another breakthrough when it persuaded the owners to provide a pension plan for the players.

The NFLPA was registered with the U.S. Department of Labor as a labor union in 1968. At this time, the player representatives from the sixteen NFL teams voted unanimously to reject an attempt by the Teamsters Union to organize the players. Creighton Miller resigned and was replaced by Chicago lawyer Daniel S. Schulman, who became the chief negotiator and legal counsel for the union. Despite his resignation as the union's legal counsel, Miller continued to be active in football labor relations as an agent representing players.

Edward R. Garvey became executive director of the NFLPA in 1971. Under his leadership, the union became more aggressive at the bargaining table and in the courtroom. He led the union when it shut down training camps for forty-two days in 1974, and as a lawyer, he was also instrumental in getting the courts to nullify the Rozelle Rule, discussed later. In 1979 the NFLPA became the first professional sports organization to receive a charter as an affiliate of the AFL-CIO, and Garvey was chosen to be the head of a new organization within the AFL-CIO, called the Federation of Professional Athletes, an umbrella group for the welfare of sports unions.

Garvey represented the union in other skirmishes with the NFL and its commissioner, acting to enhance the union's ability to bargain over certain issues and to check the power of the commissioner over players. Throughout collective bargaining during Garvey's tenure, the NFL owners refused to negotiate over numerous issues the players felt affected their working conditions. In one case, the National Labor Relations Board determined that the issue of artificial turf on playing fields was a mandatory subject for bargaining. The union had argued that artificial turf was a working condition in that players sustained a higher number of injuries on this kind of playing surface. Although the NLRB found the issue to be one that had to be negotiated, it did not find that management had failed to bargain in good faith on this issue.[3] The upshot of this ruling was that, while the union has the right to bargain over artificial turf, management's obligation is to negotiate sincerely on the subject in good faith, not necessarily to agree to change its policy. A later NLRB decision reinforced the union's right to negotiate over football rules that involve player safety.[4]

Another decision by the NLRB determined that the commissioner has power to enact a rule prohibiting players from leaving the bench area during fights and automatically fining those players who do. This decision, however, was appealed to the courts, which overturned the NLRB decision and found the NFL guilty of an unfair labor practice.[5] This decision further underscores the general rule that management has to negotiate with the union on matters affecting their wages, hours, or working conditions. Unilateral actions by management, without consultation with the union, will not be allowed if they encroach on the subjects over which the union has rights of representation.

An important function performed by unions is enforcement of the collective bargaining agreement through the grievance procedure. A union tries to settle disputes over the interpretation or application of the contract with management in a process in which unresolved grievances move upward through the steps of the procedure to higher levels of labor and management authority. In nearly all grievance procedures negotiated by unions, the final step is arbitration by an outside neutral. In baseball negotiations, the union was successful in winning the right to arbitrate and then using the arbitration step of the grievance procedure to preserve and even expand its status as a player representative.

The NFLPA has limited rights to arbitrate grievances, which have been established in its collective bargaining agreements through the years. Before these changes, the commissioner had the final say on all grievances. Even today, authority for certain areas of contract interpretation and discipline, which are usually under the purview of arbitration clauses in other sectors of private industry, remains in the hands of the commissioner. A case in point is discipline for drug-related violations.

In the 1970 agreement, arbitration was provided for disputes over player injuries. Although Ed Garvey was not executive director of the NFLPA at the time this contract was negotiated, he worked for the law firm that served as legal counsel to the union and thus was involved in negotiations. Under the negotiated agreement, a list of neutral orthopedic physicians was selected by management and the union. Employer defenses to paying injured players included demonstration that the player did not pass his physical examination, that the injury occurred from nonfootball causes, and that the player had not aggravated an old injury. If a dispute arose involving an injury, it was submitted to an impartial arbitrator, who decided whether the player was entitled to compensation under his contract with the team. The provision for arbitration of injury grievances has been continued in later agreements.

In 1977 the scope of arbitration was extended to include noninjury grievances. Although a grievance was defined as "any dispute . . . involving the interpretation or application of, or compliance with, provisions of this Agreement," various exclusions were made to the definition of a grievance and therefore to the kinds of grievances that could be submitted to arbitration.[6] For instance, the commissioner retained the right to rule on matters affecting the "integrity of or public confidence in" football and disciplinary matters involving players as stated in their standard player contracts. These provisions were continued in the 1982 collective bargaining agreement.

An important new section included in the 1982 agreement involved screening of player agents by the NFLPA. Unlike its practice in past agreements, the union did not waive its right under the National Labor Relations Act to negotiate with teams over individual player salaries:

> Other Compensation: A player will be entitled to receive a signing or reporting bonus, additional salary payments, incentive bonuses and such other provisions as may be negotiated between his club (with the assistance of the Management Council) and the NFLPA or its agent. The club and the NFLPA or its agent will negotiate in good faith over such other compensation; provided, however, that a club will not be required to deal with the NFLPA or its agent on a collective or tandem basis for two or more players on that club.[7]

What this provision meant is that if the NFLPA had chosen to do so, it could have negotiated individual player salaries. But it never did so. In 1984 the NFLPA had a policy that no staff member may represent a player in individual contract negotiations. It does, however, require agents to get approval from the NFLPA to represent players. The reason for this screening is to help ensure that the provisions of the agreement and the law are complied with and that players receive effective and responsible agent representation in their individual salary negotiations. Another provision of the 1982 agreement required that the NFLPA receive copies of all individual player contracts. This enabled the union to have complete salary data on players for the first time.

Over the years, Ed Garvey survived several attempts by the membership in the NFLPA to oust him as executive director. Controversy over his leadership peaked after the fifty-seven-day strike in 1982. Despite what appeared to be his imminent dismissal by the players, the union's executive committee, composed of player representatives, voted twenty to seven to retain Garvey in office. This committee decision in support of Garvey meant that a vote of the entire union membership was not required. Although he could have stayed on as executive director, the strike and lack of solidarity among the entire membership over his leadership placed a heavy strain on him. Garvey resigned from the union in 1983 to become deputy attorney general in his home state of Wisconsin.

He was replaced as executive director of the NFLPA by Gene Upshaw, who for the previous three years had been president of the NFLPA and was a former star player for the Oakland Raiders. Upshaw has taken a far more moderate tone in dealing with management. As he described the situation, "It's reconstruction, sort of like after the Civil War. . . . We need a change in philosophy . . . I want our image changed."[8] Upshaw's softer line became evident when he took a mild approach on the suspension of players by Commissioner Rozelle for drug abuse. He has also been in close touch with the commissioner and management representatives, indicating that he is trying to build a relationship of trust through more open communication. Grievances that would likely have gone to arbitration in the past have been settled by Upshaw. The union's heavy financial debt has been reduced under his leadership, its costs of operation have declined, and its public image as a particularly fractious organization has changed for the better. Although Upshaw's leadership was criticized as a result of the 1987 strike, discussed later in the chapter, he continues to be supported by most football players.

The principal challenge to Upshaw's leadership came in 1990. By that time the NFLPA had gone four years without being able to negotiate a new collective bargaining agreement. Also, the union was trying to decertify itself as the players' representative in order to facilitate an antitrust suit by players against the league. Into the breach stepped Larry Csonka, Hall of Fame running back. Csonka wrote a letter to twelve hundred veteran players urging them to join him in forming a new union called the United Players of the National Football League. Had a majority of the players signed an authorization card enclosed with the letter, Csonka's organization might have replaced the NFLPA. But the NFLPA countered with its own arguments to the players, and the rival group never got off the ground.

Adversary Bargaining

Collective bargaining in football has been characterized by a curious blend of workers who find strikes to be antithetical to their image of professional dedication and an adversary relationship that impels workers to withhold their services if necessary to enhance their economic well-being. Perhaps the closest analogy to football players in other sectors is certain public employees, especially those involved in health and safety services. Police officers, firefighters, and nurses, for example, have a keen sense of psychological attachment to their professions, but also realize the need to seek to maximize their economic reward by opposing the employer with pressure tactics in bargaining.

These incongruent objectives were brought into sharp focus during the fifty-seven-day football strike in 1982. Conflict can cause lack of solidarity among workers if they differ in the values assigned to maintaining public service on the one hand and financial gain on the other. Like public employees, however, professional athletes usually tend to allow their economic objective to overshadow the dedication to job and public if the stakes are high enough. But this does not make the reconciliation of opposing philosophies any less difficult for the participants.

Attitudes

The conflict between financial and professional service goals is particularly acute for football players. The sociocultural environment of their sport promotes obedience and dedication. Football is a team game that does not encourage individuality. Unlike other professional athletes, most football players rarely handle the ball. The running of plays is a highly coordinated effort that emphasizes the interdependence of individuals in the unit and their sacrifice for a common objective.

It is unusual for football players to defy authority. Their environment is paramilitary, well ordered, and authoritarian. It is distinctly two-dimensional, with the coach at the top and the players on the bottom. Youngsters who aspire to careers in the sport are taught the rigid organizational structure and the need for discipline from Pop Warner kid leagues through high school and college. It would be difficult for a player to move through this ritualistic progression without deriving a potent sense of identification with team play and the football establishment.

Players generally view themselves as athletes, not union men, as quite apart from machinists, plumbers, coal miners, and other organized workers. Members of other unions that strike can afford to take a longer view. They have more time to recoup the losses. But football players, who have the shortest career expectancy of any professional athletes, are reluctant to strike because they have more to lose and less time to make it up. They also feel less compunction about breaking a strike by returning to work, since they can be replaced by other players who are willing to work. Only if there is unusual solidarity among all players could they expect to achieve gains by striking.

In addition to the rigid organizational roles football players are molded into, they are also captives of their own image. Players are lionized by the broadcast and print media and worshiped by a legion of fans; yet they are fearful of the encroachment of age and the fragility of their skills and bodies. Thus the delicate balance of adulation, fear of failure, and a team's control over its players creates an environment in which it is difficult for players even to contemplate a strike.

Tactics

Despite the players' inherent aversion to strikes, they belong to a union that became increasingly militant under Ed Garvey's leadership. The evolution of the NFLPA into a strident force against management control was a major cause of the 1982 strike. For several years before the strike the union had shown a growing willingness to use pressure tactics to achieve its objectives. Collective bargaining between the NFLPA and NFL is characterized by an adversary relationship, and underlying this relationship is the assumption that the goals of labor and management are in conflict. The NFLPA is seeking to maximize the economic return to players. Management in the NFL is seeking to preserve and protect its revenue sources from interference by the union.

At bottom, the conflict between the adversaries is over players' salaries: how much they are going to get and how much the owners will have to give up. There are other issues of importance, such as player health and safety, but compensation is predominant. This is similar to bargaining in industries outside sports characterized by adversary bargaining in which the philosophies of union and management negotiators emphasize that division of the wealth of the industry will result from confrontation, or a strike if necessary. The history of the relationship of the adversaries influences their stance. If strikes and other acts of defiance have typified their past dealings, agreement on contract terms may be harder to reach.

The adversary approach in collective bargaining often results in economic loss to both sides. The parties' tactics are calculated either to increase the ability to inflict damage on the opponent (offensive factors) or to enhance one's own ability to withstand pressure from the other side (defensive factors). Figure 3.1 lists offensive and defensive tactics that might be used in football negotiations.

The offensive and defensive tactics indicated in Figure 3.1 are illustrative, rather than inclusive, of the available tactics. Some of these tactics—such as secondary boycotts, releasing players because of their union activities, and fines—may be challenged in proceedings with the NLRB or the courts as violating federal labor law. Some of these tactics have been used by the adversaries in football, e.g., strike, lockout, and picketing; others have not been used thus

NFLPA	NFL Management
Offensive Tactics	
Strike	Lockout
Picket	Layoff (cut dissident players)
Urge direct boycott by fans	Withhold benefits
Urge secondary boycott by firms doing business with owners	Fine players
Influence public opinion against management through the media	Influence public opinion against the union through the media
Form a new league	Cancel the season
Defensive Tactics	
Set up strike fund	Obtain strike insurance
Obtain financial aid from other unions, e.g., AFL-CIO affiliates	Set up strike fund
Arrange loans for strikers	Hire strikebreakers
Help strikers find temporary jobs	Obtain mutual aid, e.g., a strike against one club is a strike against all
Sponsor all-star games	Provide loans to financially ailing clubs
Defend the righteousness of the union's position to media	Defend the righteousness of the owners' position to media

Figure 3.1. Offensive and Defensive Bargaining Tactics

far, e.g., strike insurance, and union strike fund. The point is that there is an arsenal from which the parties can choose weapons to promote their objectives.

Strike of 1982

NFL players first struck in 1968 over pension fund contributions. Players boycotted training camps, and the owners retaliated with a lockout. After ten days, a compromise agreement was reached, and the job action had no effect on the regular season. Another strike and lockout of training camps, this time for twenty days, occurred in 1970 when pensions, postseason compensation, and a grievance procedure for players were in dispute. These early walkouts were relatively mild forms of protest and were not characterized by much hostility and acrimony between the contestants.

In 1974, however, with a full slate of demands on the bargaining table, the players struck training camps for forty-two days in a bitter dispute. They were particularly upset over freedom issues, including the hated Rozelle Rule, which allowed the commissioner to award compensation for the signing of free agents. This walkout was especially hard on the NFLPA because player solidarity broke down when numerous veteran players crossed picket lines to start training. Most of the disputed issues remained unresolved, and the owners won a clear victory that gave them a heady feeling of power over the union in the 1982 negotiations.

The players' most controversial demand in 1982 was that 55 percent of the gross revenues in the NFL be placed in a fund for distribution to them in salaries and pensions. Adopting a rigid posture, the owners hired Jack Donlan, a tough veteran negotiator, to represent them and arranged a $150 million line of credit to cushion the impact of a strike. As the fruitless talks continued, the players modified their demand for a fixed percentage to a demand for a wage scale that would base compensation on seniority and be funded out of television revenues. This demand was also met with stiff resistance from the owners. In the face of little progress, the union indicated it would strike between the second and fourth weeks of the regular season, and after completion of the second week of games, the players walked out.

As the strike progressed, the NFL offered $1.6 billion of guaranteed money to the union, in effect accepting a version of revenue sharing. But how the money was to be divided among players and the period to which it would apply remained in dispute. The parties tried mediation, bringing in Sam Kagel, a distinguished neutral from San Francisco. Confronted with the antagonisms of the chief negotiators and the chaotic scene at the bargaining table, there was little that Kagel could do. Successful mediation depends on a willingness of the parties to respond to prodding, which did not exist during Kagel's efforts.

The players showed surprising solidarity for much of the strike. They even staged all-star games and threatened to form a new league. Their efforts at offsetting the financial deprivation of the strike were not successful, however. Dissent in the ranks over continuing the strike and disenchantment with Ed Garvey's leadership of the union began to mount.

As happened in the baseball strike of 1981, real pressure for settlement of the impasse occurred only when it became likely that the rest of the season would have to be forfeited if the strike continued much longer. Unlike the baseball strike, however, football player solidarity eventually showed signs of crumbling completely, with some players appearing on television to urge the others to return to play. Paul Martha, a former player and executive with the San Francisco Forty-Niners, made a last-ditch attempt to mediate the dispute. His efforts were successful because, by this time, the parties were willing to come to terms.

The players gave up their demands for a wage scale based on seniority, but achieved a total compensation package of $1.6 billion over five years with a $1.28 billion guarantee. There is little doubt that the owners won the fifty-seven-day strike. While the settlement appears generous, it was far less than the owners could have afforded, given substantial income from attendance and television. The continuation of the old system with little change for another five years made NFL franchises more profitable than ever.

Strike of 1987

The chief protagonists in the 1987 negotiations were Donlan and Upshaw.[9] The old five-year agreement expired on August 31, 1987. Even before this, there were several reasons to expect negotiations to falter and end in a strike. First, the union had always struck in formal negotiations with the owners. Thus a strike should have been considered likely. Second, there had been a strike in baseball in 1985. Although this strike lasted for only two days, there is a certain imitative quality about the NFL players' association in following its baseball brethren. The long football strike of 1982 followed the long baseball strike of 1981. In addition, the incidence of strikes is far higher under new leaders, and Upshaw was the new executive director of the players' association. Also, the USFL had discontinued operation the year before. Had the USFL kept playing, NFL owners probably would not have allowed a strike for fear of losing players and public support to the rival league. Perhaps most important were the perceived inequities by the players—that they were not paid what they were worth, while the owners reaped large profits from the game.

Despite these ominous portents, a strike seemed unlikely. While important issues were on the table, there did not appear to be anything worth striking over. There had been too much suffering in 1982, and the level of acrimony in 1987 was down. Moreover, instead of bargaining in one place, the negotiations moved around, with sessions in Tampa, San Francisco, Washington, D.C., New York, and Philadelphia. The purpose of moving the negotiations was to get more privacy. Also, an attempt was made to avoid the glare of the media. The twice-daily news conferences of the 1982 strike were not held. Though perhaps entertaining for the public, they proved counterproductive as the two parties resorted to insulting each other. This caused attitudes to deteriorate and polarized the negotiators. In 1987 no public announcements were made ahead of negotiating sessions, and news stories emanating from the parties were kept to a minimum. (This policy later broke down.)

What became disquieting to observers, despite all the optimism about a strike-free settlement, was the lack of progress in negotiations. It is customary for negotiations to start well before the expiration of the agreement. The parties in football had several negotiating sessions in the early summer, but progress was negligible and it seemed that the sides were not going to enter serious discussions until late August. By this time, though, the contract had almost expired and the regular season was ready to start. By mid-September strike talk began to circulate. At this point, the union may have been well advised to make major concessions because it had never won a battle with the owners outside of court and there was little reason to expect it would do so in 1987 by striking.

Nevertheless, the players' association went forward with a vote to strike on September 22. Both Donlan and Upshaw appeared before television viewers to plead their case. Donlan observed that Upshaw had not been to the bargaining table in two weeks and was instead out conferring with the players. The owners charged that the players were not bargaining in good faith and filed a complaint with the National Labor Relations Board. This pointed out the dilemma Upshaw was in. He had to try to maintain solidarity among the players by making personal appearances around the country, but in so doing he had to sacrifice his duties as a negotiator with management. The prolonged absence by Upshaw may have allowed the owners to stiffen their negotiating position. When the union refused to accept a request by the owners to extend the strike deadline by thirty days, the strike became inevitable.

The owners' revised strategy seemed simple: (1) stonewall in negotiations; (2) use the NFL's public relations program to persuade the fans of the rightness of their position; and (3) divide and frustrate the players by proceeding with the regular schedule, using strikebreakers.

This strategy, a throwback to the early twentieth century, was calculated to wear down the union. The owners were taking a long-term view. This approach was effective because, unlike 1982, the games went on. Coupled with the breakdown in player solidarity, this tactic probably won the strike for the owners.

Impact of the Strike

The owners were far better prepared for a strike than the players. About two-thirds of the teams signed replacement players, who promised to continue the season in the event of a strike. Just two weeks before the start of the season there had been one hundred players on each NFL team's training camp roster. Eager to play in the NFL, if only for a short time, they gladly took the $1,000 proffered by the owners for standing by as potential replacements.

Although the players should have realized from the 1982 experience that they needed to take steps to insulate themselves from the impact of a strike, not much was done. There was no union strike fund from which to draw benefits. No line of credit was available for player loans. As a member of the executive council of the AFL-CIO, Upshaw was able to get support from organized labor in NFL cities. This support, which included AFL-CIO picketing, hurt the owners by reducing attendance at games but did nothing to alleviate the players' financial plight.

In the first week of the strike games, television ratings were down three to four rating points from the usual network average of fifteen. Most observers were surprised that the ratings were that high. Many viewers tuned in to the games out of curiosity. Interest declined, however, and television ratings dropped further as the strike continued. In contrast, gate receipts went in the opposite direction. An average of seventeen thousand fans, 28 percent of usual, attended the first week of the strike games. Attendance climbed to twenty-five thousand in the second week.

What was the impact on players and owners? The strikers lost an average of $15,000 per game, and approximately $80 million altogether. All teams refunded monies to fans who had purchased tickets but did not attend strike games. Although gate receipts and television ratings were down, the owners saved on salaries by paying the replacement players comparatively little. The average owner's profit per game actually rose from $800,000 before the strike to $921,000 during the strike. This profit was temporary, however, because the league had to refund $60 million to the networks over the next two seasons for the one missed weekend of play, the reduced ratings, and the decline in advertising revenues.

The strike also affected public opinion of the union. A poll by ESPN found that fans favored the owners over the players by about three to one. Although the games were played mostly with unknown players, they had the appearance of major league football. NFL officials crossed the picket lines to referee games, and the regular television announcers were on hand to provide commentary. Although many of these announcers were former players, their sentiments appeared to be on the side of the owners.

Also harming the union position was the erosion of player solidarity. In the first week of the strike several veteran players crossed picket lines. The number of defectors increased as the strike continued. Although about 84 percent of the 1,585 regular players stayed out for the duration, at the time the strike was called off it looked like many players would be returning. The owners, however, maintained their solidarity. The NFL Management Council spoke with a unified voice, and no owners negotiated separately.

End of the Strike

On the twentieth day of the strike Upshaw appeared on television during the Monday Night Football game to propose an end to the strike. This was a desperate effort by the union to settle, because players on a majority of teams were poised to return to work if the strike was not settled before the upcoming weekend of October 18. The executive director's proposal contained three parts: (1) all strikers would be reinstated for the rest of the season, and all player representatives and alternative player representatives would be protected; (2) the 1982 collective bargaining agreement would remain in effect; and (3) all current bargaining issues would be submitted to mediation for six weeks, and, after that, all remaining unsettled issues would be submitted to arbitration.

The owners indicated a willingness to protect the player representatives, submit to mediation, and continue the 1982 agreement, but guaranteed the strikers' salaries for only two games and rejected arbitration. Historically, the owners have been wary of arbitration. Arbitration is commonly used in football for grievances and injury disputes, but the owners have never allowed arbitration of provisions that go into a collective bargaining agreement. This points up one of the reasons why arbitration of interest disputes is rare throughout American industry. In negotiations, one of the parties typically has a position of strength. That party would rather go to the bargaining table than allow an arbitrator to decide its fate.

Faced with the owners' rejection of its proposal, the union decided to end the strike on October 15. It is customary when a strike is over for management to welcome back the strikers and get on with business as usual. But the owners surprised the returnees. The owners had established October 14 as the deadline for players to return to be eligible for play in that weekend's games. Because the players ended the strike a day late, the owners refused to allow them to play on October 18 and 19. Some players saw this as a violation of trust, and the union protested the legality of the action with the NLRB. The owners reasoned publicly, however, that the players were out of condition and would risk injury. In 1994 the NLRB ruled that about thirteen hundred players would share a $30 million award. The board found that by not allowing the returning strikers to play or be paid, the NFL committed unfair labor practices in violation of the National Labor Relations Act. This victory by the players was the only thing they won in the strike.

In retrospect, there was no real question about who would win the 1987 strike. The players struck reluctantly, without a significant issue to rally behind. When the union leaders were asked to identify their big issue, they named free agency, for which few players had much enthusiasm. By striking when so many players preferred not to, the union harmed itself. As a result of the strike, the players' association lost its dues checkoff privilege. So, rather than having the clubs automatically deduct the $2,400 in union dues, the union had the difficult task of collecting the monies from disgruntled players. But as incensed as some players were with their union, they were also bitter toward the owners, especially for not letting them play after they had capitulated.

Player Salaries

Until the formation of a rival league such as the USFL, there was little reason for NFL teams to spend lavishly on player salaries. Except for playing in Canada, threatening not to play at all, and very limited opportunities for free agency, NFL players had no alternative to accepting the club's salary offer at terms favorable to the owner. Unlike other professional team sports in which teams are smaller and the value of personal performance is magnified, individual football players have less influence on overall team success. Stadiums are already filled to near capacity, and television revenues are guaranteed.

Table 3.2 shows average salaries in the NFL for selected years since 1967. In 1967 NFL players were paid significantly more than players in any other professional sport, having been elevated as a result of the bidding wars between NFL and AFL teams. Over the years, football players' salaries rose, but not nearly so fast as those of athletes in other sports. In 1982, however, as a result of higher salary minimums negotiated by the NFLPA and the renewed upward pressure from a competitive league, NFL salaries began to rise sharply again.

The USFL influence on NFL salaries worked two ways: NFL teams had to pay their present players more to keep them from jumping to the new league, and they had to pay more to top players leaving college to sign them as draft choices, since these players were also sought by the USFL. John Elway, a rookie in 1983, became the highest paid player in the NFL when he signed a five-year, $5 million contract with the Denver Broncos, and salaries of first-round draft choices in 1983 were up about 60 percent over 1982.

Table 3.2 Average NFL Salaries, 1967–94

Year	Average	Year	Average
1967	$25,000	1989	300,000
1972	35.000	1990	352,000
1977	55,288	1991	415,000
1982	90,412	1992	488,000
1983	112.967	1993	700,000
1984	158,600	1994	650,000
1985	190,000		
1986	203,565		
1987	230,000		
1988	238,490		

Sources: 1967, 1972, 1977 data from Ray Kennedy and Nancy Williamson, "Money: The Monster Threatening Sports," *Sports Illustrated,* 17 July 1978, 46. Data for 1982 to 1994 from the National Football League Players Association. The average for 1993 is higher than for 1994 because contracts were frontloaded to avoid the salary cap.

Table 3.3. Percentage of Black Players in the
NFL, 1969–94

Year	Percentage
1969	33.7
1979	48.8
1984	52.0
1988	56.0
1990	60.0
1994	65.0

Sources: Sports Illustrated, 17 September 1984, 63; 8
February 1988, 9; author's data.

Professional football has been a source of economic advancement for blacks. The first black players in modern professional football were Kenny Washington and Woodie Strode, who signed with the Los Angeles Rams in 1946. For many years, the number of blacks on NFL rosters remained small, but by the mid-1960s their proportion began to become significant, and today they constitute a majority of NFL players. Table 3.3 shows the percentage of blacks in the NFL for selected years since 1969. Except for hockey, which has only a handful of black players, all major professional team sports have high proportions of blacks; the percentage of black players is highest in basketball, which also pays the highest average salaries of any team sport.

Despite the sizable proportion of black players in the NFL, there are relatively few black coaches and front office personnel. In a controversy similar to the one that occurred as the result of remarks made by Al Campanis of the Los Angeles Dodgers, Jimmy ("the Greek") Snyder was fired in 1988 for racist comments. Snyder, a CBS football sportscaster, had indicated that black athletes excel because of breeding during the slavery era and that eventually there will be no whites in professional sports. His remarks sparked a controversy that called public attention to the lack of blacks in off-field positions and put pressure on the NFL to increase the participation of blacks in these positions.

In 1989 Art Shell, Hall of Fame offensive lineman for the Oakland Raiders, became the first black head coach in modern NFL history. He was hired by Al Davis of the Los Angeles Raiders. The only other black coach in the NFL had been Fritz Pollard, who was a player-coach in 1923–25 for the Hammond (Indiana) Pros. Following Shell, Dennis Green was hired as head coach by the Minnesota Vikings. In 1995 Shell was fired by the Raiders, but Ray Rhodes became the third black head coach when he was hired by the Philadelphia Eagles.

Antitrust Issues

The Sherman Act of 1890 is the principal antitrust law in America. It was passed by the federal government to control the growth of trusts, powerful business firms that engaged in monopolistic practices to stifle competition. The key language of this law, which is applied to the regulation of business, including professional sports, is, "Every contract, combination in the form of trust or otherwise on conspiracy in restraint of trade or commerce among the several states . . . is hereby declared illegal." The Sherman Act provides for treble damages in cases of violation of the law.

The NFL has an exemption from Congress that allows it to pool television rights without violation of the antitrust law. The merger between the NFL and AFL was also exempted. Except for these exemptions, however, antitrust law has been applied to football in several instances, involving such issues as free agency, drafting of players, and movement of franchises.

Free Agency

Before 1976 professional football had the same kind of reserve system as other sports. That is, players entered into the game through drafting by single teams. Players signed standard contracts that bound them to their teams for their careers unless they were traded, sold, or put on waivers. There was hardly any freedom for players to initiate movement from one team to another.[10] Having only one choice of employer, players were in a weak bargaining position.

The first important legal case challenging the owners' control over players was *Radovich*, decided by the U.S. Supreme Court in 1957.[11] William Radovich had been a guard for the Detroit Lions. He contended that he had been blacklisted by the NFL and prevented from earning a living in his profession. He charged the league with a conspiracy to monopolize and control professional football in violation of the Sherman Act of 1890. The Supreme Court's six-to-three decision did not award damages to Radovich, but it did establish the principle that professional football comes under the coverage of the antitrust laws because of the volume of interstate commerce involved in the sport. After this decision, the NFL tried to get Congress to give it a complete exemption from the antitrust laws, but such a law was not passed.

In 1962 a crack opened in the control of owners over players when R. C. Owens of the San Francisco Forty-Niners played out his option and signed a contract with the Baltimore Colts. The crack was temporarily repaired by the owners the following year by establishment of what became known as the

Rozelle Rule. This rule allowed NFL commissioner Pete Rozelle to award compensation (players, draft choices, money) to a player's former team when he signed a contract with a new team. From 1963 to 1976, only four players played out their options and signed with other clubs—Pat Fischer, David Parks, Phil Olson, and Dick Gordon. In effect, the Rozelle Rule denied players the opportunity to sell their services to other teams. To sign a player who played out his option was risky, because it was uncertain what penalty would be imposed on the club by the commissioner. For example, Dave Parks, an all-pro receiver for the San Francisco Forty-Niners, played out his option and signed with the New Orleans Saints. Commissioner Rozelle ordered the Saints to give the Forty-Niners their first-round draft choices in both 1968 and 1969. This was a very harsh penalty for the Saints.

A challenge to the Rozelle Rule was first made by Joe Kapp.[12] Kapp was a quarterback for the Minnesota Vikings, and when his contract expired, the club invoked its option clause for the 1969 season. Kapp then agreed to play for the New England Patriots in 1970, but did not sign a standard player contract with the Patriots. When he refused to sign such a contract for the following year, he was not allowed to play. His lawsuit sought damages from the NFL for terminating his playing career. Although the federal court rejected Kapp's claim that the Rozelle Rule was an illegal conspiracy to restrain trade and monopolize football in violation of the antitrust laws, it did find that the NFL's enforcement of the rule was too severe and caused undue hardship on the players.

In the *Mackey* case, a second court challenge was made to the Rozelle Rule under the antitrust laws.[13] John Mackey was a tight end for the Baltimore Colts and president of the NFLPA who alleged that the rule violated the Sherman Act by denying players an opportunity to contract freely for their services. The federal courts agreed with this contention, finding that the Rozelle Rule was an unreasonable restraint of trade because it acted as a prohibitive deterrent to player movement in the NFL.

With the decision in *Mackey*, NFL players were able to become free agents by playing out their options with the barrier of a compensation penalty to their new team no longer in the way. The NFLPA, however, bargained away the rights won in the courtroom and locked itself into a new method of determining compensation payments for signing free agents. This provision, negotiated in the 1977 collective bargaining agreement, allowed scarcely more free agent mobility than the Rozelle Rule. The 1982 agreement liberalized free agency somewhat, but compensation penalties remained severe.

There is probably no better evidence of the restriction on free agency in the NFL than the fact that from 1977 to 1987 only one free agent, Norm Thompson of the St. Louis Cardinals, signed with another club. In 1988 Wilber Marshall of the Chicago Bears signed as a free agent with the Washington Redskins for a reported $6 million over five years. Although the 1987 agreement had expired, the free agency provisions continued in effect, pending the outcome of antitrust litigation filed by the NFLPA against the NFL as an outgrowth of the 1987 strike. The Redskins had to give up their first-round draft choice in 1988 and 1989 as compensation to the Bears. Thus Marshall became only the second free agent in eleven years to change teams. The Redskins had to pay a steep price in draft choices to get Marshall, a consideration that deterred clubs from signing free agents. As winners of the previous Super Bowl, the Redskins had the last, or twenty-eighth, choice in the first round for 1988, so they figured Marshall was worth the penalty.

What temporarily broke the free agency logjam was the opportunity for an NFL player to play out his option and then sign with a USFL club. In this case, compensation was not required because the USFL was a separate league not bound by the contract between the NFL and NFLPA. The USFL presented a way not only of dodging the compensation bullet, but of achieving a richer contract as a free agent. At the same time, a free agent NFL player was still able to sign another contract with his NFL club, but at far higher pay because of the opportunity to jump leagues. One player, Billy Sims of Detroit Lions, signed a contract with his NFL team and then tried to get out of it by signing two contracts with the USFL. (A bumper sticker appeared on automobiles in the Motor City saying "Honk if you have a contract with Billy.") After litigation, Sims wound up staying with the Lions.

On the day the 1987 strike ended, the union filed an antitrust suit, seeking to use a weapon that had proved menacing to the owners in the past. The suit was brought by Marvin Powell, who was the player president of the NFLPA. It challenged the restraints on free agency and also the college draft and other practices that the union alleged were unfavorable to competition in the football labor market.

A priority with the union in the antitrust suit was to get free agency for players whose individual contracts with their clubs had expired. Judge David Doty, hearing the case in U.S. District Court in Minneapolis, refused the union's initial request for an injunction to release the players, because he was waiting for an NLRB ruling on good faith bargaining. Meanwhile, ruled Judge Doty, the 1982 agreement would remain in effect. When the NLRB dismissed the owners' charge that the union had failed to bargain in good faith, Judge Doty found that an impasse existed. This finding allowed for the chance that approximately 280 players without contracts would be declared free agents when the judge finally ruled on the union's injunction request in mid-July, just before the opening of training camps for the 1988 season. Judge Doty denied the injunctive relief, however, indicating that the potential change of teams by so many players could have had a devastating effect on the competitive balance of the NFL. The judge urged the parties to return to the bargaining table.

Before 1987 the NFLPA was handicapped on antitrust litigation. As long as the NFLPA and NFL had agreed to a free agency system in collective bargaining, the league had a "labor exemption" from the application of the Sherman Act. In the *Powell* suit the union reasoned that without a contract the labor exemption would not apply, and therefore the limits on free agency would be illegal under antitrust law. Judge Doty ruled in favor of the NFLPA in the *Powell* case, but his decision was reversed by the U.S. Court of Appeals, which found that even though the contract had expired and the parties were at impasse in negotiations, the labor exemption from the antitrust law continued to apply.[14]

This setback prompted the NFLPA to decertify itself as the players' representative, reasoning that without a bargaining relationship the league could not shield itself from application of the antitrust law. The NFL, sensing its vulnerability on this ground, unilaterally established a new free agency system called Plan B. This allowed a team to protect 37 players on its roster, with the remaining players able to become free agents without compensation. A protected player could sign as a free agent, but the old practice of contractual free agency compensation continued to apply. As a result, opportunities for free agency improved but not for the most talented players and not nearly as much as the union wanted.

Freeman McNeil, a running back with the New York Jets, joined together with seven other players in a challenge to Plan B. These players were restricted free agents whose old teams would have to be compensated if they were signed by new teams. They contended that Plan B restricted their movement in violation of the antitrust law. Technically, the NFLPA was not a party to the lawsuit because of its voluntary decertification as the players' representative, but the association funded the suit and was its moving force.

The league's defense was primarily that Plan B was necessary to maintain the competitive balance among teams and contributed to the prosperity of the game. They also claimed that Plan B had stimulated free agency and worked to the players' advantage in raising their average annual salaries to $440,000. The trial in *McNeil*, however, revealed that team profits were much higher than the owners had claimed. There was also testimony about how the league had frozen pension benefits, eliminated severance pay, added games to the season, and raised health insurance deductibles.

The jury of eight women found that Plan B was much too restrictive on player mobility and therefore violated antitrust law. Four players were awarded a total of $543,000, which was trebled under the antitrust law to $1.63 million. The other four, including McNeil, were not awarded damages because the jury could not find enough evidence to justify it.

There is an interesting bottom line here. Not only was there a mixed result in damages, but the decision itself was somewhat ambiguous. Although the jury found that Plan B was too restrictive, it nonetheless agreed that it helped maintain competitive balance and that total free agency is not appropriate. Thus, neither side won an outright victory, although the decision was far more in favor of the players than the league.

The *McNeil* decision had immediate impact. After the decision, the options of the parties seemed clear enough even if it wasn't known which courses of action would be taken. Furthermore, it was clear that Judge Doty was willing to be an active presider over this matter.

Shortly after the jury decision four players who were unsigned for the 1992 season asked Judge Doty to declare them free agents. Doty obliged, and gave the players a five-day period in which to sign with new teams. As a result, tight end Keith Jackson of the Philadelphia Eagles signed with the Miami Dolphins, Garin Veris of the New England Patriots signed with the San Francisco Forty-Niners, and Webster Slaughter of the Cleveland Browns signed with the Houston Oilers. Each of these players contracted for substantially more money than they made in the previous year. The big winner was Jackson, who made $350,000 in 1991 but will be paid a reported $6 million over four years under the new contract.

On the whole, free agency is a valuable right for a union to achieve for its players. But free agency is less important to football players than it is for players in other sports. There are several reasons why this is so.[15]

For one thing, gate receipts in the NFL are divided: 60 percent to the home team and 40 percent for the visitors. In contrast, major league baseball has an 85–15 division, and in basketball and hockey the home team keeps 100 percent of gate receipts. What this means is that there is less incentive for an NFL team to sign a free agent because it has to give up a higher percentage of its gate revenues anyway, regardless of outcomes on the playing field. Besides, most stadiums are already filled to capacity.

Incentive to win, and thus to sign free agents, is also dampened by the national television contracts. Each NFL team shares equally in this television money, regardless of its won-lost record. Other sports have equal division of revenues from national television, but teams get to keep all revenues from local broadcast contracts, which the NFL doesn't have.

Thus, from a purely financial standpoint, it makes little sense for NFL teams to sign free agents. But what about psychic income to owners from winning? This may be important, but the value of free agents is limited because football has such large roster sizes that one player is less likely to have an impact on game outcomes. In contrast, one new basketball player might lift a team from mediocrity to the playoffs. Football is more of a coordinated team game with success dependent on systematic operation. A player who excels under one coach's system may not be successful in another's.

There is also less opportunity for football players to capitalize on free agency. Their career length averages only four years, the lowest of any team sport and about half the average in baseball. Given the high incidence of serious injuries to the back and the knees in football, emphasis would seem better placed on health care and insurance plans that provide lifetime protection. Free agency is just pie in the sky for the typical player, who may sign only one NFL contract in his short career.

NFL Draft

The NFL draft was challenged on antitrust grounds in the *Smith* case.[16] Yazoo Smith was a defensive back selected by the Washington Redskins as its number-one draft choice in 1968. He suffered a career-ending neck injury in the final game of that year. Smith's suit alleged that the draft denied him bargaining power and restricted him from obtaining contract provisions to protect his financial future in case of a disabling injury. In the meantime, while the case was being heard in the federal courts, the NFL changed the draft rules, so the case did not have an effect on the modified draft procedure. Nonetheless, the U.S. Court of Appeals found that the old draft procedure was illegal. Although the appellate court did not find a violation of the antitrust laws, it noted that the draft reduced competition by taking away opportunities for college players to market their talents. The U.S. District Court had earlier noted that one of the ways to decrease the anticompetitive influence of the NFL draft on college players was to reduce the number of selection rounds. This step was taken by the NFL to insulate itself from further judicial scrutiny.

When Herschel Walker signed with the USFL, other questions were raised about the draft. Before the Walker contract, the USFL indicated that it would follow the NFL's long-standing rule of not drafting players until they had completed four years of college football eligibility or for five years from the time they enrolled in college. Because Walker was a college junior with another year of eligibility when he was signed, the USFL broke its own rule to secure him.

Then in 1984 a U.S. District Court overturned the USFL's rule on antitrust grounds. The rule was challenged by Bob Boris, a former punter at the University of Arizona, who sought to play in the USFL before his class had graduated. He signed with the Los Angeles Express when the USFL waived its eligibility rule for him, as it had done earlier with Walker. At the time of the suit, Boris had been cut by the Express and was playing for the Oklahoma Outlaws. Judge

Laughlin Waters found that the rule constituted a group boycott and was a per se violation of the Sherman Act. This decision opened the door for other college underclassmen to be drafted by and sign with USFL clubs.

Player draft rules provide a scheme that is beneficial to owners in that they allow owners to collude to keep salaries low by exerting monopoly control over signings.[17] Draft rules may promote a more equal distribution of talent among teams, because teams draft in reverse order of their place in league standings the year before. At the same time, they penalize players for being talented, because the very best go to the least successful teams. The USFL draft allowed for territorial draft choices so that players could be retained in the regions where they played their college careers. It also allowed teams to cooperate on the drafting of a particular player if they felt it was in the interest of the league. The Los Angeles Express, for instance, persuaded other teams not to draft Steve Young, because if he signed in Los Angeles, the second-largest market in the USFL, the league would prosper by greater exposure. This collusive arrangement was not a disservice to Young, but might have been to other players. Such noncompetitive practices may mean that teams in the smaller markets get fewer excellent players.

Restrictions such as the draft do not exist in areas of the labor market other than sports. Advocates of the NFL rule prohibiting the drafting and signing of underclassmen note that players need a college education so that they can move on to other endeavors after their professional football careers. This argument has some merit, but it belies the fact that many college athletes matriculate in watered-down curricula. The NFL's drafting rules are far more restrictive than rules on player eligibility in any other major professional sport. Baseball and basketball, for example, permit drafting after high school, and hockey at the age of eighteen. The U.S. District Court decision on the USFL's rule signaled the beginning of the end of the NFL's rule, which many observers agree is also a violation of the antitrust laws.

In 1990 Commissioner Tagliabue changed the league rules to allow college juniors to apply for the draft, provided they renounce their remaining college eligibility. The NFL had little choice but to make this decision, because it would almost certainly have been held in violation of the antitrust laws restricting entry into the labor market. It would not be surprising if sophomores are the next group to knock on the NFL's door.

Franchise Movement

The movement of team franchises from one city to another can also raise antitrust issues. Al Davis, owner of the Oakland Raiders, sought permission under NFL Rule 4.3 to relocate his franchise in Los Angeles. Always known as an innovative, farsighted, and successful owner, Davis was interested in Los Angeles because of its larger stadium and television market. Were the NFL to sign a contract with pay television in the future, the revenues might not be shared equally among teams, so teams in big television markets would get larger shares. But Rule 4.3 prevented a team from relocating without a three-fourths vote of all teams. When Davis did not get the necessary votes, he went ahead with his plans to move the Raiders to Los Angeles anyway. When the NFL tried to block the move, Davis charged that Rule 4.3 violated the antitrust laws. In 1982 a jury in U.S. District Court in Los Angeles decided that the NFL violated the Sherman Act by trying to prevent the Raiders from moving. The U.S. Court of Appeals in San Francisco upheld the jury verdict, and the U.S. Supreme Court declined without comment to hear the NFL's final appeal in 1984.[18]

The city of Oakland persisted in its attempt to get the Raiders back by filing an eminent domain suit to allow the city to buy the Raiders as a civic asset. This was an unusual case in that eminent domain is ordinarily used by government agencies to seize property for freeways and other public works. In an aside to the main suit, the California Supreme Court found that maintenance of a sports franchise may be an appropriate municipal function for exercising eminent domain rights, thus clearing the way for the case to proceed on the issue of whether the city of Oakland could exercise this right in the matter of the Raiders.[19] The California courts decided against the city, however, reasoning that allowing it to seize a team in a nationwide football league would violate the U.S. Constitution by interfering with the NFL's right to engage in interstate commerce.

For several years legislation has been introduced in Congress to protect communities that support their franchises by allowing the NFL to disapprove relocation of franchises without running afoul of antitrust law. This legislation would recognize the long and faithful support that the people of Oakland gave the Raiders and the important emotional and financial stake that the city has in the team. This proposed legislation has gained more support in recent years, as discussed in Chapter 6.

Following Al Davis's lead, Baltimore Colts owner Robert Irsay moved his team to Indianapolis. This deprived another proud city with a long professional football tradition of its team. Commissioner Rozelle indicated that in view of the enormous expense of trying to stop Al Davis (estimated at about $50 million), the NFL would not oppose the move by Irsay. Thus the league seems to have entered into a "free agency" era for franchise movement. In 1988 the St. Louis Cardinals moved to Phoenix, although owner William Bidwill did get permission to relocate from the NFL. The Los Angeles Rams' attempt to relocate in St. Louis was initially rebuffed by the NFL in 1995, but later allowed, as discussed in Chapter 6. Also in 1995, mirabile dictu, the mercurial Davis moved the Raiders back to Oakland.

USFL Suit

In October 1984 the USFL filed a $1.32 billion antitrust suit against the NFL, in the largest lawsuit yet filed in professional sports. (The USFL sought $440 million in damages, which under the Sherman Act would be tripled if the USFL prevailed in the litigation.) The crux of this suit was the allegation that numerous predatory and unlawful actions were undertaken in a conspiracy by the NFL to perpetuate its monopoly power and prevent successful operation by a rival league. Named as an "involuntary co-conspirator" in the suit was ABC, the network on which USFL games were presented. A few months before the suit, ABC's initial $18 million, two-year contract with the league expired. The network had the option under this contract to pick up games in the 1985 season for $14 million and in 1986 for $18 million. It exercised its option for 1985. ABC was included in the litigation because it allegedly refused to negotiate in good faith on the 1985 option year renewal, failed to promote USFL games during its other programming, and made disparaging remarks about the USFL.

In its complaint against the NFL, the USFL alleged that the NFL (1) entered into long-term, exclusive agreements with stadium operators that froze out competitors; (2) exercised unfair control over the major television networks, with the objective of excluding the USFL from competitive programming; and (3) controlled the available pool of player talent by practices such as signing free agents to play for future seasons during the current season. Had it been successful, the USFL suit would have broken the NFL's network television and stadium contracts. Similar antitrust actions against the NFL in the past, by the American Football League and the World Football League, were unsuccessful.

In a sense the USFL won the suit, but it was a hollow victory. A federal court jury ruled in 1986 that the NFL did have a monopoly on the overall professional market, but that it did not monopolize the market for fall football telecasts or exert pressure on the three major television networks to stop them from offering a contract to the USFL. For all its trouble, the USFL won a one-dollar award, which was tripled under the antitrust law to three dollars.[20] In effect, the jury found that the USFL's problems were the result of its own mismanagement. Several attempts were made by USFL attorneys to get the decision modified or overturned, and it was not until 1988, long after the league had stopped play, that the last of the appeals was rejected by the federal courts.[21]

1993 Agreement

In January 1993, after five years of impasse, the NFL and NFLPA reached a new collective bargaining agreement. More than any other factor, the *McNeil* case opened the door to agreement. *McNeil* declared the owners' Plan B system of free agency in violation of antitrust law. Although the NFL could have appealed *Mc-Neil* and perhaps won a reversal, the long time that an appeal would take was daunting to both sides. Also, Judge Doty pressured for an agreement, threatening to impose conditions on the parties if they did not come up with their own.

The new seven-year agreement contains a quid pro quo on two key issues: (1) free agency, which benefits the players, and (2) a salary cap limiting spending, which benefits the owners. These features are major breakthroughs from which each side should gain significantly over the course of the agreement.

On free agency, players with five years of NFL service were initially able to change teams without restriction when their contracts expired. When the salary cap ceiling was reached, however, eligibility for free agency dropped from five years of play to four years. Each team is allowed to exempt one "franchise" player from free agency for his career, provided that player is offered the average of the five top salaries at his position. Also, a team was granted a right of first refusal, i.e., to match another team's offer, for two free agents in 1993 and one in 1994. From 1995 throughout the remainder of the agreement, however, the only restriction on free agency, apart from the salary cap, is for the franchise player.

The salary cap is a boon to the owners. As in a similar practice begun in the National Basketball Association, players get a salary guarantee: a minimum of 58 percent of designated gross revenue (about 95 percent of total revenue) goes to player salaries. As provided under the agreement, because NFL teams spent 67 percent of their revenues on player salaries during the 1993 season, the salary cap went into effect in 1994 for the final six years of the agreement. The cap thereafter dropped for three consecutive years, to 64 percent for 1994, 63 percent for 1995, and finally to 62 percent for 1996, where it remains for the duration of the agreement.

Apart from limiting overall expenditures, the salary cap forces traditionally low-paying teams to spend more on salaries, while the big-spending teams must curb their generosity. Individual players have been hurt by the cap. The Indianapolis Colts, in order to sign rookies Marshall Faulk and Trev Alberts, had to waive seven veteran players to comply with the salary cap in 1994. New York Giants quarterback Phil Simms was waived in order to make room for new players. Other players had their salaries cut significantly. This caused some players to complain that while they have the ability as free agents to change teams, as a practical matter movement is restricted because of the salary cap. Still, many players have changed teams—120 during the first year alone.

The bugaboo of teams in the big media markets buying up all the talented players and wrecking competitive balance has not occurred. A team needs only a certain number of players at each position, and star players do not like to ride the bench. As player agent Leigh Steinberg points out, players are motivated by a host of factors in signing with a club: geography, lifestyle, endorsement opportunities, coaches, organization structure, and a team's style of play.[22] The top free agent in 1993, Reggie White, signed with the Green Bay Packers, the team with the smallest market. Although players in big-market cities may get more media attention, the long reach of cable television today means that a player's home team is less important in endorsement marketability.

Just as free agency stimulates some owners to open up their pocketbooks to produce winning teams, certain players are strongly motivated to play with a winner. A good example is the San Francisco Forty-Niners. Under owner Eddie DeBartolo and president Carmen Policy, the Forty-Niners became the most successful team in football, spending liberally on players. The team payroll in 1993 was about $50 million, highest in the league. Because the salary cap came into effect in 1994, however, the payroll had to be reduced to $34.6 million. Consequently, a few high-salary players were traded or waived and several free agents were signed. Some free agents, such as Rickey Jackson, Deion Sanders, and Bart Oates, signed with the Forty-Niners for less than their market value because they wanted to play with a winner. They were rewarded when the team won the Super Bowl in 1995.

Besides free agency and the salary cap, the 1993–97 collective bargaining agreement contains other notable features. NFL players were polled by *Sports Illustrated* in 1991 on their priorities in collective bargaining. Of the 205 players who responded, 56 percent ranked improved benefits as their number-one objective, while 39 percent rated free agency as their top priority.[23] Accordingly, benefits were emphasized in the new agreement. Pensions were raised so that players with three years of NFL experience in 1997 get $300 a month for each year played, beginning at age fifty-five. The annual deductible for full family health insurance was reduced from $2,800 to $400. Disabled players get an extra $4,335 per month by 1997. A 401(k) plan was established with teams matching $7,500 annually per player in pretax savings for retirement. There is severance pay of $30,000 for each year of play.

Other terms of the agreement include $195 million in damages to about two thousand players in various lawsuits that were settled. The addition of two new teams was provided, and the cities ultimately selected, Charlotte (Carolina) and Jacksonville, began play in 1995, raising the number of teams in the league to thirty. The NFL's developmental World Football League (discussed in Chapter 6) was revived and resumed play in the spring of 1995.

Substance Abuse

Drug abuse has become a serious concern in professional team sports. Until recently, however, little effort was made to deal with the problem. Amphetamines, stimulants to the central nervous system, have long been part of the culture of football players. As we are frequently reminded by broadcasters, football is a game of emotion, and the team that reaches a higher level of emotional intensity if more likely to win. Players have long relied on painkillers to enable them to play with minor injuries, and some football players have used anabolic steroids to develop their muscles and gain strength.

Widespread use of amphetamines in football came to light in 1973, when it was estimated that between one-third and one-half of the players on the Washington Redskins team used the drug to get up for games. Because amphetamines were sometimes distributed by team physicians and were otherwise easily available to players, the NFL for several years required that a bulletin be posted in locker rooms to the effect that the NFL did not condone the use of pep pills and warned players against their use. The NFL also had security representatives make annual visits to teams to express its disapproval of drug misuse. Spot checks were occasionally made by security personnel, and a physician was hired by the league to evaluate bills of drug purchases submitted by teams. In 1974 Commissioner Rozelle fined the San Diego Chargers, its general manager, and eight of its players for improper use and distribution of drugs to the team. These measures for drug control, however, were aimed primarily at the use of amphetamines and other mild forms of abuse. More serious drug abuse problems involving possible criminal penalties had not emerged yet.

A public disclosure by Don Reese in 1982 brought to light widespread use of cocaine by football players. A former player for the New Orleans Saints, Reese was convicted for dealing in cocaine, and he revealed the considerable use of this drug by NFL players. Although there had been some earlier evidence of a cocaine problem among NFL players, players who disclosed their problems, such as Carl Eller of the Minnesota Vikings, were thought to be isolated cases. Few people realized the dimensions of cocaine use in football. Commissioner Rozelle had down-played the drug problem by taking the position that football players had no greater drug problem than does society. With Reese's disclosure, Commissioner Rozelle mounted a public relations campaign to express the NFL's concern and intention to take action.

The NFL's revised program emphasized education and rehabilitation. Players were informed of treatment programs and given counseling and warnings by officials of the Drug Enforcement Administration and the Federal Bureau of Investigation. Gene Upshaw of the NFLPA became active in talking with play-

ers about drug abuse, as did some team coaches. The centerpiece of the rehabilitation phase of the program was to send players who requested help to the
Hazelden Clinic in Minnesota, with the NFL paying the bills and not disclosing
names of players. But few players came forward to admit they had problems,
and stories of cocaine use continued. According to a story in the *New York Daily
News*, which was widely referenced in the media, cocaine was used by as many
as 50 percent of NFL players, with about 20 percent qualifying as "hardcore"
users.[24] Commissioner Rozelle responded that, according to NFL security reports, the figures were exaggerated. Public pressure for action kept growing after five members of the Dallas Cowboys were investigated for suspected cocaine
violations and Tony Peters of the Washington Redskins was arrested and later
imprisoned for acting as a go-between in a cocaine sale.

The NFL's drug policy acquired a punitive aspect when the NFL began enforcing the law as well as providing education and rehabilitation. Before the
start of the 1983 season, the NFL suspended four players without pay for four
games. Ross Browner and Pete Johnson of the Cincinnati Bengals had admitted
in federal court to purchasing cocaine from a drug dealer; in separate incidents,
E. J. Junior of the St. Louis Cardinals and Greg Stemrick of the New Orleans
Saints had both pleaded no contest and were convicted on cocaine felony
charges. None of the players was imprisoned. In his announcement of the suspensions, Rozelle noted,

> NFL players occupy a unique position in the eyes of the public. They are objects
> of admiration and emulation by countless fans, particularly young people. In-
> volvement with illegal drugs poses numerous risks to the integrity of professional
> football and the public's confidence in it. Thus, every player must adhere to cer-
> tain standards of personal conduct both on and off the field. Every player agrees
> by his employment contract to not engage in activities detrimental to the sport.[25]

Under Ed Garvey, the NFLPA would probably have attacked Commissioner
Rozelle for taking such harsh action against players, arguing double jeopardy
because Rozelle imposed his own sentence after the players had been dealt with
in court. By the time of the cocaine busts, however, Gene Upshaw had taken over
as the union's executive director, and he took a noncombative stance on the issue. In any event, there was little the union could do, because the collective bargaining agreement provides the commissioner with control over the integrity of
the game, and players are subject to discipline under their individual contracts.

Despite the punishment of players by the NFL, reports of drug use continued
to surface. The most tragic of these incidents involved the death of Cleveland
Browns safety Don Rogers from cocaine intoxication in 1986. Later that year
Commissioner Rozelle, unable to reach agreement on revisions to the drug

program with the NFLPA, announced his intention to require two random regular-season urinalysis tests for cocaine, marijuana, opiate, and amphetamine use. Under this program a first positive test would require a player to receive thirty days of counseling at half pay; a second violation would lead to a thirty-day unpaid suspension; and a third would result in banishment from the league.

With a majority of players opposed to random testing, the NFLPA sought a court injunction to prohibit the NFL from implementing the program. The NFLPA also filed a grievance. The players had earlier agreed in collective bargaining to testing during preseason training camps (but not during the regular season) and to subsequent testing when management had "reasonable cause" to believe that a player was using drugs.

To avoid a court battle, the league and union agreed to submit the validity of the commissioner's proposal to arbitrator Richard Kasher. In late 1986 Kasher ruled that the program violated the collective bargaining agreement. Although he acknowledged the commissioner's power to take action to protect the integrity of the game, the random regular-season testing proposal went beyond the provisions for preseason and "reasonable cause" testing in the negotiated agreement.

At about the same time that Kasher's decision came out, another arbitrator, Sam Kagel, ruled that about two hundred players had been improperly fined $1,000 by their clubs for refusing to submit to drug tests after the 1985 season. Arbitrator Kagel determined that preseason tests, but not postseason tests, were allowed by the collective bargaining agreement.

Thus the NFL was thwarted twice by arbitrators over drug policy. Nevertheless, in response to public pressure, the league kept trying to impose change. Following the arbitrators' rulings, the NFL announced that it was going to expand its preseason tests to include anabolic steroids. The league had long been criticized for its inaction on steroids. Steroids have a number of dangerous side effects, such as liver and kidney disorders, hypertension, sterility, and cancer. Even a few players had begun to speak out against steroids, and some insurance companies stopped writing new policies against career-ending injuries for football players. Also, chemical laboratories had indicated a willingness to improve the techniques for steroid testing, making action by the league seem prudent. Testing for steroids began before the 1987 season.

Although several players tested positive for steroids in 1987 and 1988, none was disciplined. In 1989, however, thirteen players were given a four-game suspension for testing positive. This crackdown led to a sharp drop in penalties to only four in 1990, one in 1991, and very low numbers since.

In response to steroid and other drug problems, the NFLPA established a drug prevention committee. Its chairman, guard Bill Fralic of the Atlanta Falcons, testified before a U.S. Senate Judiciary Committee in 1990 that as many as 75 percent of NFL linemen, linebackers, and tight ends had used steroids. A problem is that one can use steroids but then stop before testing so as to avoid detection. This problem was countered by Commissioner Tagliabue in 1990 when he imposed random testing on up to four occasions during the regular season (in addition to the two training camp tests). Under the revised policy players testing positive for steroids are suspended for thirty days, and a second violation results in a one-year suspension. Dr. John Lombardo heads up the league's steroids program.

The NFL's policy on drugs other than steroids has been changed somewhat since the 1986 revision. As of 1994 the rules were that a first violation results in random testing, a second violation gets a six-week suspension, and a third violation results in at least a year without pay. Occasional third violations have occurred. In 1988 running back Tony Collins of the Indianapolis Colts was banned for two years. In 1989 Stanley Wilson, running back of the Cincinnati Bengals, was permanently banned and defensive lineman Dexter Manley of the Washington Redskins was suspended for a year. New Orleans Saints defensive end Frank Warren was suspended for a year in 1990. In 1993 Los Angeles Raider defensive back David Waymer died of cocaine ingestion.

Since 1988 testing of players in training camps and in random situations has been in the hands of the NFL's drug expert. Before that time testing was carried out by team doctors, who were beholden to their clubs and did not regularly report negative results. The first drug expert was Dr. Forest Tennant, a professor of public health at UCLA. He was succeeded in 1990 by Dr. Lawrence Brown, Jr., an instructor in clinical medicine at Columbia University's College of Physicians and Surgeons.

In 1991 the NFL became the first major professional sports league to have a disciplinary policy for alcohol-related misconduct. Under the policy, established by Commissioner Tagliabue, a first offender can be suspended for as much as five weeks without pay, a second offender for six weeks, and a third offender for a year. Discipline is for serious misconduct, such as drunk driving.

Players, coaches, and other league personnel have become more sensitized to drug and alcohol issues. Considerable progress has been made. This may be partly due to a slowing in the use of drugs and alcohol throughout society. Also, during the years that the NFLPA was without a collective bargaining agreement, it did not seek to defend guilty players, which may have strengthened the deterrent factor of punishment. Over the years the league has revised its policies to adapt to problem areas and has become more consistent in applying its rules.

Basketball   4

Few persons who watch professional basketball are not impressed with the grace, skill, and quickness of the magnificent athletes who play the game. Off the court, these players are motivated by the same economic objective as athletes in other major professional sports, to maximize their financial returns over short playing careers. As in other sports, players have formed a union, the National Basketball Players Association (NBPA), to promote their collective interests, and they are usually represented by outside agents in their individual salary negotiations with clubs. The NBPA has been active in legal affairs, helping to establish free agency for greater player mobility and bargaining power. The union confronts a league, the National Basketball Association (NBA), that bargains on behalf of team owners through the familiar multiemployer structure. Industrial relations in professional basketball have not had the prominent media exposure that baseball and football have. There has never been a strike by players, yet there are a number of interesting developments, many of which are unique to the sport.

Baseball had its forerunner in the game of rounders in England, the country that also developed football's predecessor, rugby. Hockey has Canadian origins. But basketball is a distinctly American game. It was the creation in 1891 of Dr. James Naismith, an instructor at a YMCA training school in Springfield, Massachusetts.[1] Naismith was asked by the director of the school to devise a game that would occupy the attention of a fractious group of physical education students. After some experimentation, he hit on the idea of nailing two peach baskets to the balcony of the gymnasium. The object was to throw a ball into the basket, and the players were not allowed to run with the ball or use roughhouse tactics. A ladder was used to retrieve the ball. By 1912 an open net was used.

Colleges took up the game, and the YMCA did much to promote it. Although the game changed substantially over the years, twelve of the original thirteen rules laid down by Naismith still survive.

Professional basketball began in 1898 with the formation of the National Basketball League. It folded after the 1902-3 season. Numerous other leagues were established in the early years, but it was not until the American Basketball League (ABL) started play in 1925 that something of a lasting foundation was laid. The ABL initially had nine teams, including the original Celtics, which played their home games in New York (two of the stars of this team were Nat Holman and Joe Lapchick, who later became renowned coaches). But the ABL and other early leagues were poorly organized and managed. Players rarely had binding contracts and would jump back and forth between teams. Fan interest was minimal. A more stable league format was created when the National Basketball League began in 1937 and the Basketball Association of America in 1946. In 1949 these leagues merged to form the National Basketball Association, which continues today as the major professional league.

Economics of Basketball

The economics of basketball indicate that the sport is in the midst of an era of unprecedented growth and prosperity. Although the league looked shaky in the early 1980s, as attendance and profits dwindled, there is no doubt that the NBA is on a roll.

NBA basketball is in a relatively favorable position to be packaged for spectators. With the demise of the ABA, there is no rival league to dilute fan appeal and drive salaries upward. There are considerable opportunities for exposing the sport to potential spectators, with a regular-season schedule of eighty-two games plus extended playoffs and twenty-nine teams operating in markets that extend to nearly all the large population centers of the nation. Moreover, the game presents an attractive product for television. It has a compact playing area, few players to follow, and a highly visible ball. Although there is some overlap with the seasons for other sports, product competition during the winter months is not extensive. With only twelve players on a team, high salaries are justified because relatively few players must be paid.

Professional basketball teams have three major assets: the right to present games in a particular geographic area, player contracts, and access to an arena for staging games.[2] These are essentially contractual agreements that protect teams from competition. Profitability is determined by a number of factors, among them the inherent attraction of the game. Professional basketball has a constant flow of new, exciting players coming into the game who have already developed strong public recognition during their college careers, but the large number of games played and frequent travel sap players' vitality. Perhaps many fans have the perception that NBA games do not get interesting until the closing minutes, when players go all out to win, because it is difficult to maintain a fast pace over the entire game during the long season.

The financial success of individual teams depends primarily on the demand for games in the team's home city, the team's success, costs of operation, the club's tax liability, and how efficiently the franchise is managed. The greater the population in the team's home area and the larger the arena size, the greater will be the potential market and gate receipts. Like other professional sports, basketball has its rich-poor dichotomy, with teams in New York and Los Angeles having great market advantages over teams in Utah and Sacramento. A team's win-loss record is important in attracting fans and justifying higher ticket prices, and because the addition of a single superstar player can make a significant difference in the team playing success, top free agents are in great demand. When owners try to gain an edge by raising salaries, the costs of operation can rise quickly. In the late 1970s and early 1980s, the increases in gross income did not come close to keeping pace with the increases in player salaries. Several teams consistently lost money during this period. In a classic case of poor management, Ted Stepien, owner of the Cleveland Cavaliers, paid enormous salaries to free agents and traded away draft choices only to acquire a team with players of limited skills. When he finally sold the team, the NBA voted to allow the new owners to regain four first-round draft choices in an effort to revitalize the wrecked franchise.

Do big cities have better teams? Roger Noll, a Stanford University economist, answers this question by historical analysis, showing that teams in major metropolitan areas—Boston, Los Angeles, Philadelphia, New York, and Chicago—have won a disproportionate share of league championships.[3] Noll cites as one reason for this dominance the attendance effect, causing better entrepreneurs to locate in or move their franchises to large cities. Another reason he gives is the incentive created by national broadcasting, because the audience for national telecasts is larger if successful teams are in big-market areas. Although some parity among teams in a league is desirable because it creates uncertain outcomes that keep all fans interested, overall league financial strength is greater if big-market teams win championships.

The home team in basketball keeps 100 percent of the gate receipts. This creates an incentive to replace older, smaller-seating-capacity arenas with big new facilities that include luxury boxes. As shown in Table 4.1, average attendance in the NBA has increased steadily over the past several years. Arenas are filled to

Table 4.1. Average Attendance at NBA
Games, 1976–95

Season	Attendance
1976–77	10,974
1977–78	10,947
1978–79	10,822
1979–80	11,017
1980–81	10,021
1981–82	10,567
1982–83	10,220
1983–84	10,620
1984–85	11,141
1985–86	11,893
1986–87	12,795
1987–88	13,419
1988–89	15,088
1989–90	15,690
1990–91	15,245
1991–92	15,689
1992–93	16,060
1993–94	16,246
1994–95	16,727

Source: National Basketball Association.

nearly 90 percent of capacity during the regular season and are typically sold out during the playoffs. This success has occurred despite high ticket prices and competition for fan interest from college basketball, professional hockey, and indoor soccer. Although the NBA is riding a wave of prosperity, it is always appropriate to be cautious about the future of any professional sport. The history of major sports leagues is riddled with failed franchises and disappointed investors. Inflation bubbles can burst and golden ages end. One is reminded of an interview with Frank Layden, former coach of the Utah Jazz. When asked how someone could make a small fortune in professional sports, Layden said, "You start out with a large one."[4]

League Expansion

The continued success of the NBA, as with other leagues, depends in part on expansion of new franchises. Growth in a league discourages rival leagues from forming, maintains monopoly control of the sport, adds to league revenues, and stimulates fan interest in new competition. In the 1988–89 season the NBA added teams in Charlotte and Miami, and in 1989–90 in Minnesota (with the franchise located in Minneapolis) and Orlando. Each of these new franchises paid an entry fee of $32.5 million, with each of the previous twenty-three teams sharing equally in the total $130 million paid. In the 1995–96 season the NBA expanded to Canada with the addition of teams in Toronto and Vancouver. These new teams each paid an entry fee of $125 million, nearly four times that paid by the teams joining the league in the late 1980s.

Although some observers are concerned about diluting the number of talented players as a result of expansion, the value of NBA franchises has skyrocketed. In 1986 the Boston Celtics became the first publicly traded NBA team when 40 percent of its stock was sold on the equity market. The following year the Denver Nuggets went public with a stock sale. In 1991 the Orlando Magic sold for $85 million, up from $32.5 million in 1989, and the Houston, Minnesota, and San Antonio franchises were later sold in the $80 million range. In 1995 the Golden State Warriors were sold for a record $126 million. These numbers indicate that NBA teams are almost as valuable as franchises in baseball and football.

Television

Although basketball is well suited to television coverage, it has traditionally ranked a poor third to football and baseball in television ratings. The first nationally televised professional basketball game, between the New York Knickerbockers and Boston Celtics, was shown on NBC in 1954. The owners recognized the importance of television exposure to expanding interest in and profitability of the game, and they began to negotiate network and local television agreements. A three-year agreement was reached with CBS to televise thirty-eight games each season, beginning in the 1973–74 season. In 1976 this agreement with CBS was extended for two years in a $10.5 million deal arranged by Commissioner Lawrence O'Brien.

Beginning in the 1982–83 season, a four-year $88 million television agreement with CBS paid each team about $1 million a season. In addition, each team received another $240,000 annually from league contracts with the USA and ESPN cable networks, plus anywhere from $100,000 to $1 million from local television agreements, on either free television or cable. National cable television revenues doubled for the 1984–85 and 1985–86 seasons under a contract with WTBS, Ted Turner's Atlanta-based network, to show fifty-five regular-season and twenty playoff games each year. In 1986 the NBA agreed to a new four-year agreement with CBS for $170 million, which provided about $2 million per team annually. The cable television contract also doubled, with WTBS agreeing to a $50 million deal covering 1988–89 and 1989–90.

In 1989 NBC replaced CBS as the league's primary network by paying the NBA $600 million over four years. NBC also agreed to spend another $50 million to promote the NBA on television and radio. Rights fees thus more than tripled over the previous contract. NBC got an increased number of regular-season games to telecast, from sixteen to twenty, with the right to air up to twenty-six games during the last three years of the contract. All-star game and playoff rights were also part of the package. The NBA sold cable rights to seventy-five games to Turner Broadcasting System in a four-year deal for $275 million, quadrupling the price of the prior contract. In 1988 Turner had established a new venture called Turner Network Television (TNT). Part of the motivation for paying such a high price to the NBA for cable rights was to attract new subscribers to TNT.

An important change in the structure of sports television contracts occurred in 1993 when the NBA renewed its agreement for four years (through the 1997–98 season). The rights fees increased to $750 million, up 25 percent over the prior agreement. Although this is a substantial increase, it is less than the doubling and tripling of revenues in the past. What makes the new contract unique is that the league has the potential for increasing its revenue in a partnership arrangement with the network. NBC agreed to share advertising revenues equally above a certain level with the league during the fourth year of the contract. This revenue-sharing feature is a hedge against risk for both sides. In 1993 the NBA also reached a four-year cable agreement with TNT for $352 million, providing rights to televise seventy regular-season games and at least thirty-five playoff games.

In 1990 the NBA board of governors passed a resolution to phase out broadcasts of games by television superstations, stations whose signals are picked up by cable companies throughout the nation. The league figured that the superstation telecasts invaded the media markets of NBA teams and diminished the value of league contracts with NBC and cable companies. In the past the NBA had allowed limited superstation telecasts. But its attempt to reduce and eventually eliminate superstation telecasts prompted a lawsuit by the Chicago Bulls and WGN, the Chicago-based superstation that televises Bulls games. In 1991 Hubert Will, a federal district court judge in Chicago, ruled that the NBA violated antitrust law by restricting the number of games a franchise can broadcast on superstations. Judge Will reiterated this conclusion in 1995 when he ruled that WGN could telecast at least thirty Bulls games in the 1994–95 season. These rulings may have a broader implication in that they interpret the Sports Broadcasting Act, which states that federal antitrust law does not apply to leagues that seek to protect the television rights of small-market teams. By finding that the

NBA violated antitrust law in the Chicago case, the court opened the door to more superstation telecasts of other major league sports as well as basketball.

Structure of Employment

NBA and the ABA

The NBA had seventeen teams in its inaugural season, but lost six teams for the second season and was down to only eight teams by 1957. Since then, the league has steadily expanded to twenty-nine teams in 1995–96, each of which plays an eighty-two-game schedule. There are also a good number of postseason playoff games, with eligibility determined by placement among the top sixteen best won-lost records. The NBA is a joint venture. Most clubs are owned by corporations, but authority is exercised by a single dominant owner who is usually the majority stockholder. Club owners join together to make policy decisions on rules and other matters of common interest through the board of governors of the NBA. The league also has a labor relations committee, composed of owners, which is primarily responsible for collective bargaining.

After the merger of the two leagues to form the NBA in 1949, there was no serious threat to its hegemony over professional basketball. In the 1960s, however, two leagues were formed that caused competition for acquisition of players and fan attention and provided stimulus to NBA salaries. The first of these rivals, the American Basketball League (ABL), was formed in 1961 by Abe Saperstein, owner of the Harlem Globetrotters.[5] Despite such innovations as awarding three points for field goals initiated from more than twenty-five feet from the basket, the ABL never really caught on among fans and had very limited television exposure. After only one full season and part of another it collapsed. Before the start of the ABL's truncated second season, the best team in the league, the Cleveland Pipers, was absorbed into the NBA. Losses to the league's eight teams were estimated at $1.5 million in the first season, and no team was profitable when the league folded. About one hundred players lost their jobs.

In 1967 a more formidable rival for the NBA emerged. The American Basketball Association (ABA) was far better financed and organized than the ABL. Creation of the league was largely the work of Gary Davidson, a maverick sports entrepreneur who also founded competitive sports leagues in football and hockey. The commissioner of the new league was George Mikan, formerly a great player with the Minneapolis Lakers. A key ABA strategy was to avoid head-to-head competition with NBA teams by establishing as many ABA franchises as possible in non-NBA cities. The league began play in the 1967–68 season with teams in Anaheim, Dallas, Denver, Houston, Indianapolis (called Indiana), Louisville (called Kentucky), Minneapolis (called Minnesota), New Jersey, New Orleans, Oakland, and Pittsburgh. Only three of these franchises—New Jersey, Anaheim, and Oakland—competed for spectators with teams in nearby NBA cities (New York, Los Angeles, and San Francisco). Another tactic to preserve the financial strength of ABA teams was to avoid bidding wars for players with NBA teams. This policy did not hold for long, however, since ABA teams soon began to draft and sign top college players. To spice up play, the ABA had three-point field goals (from more than twenty-five feet), a thirty-second shot clock, and a resplendent red-white-and-blue basketball.

Many of the initial ABA players were NBA rejects or marginal players who jumped leagues. An exception was the brilliant forward Rick Barry, who went from the NBA's San Francisco Warriors to the Oakland Oaks of the ABA. In later seasons, several other outstanding NBA players jumped leagues, including Zelmo Beatty, Billy Cunningham, and Dave Bing. Some talented players—for example, David Thompson, Dan Issel, Bobby Jones, and Artis Gilmore—also joined the ABA's teams directly from college, with more coming as the league became better established. What gave the ABA a leg up on the NBA in attracting potential superstars was that the new league did not adhere to the NBA rule of waiting until a player's college class had graduated before making him eligible for drafting. Thus the ABA picked off such plums as Moses Malone, who signed out of high school, and Julius ("Dr. J") Erving, George McGinnis, and George Gervin, who all left college early. Another interesting star in the ABA was Connie Hawkins, who was at first barred from the NBA because of a collegiate gambling scandal.

The ABA struggled through the first year without a television contract. In ensuing years local TV contracts were signed with ABA teams, but the big national network coverage never materialized. Nevertheless, the ABA enjoyed a measure of respectability, and many observers felt that overall its players nearly achieved parity with those in the NBA. After its first season, league players formed the American Basketball Association Players Association in Denver. Larry Jones of the Denver Rockets was its first president. The ABA union never became a dominant force against the owners. Its most significant accomplishment appears to have been a licensing and merchandising agreement with the league and Metro-Goldwyn-Mayer to arrange deals with companies in the food, toy, and other industries for use of the ABA name.

The opening round in the bidding war between the leagues began in 1968, when the NBA stole a march on its rival by holding an early draft for first-round choices. Competition between the leagues for players caused a tremendous surge in salaries, making basketball players by far the highest paid professional team athletes. It was estimated that owners of ABA teams lost $50 million during the nine years of the league's existence, and the competition also cut deeply into NBA profits. After just two years of bidding wars, the rival leagues realized that further competition would be difficult to sustain.

In 1969 officials of the leagues began talks directed at merger or, at the least, establishment of a common draft. The NBPA quickly announced its vigorous opposition to any kind of collusion between the leagues, arguing that a merger or common draft would restrict a player's ability to earn a living. But after several months of discussions, ABA owners agreed to pay an indemnity of $11 million to merge with the NBA and to have limited interleague play, playoffs, and an all-star game between the two leagues. This prompted the NBPA to file an antitrust suit in federal court to stop the merger as well as to challenge the draft, uniform contract, and the reserve clause that tied a player to one team within the NBA. A temporary restraining order and later a preliminary injunction were issued by the federal courts to prevent the merger pending determination on the merits of the suit.

Despite the injunction, the leagues proceeded with plans to merge, and in 1970 both voted in favor of a merger, subject to approval by Congress. Congress had approved a merger of the National and American Football Leagues in 1966, but at that time there was no opposition from the players of either league. Thus the basketball leagues, in the face of opposition from NBA players, sought congressional exemption from the antitrust laws to allow them to merge in order to stop the bidding war by establishing a common draft and arrangements for the signing of free agents. United States Senator Sam J. Ervin, Jr., called for a careful review of the antitrust issue in basketball and sponsored legislation applying the Sherman Act to professional sports.[6] This legislation was not enacted by Congress, however, so the problems continued.

The potential merger of the ABA and NBA was complicated by the fact that each league negotiated with a union representing its players. With separate bargaining units, the question arose as to whether the leagues needed approval from both players' associations in order to establish a common draft. If the merger was approved, the players would clearly suffer because competition for their services would be eliminated. Had Congress granted approval for exemption from the antitrust laws, the merger of the leagues would have gotten around the meddlesome players. But the failure of Congress to sanction the merger placed the determination of the issue back in the hands of the courts, where it was to languish for several years. During this period the merger agreement between the leagues expired, and the leagues awaited the outcome of litigation before resuming efforts to merge.

When the legal issues barring a merger were finally removed, the door was opened for resumption of talks. In June 1976 the NBA and ABA consolidated into a twenty-two-team league. Four of the six surviving teams in the ABA were absorbed into the NBA and began play in the 1976–77 season. These teams—New York Nets, Indiana Pacers, Denver Nuggets, and San Antonio Spurs—were each required to pay $3.2 million in cash to the NBA. In addition, the Nets were required to indemnify the New York Knickerbockers by cash payments over several years for moving into their territory.

The Kentucky Colonels and Utah Rockies were left out of the merger and were paid about $3 million each by the four teams that were accepted in the NBA. Kentucky and Utah players were dispersed in a special draft involving all twenty-two teams. Because they had the worst record in the league, the Chicago Bulls had first choice in the dispersal draft of twenty players and selected Artis Gilmore from Kentucky. Other outstanding players available through this draft were Moses Malone and Maurice Lucas. Although numerous league and team officials played an important role in the merger, the principal architects were Larry O'Brien, commissioner of the NBA, and David DeBusschere, commissioner of the ABA.

The Commissioner

The NBA commissioner, who holds a position formerly known as president of the NBA, is influential in labor relations. The first president of the league was Maurice Podoloff, who is credited with holding the league together in the difficult early years. In the infancy of the NBA, the most visible labor relations function of the president was to uphold the integrity of the game by investigating charges of gambling by players. Podoloff was succeeded as president in 1963 by Walter Kennedy, former mayor of Stamford, Connecticut. When Kennedy retired as commissioner in 1975, he was replaced by Lawrence F. O'Brien. At the time O'Brien was chosen by the owners, the NBA was embroiled in litigation over the proposed merger with the ABA and was active in congressional lobbying for antitrust law exemption. He seemed a perfect choice for the job because of his previous political experience as campaign manager for John F. Kennedy, Lyndon B. Johnson, and Hubert H. Humphrey and his service as national chairman of the Democratic party and as postmaster general.

Larry O'Brien proved to be a great leader during a very hectic period of the NBA, but not always in the way the owners wanted. He took a more sympathetic stand toward players' rights than was expected, although he was a strict disciplinarian on matters such as player fighting and drug abuse. O'Brien's major accomplishments were (1) resolution of an antitrust suit by players, (2) signing of three collective bargaining agreements that were among the most progressive in professional sports, (3) finalizing the merger with the ABA that resulted in the addition of four teams to the NBA, (4) negotiating major television contracts, and (5) instigation of a new drug control policy. When O'Brien resigned in 1983 he was succeeded as commissioner by David J. Stern. Stern had begun service with the NBA in 1967 as an attorney with the New York law firm that represented the league. In 1978 he became the NBA's general counsel and later an executive vice-president for business and legal affairs. Stern worked closely with O'Brien over the years and was O'Brien's choice for the commissioner's post. Stern has proved to be an inspired choice who has excellent skills in negotiation, marketing, finance, and public relations.

Players and Their Union

There are about three hundred and fifty players in the NBA. Nearly all of them are recruited from colleges, and NBA rosters are dominated by black players. In 1954 only about 5 percent of the league's players were black; by 1962 the percentage had risen to 30 percent and by 1970 to 57 percent.[7] In 1995 about 80 percent of the players on the NBA rosters were black, a larger proportion than in any professional sport.

In the early years, professional basketball was segregated. The greatest black team was the Renaissance Big Five, organized in Harlem in 1922. The Rens, as they were popularly known, played against the best all-white teams in the 1930s and were considered the best team in the nation.[8] Another successful early black team was the Harlem Globetrotters, known primarily today for their clowning techniques that delight fans.

Baseball was the first major professional sport to break the color line when Jackie Robinson played for the Brooklyn Dodgers in 1947. Three years later, Earl Lloyd and Chuck Cooper became the first black players in the NBA, signing with the Washington Capitols and Boston Celtics, respectively. In 1966 basketball became the first sport to employ a black coach when player Bill Russell succeeded Arnold ("Red") Auerbach as coach of the Boston Celtics, and since then other black players, such as Lennie Wilkins, Alvin Attles, K. C. Jones, Wes Unseld, and Bob Lanier, have coached NBA teams. A black lawyer, Simon Gourdine, served as deputy commissioner in the NBA. Despite the high percentage of black players, only about 30 percent of the front office positions were occupied by blacks in 1987; toward reducing this disparity, the NBA entered into an agreement with the National Association for the Advancement of Colored People to increase minority off-court employment. This has resulted in an increase in jobs for blacks, recently to about 20 percent for head coaches and general managers. Black ownership came to the NBA in 1990 when Bertram Lee and Peter Bynoe purchased 37.5 percent of the Denver Nuggets.

Various factors contribute to the prominence of blacks in professional basketball. Unlike such sports as golf or tennis, in which economic constraints have prevented high numbers of blacks from participating, basketball is a playground game that is readily accessible to most youths. Open university admission policies have given blacks greater opportunities to play at the college level. The NBA not only encouraged black players to participate through its draft but also protected them from racial harassment; for example, in 1959 the NBA board of governors established a policy to insulate black players from embarrassment stemming from segregated housing and dining facilities.[9] Formation of the rival ABA created additional jobs in basketball and unprecedented opportunities for black players.

The National Basketball Players Association (NBPA) was formed in 1954 by Bob Cousy, a star player for the Boston Celtics. He was assisted by his close friend and insurance agent, Joseph P. Sharry, who served as secretary-treasurer. Cousy selected an outstanding player from each team to serve as the initial player representatives. When its grievances were ignored for two years by league president Maurice Podoloff, the NBPA threatened coercive action. There were rumors of a strike if the league did not recognize the association. Unable to get satisfaction from Podoloff, Cousy met with a representative of the American Guild of Variety Artists to consider affiliation with this labor union. Podoloff indicated that he was not opposed to the players organizing but felt that their association should be limited to players only.[10] In response to the players' threats, Podoloff invited their representatives to a joint meeting with the owners in 1957. Recognition was granted the NBPA at this meeting.[11]

After its recognition by the owners, the NBPA seemed to lose its vitality and cohesiveness. Organization was poor because there was no constitution or bylaws, and meetings were infrequent. This lack of organization as well as a shortage of funds made it difficult to mount a sustained membership drive, and no affiliation with another labor union was accomplished. Then in 1962 the players hired attorney Lawrence Fleisher as general counsel. Fleisher undertook a spirited organization campaign and tightened up the operation of the NBPA so that it could stand as a strong union without outside affiliation. He confronted the owners as an antagonist. With strike threats and a majority of the players behind him, Fleisher achieved significant gains. He was criticized for serving as a players' agent in individual salary negotiations with teams while simultaneously leading the union (among his clients were John Havlicek, Jerry West, and Bob Lanier), raising legitimate questions of conflict of interest. Yet his loyalty to all players was never in doubt. Fleisher negotiated pioneering collective bargaining agreements that created free agency, an antidrug program, reduction in the draft to just two rounds, and a 53 percent revenue guarantee for players. During his twenty-seven-year tenure average basketball player salaries rose to the highest level in sports, and he accomplished this without ever calling a strike. Fleisher retired in 1988 and died of a heart attack the following year.

Charles Grantham, a black, was named to the newly created position of executive director of the NBPA when Fleisher retired. For the past decade Grantham had been the union's executive vice-president. A former basketball player at Cheyney State University, Grantham served as director of admissions at the University of Pennsylvania's Wharton School and held personnel jobs at General Electric and RCA before coming to the union. He was a tough negotiator on money issues but, like Fleisher, recognized the importance of the union's partnership with the league.

When Grantham resigned in 1995 he was succeeded by Simon Gourdine. A graduate of Fordham Law School, Gourdine was the NBA deputy commissioner in the 1970s. He left the league to become commissioner of the New York City Department of Consumer Affairs and later served as director of labor relations for the Metropolitan Transit Authority in New York. Gourdine returned to basketball in 1990, switching sides to become the general counsel for the NBPA.

Early Agreements

A major confrontation between the NBPA and owners in 1964 resulted in the establishment of a player pension plan. For several years the players had been trying to achieve pensions in talks with owners and the league president, and in 1962 the owners had forwarded a specific pension plan to Tom Heinsohn of the Boston Celtics, who succeeded Cousy as president of the union. Implementation of the plan was delayed, however, because Heinsohn did not realize that the owners' proposal had to be either accepted or rejected. When Heinsohn and player representatives later expressed desire to put the pension plan into effect in meetings with league president Walter Kennedy, they were frustrated by stalling tactics. The matter came to a head when players threatened to boycott the 1964 all-star game and caused the game to be delayed by several minutes. This forced the owners to guarantee that they would take action to implement the pension plan.

The NBPA again threatened a strike over pension issues in 1967. This time the players said they would strike the championship playoffs and file for certification with the National Labor Relations Board as a labor union if their demands for increases in pension plan contributions were not met. The players sought an increase in pension payments to $600 a month at age sixty-five for players with ten years' service, which they argued would bring them up to levels found in baseball and football. Shortly before the playoffs were to begin, the owners capitulated on the pension demands. In addition, the players won a new medical and insurance program, elimination of games played immediately before and after the all-star game, and limitation of the regular schedule to eighty-two games. The 1967 collective bargaining agreement was the first in all of professional sports.

In 1968 an agreement was signed by league president Kennedy and the new president of the NBPA, Oscar Robertson, to increase pay for rookies and veteran players. The following year, the players threatened to strike over the proposed merger between the NBA and the ABA, contending that the merger would violate the antitrust laws. This dispute resulted in extensive litigation in the courts. In 1970, salary minimums, monies for the playoff pool, and meal allowances were increased after negotiations between the NBA commissioner and the NBPA. Before 1971 the Uniform Player's Contract could be unilaterally renewed with a 25 percent salary reduction. In 1971 this provision was changed so that renewal was at the same salary the player received in the preceding year of his contract. It was not until 1973 that the first comprehensive agreement was negotiated between the owners and players. In this three-year agreement the pattern of increasing minimum salaries, playoff shares, and pensions was continued. But many items that were the subject of individual agreement in the past were folded into one contract, and new items, such as arbitration, made their initial appearance in a contract.

When the 1973 agreement expired, negotiations were complicated by the antitrust suit of the players against the NBA-ABA merger. Over a period of several months, only one fruitless negotiating session was held. There were rumors that players would not attend training camps as a protest to lack of progress, but the players reported as usual. It was not until the courtroom battle over the proposed merger was resolved that the parties were able to come up with a replacement agreement.

Player Salaries

Teams will make money if they pay players less than the contribution that their skills make to team revenues and will lose money if they pay players more than they bring in. That so many basketball teams reported operating losses in the early 1980s indicates that they were paying out too much in salaries. In 1967

Table 4.2. Average Salaries in the NBA,
1967–95

Season	Average Salary
1967–68	$ 20,000
1972–73	90,000
1977–78	143,000
1979–80	173,000
1980–81	189,000
1981–82	218,000
1982–83	246,000
1983–84	275,000
1984–85	340,000
1985–86	395,000
1986–87	440,000
1987–88	510,000
1988–89	601,000
1989–90	748,000
1990–91	1,034,000
1991–92	1,202,000
1992–93	1,348,000
1993–94	1,558,000
1994–95	1,800,000

Sources: Data for 1967–78 from Ray Kennedy
and Nancy Williamson, "Money: The Monster
Threatening Sports." *Sports Illustrated,* 17 July
1978, 46. For 1979–83, data from David DuPree,
"NBA: Red Ink and a Bleak Future," *Washington
Post,* 15 March 1983, D4. Data for 1983–84 from
Sports Illustrated, 2 July 1984, 14; for 1984–88, estimated from various sources; and for 1989–95,
from the National Basketball Association.

only about 30 percent of gross revenues went for players' salaries; by 1972 the
percentage had risen to 66 percent and in 1977 to 70 percent.[12] By 1983 nearly
three-quarters of revenues were allocated to salaries. During this period salaries
rose dramatically in the NBA, making players the highest paid group in any
sport (see Table 4.2).

Two principal factors have led to surges in NBA salaries: the competition with
the ABA that ignited salaries in the late 1960s and the removal of the need to
provide compensation for the signing of free agents, which began in 1981. This
points up the fact that change in player salaries is very different in situations of
open competition for players. Owners have less control over competition from
rival leagues. If they are too complacent and do not match salary levels offered
in the market created by owners in the other league, their own survival is threatened. Although free agency poses a less serious threat in that owners can tacitly
agree to keep from bidding against each other for players, there always seems to

be at least one owner who refuses to go along, such as Ted Stepien, who established the early pattern for free agents in 1981, and Harold Katz, owner of the Philadelphia 76ers, who in 1982 signed free agent Moses Malone to a six-year contract for a total of $13.2 million. As it turned out, Malone was a good investment for Katz since 76ers' attendance rose significantly and the team won the NBA championship in Malone's first year with the club. But big contracts create a ripple effect that justifies higher salaries for other players, who may turn out to be poor investments.

At one time player contracts provided for substantial deferred payments after a player has left the game, the most extreme case being Earvin ("Magic") Johnson of the Lakers, who signed a $25 million contract for twenty-five years. At the time Johnson's contract was signed, teams in the NBA were estimated to owe between $80 million and $90 million in deferred payments to current and former players. As a result of the Johnson contract and the mounting deferred payment obligations, NBA owners agreed to establish a seventy-thirty rule, meaning that a player must get 70 percent of his contract up front in cash within a period defined by the life of the contract plus two years after his last playing year. Only 30 percent of the payment can be deferred beyond this period. Johnson's contract was later renegotiated.

The high percentage of black players in the NBA and the high salary levels in the league indicate a unique, albeit small, segment of the labor market in which blacks have made significant economic progress. Yet, according to a study of NBA player salaries, there is a shortfall in the compensation of black players compared to white players.[13] In this study, Kahn and Sherer found that the average salaries of black and white players on the whole were similar. But when various performance factors were taken into account—such as minutes played, points scored, rebounds, and steals—the black players were underpaid compared to the white players by about 20 percent. Offsetting this disparity, however, the authors found that replacing one black player with an identical white player (in terms of performance) raised home attendance by eight thousand to thirteen thousand fans per season. What occurs, in effect, is customer discrimination, because most of the fans who attend NBA games are white.

Antitrust Issues

Unlike baseball, which enjoys special immunity, basketball comes under the purview of the antitrust laws. In *Washington Professional Basketball Corp. v. National Basketball Association,* a U.S. District Court found that the business of professional basketball is conducted on an interstate basis.[14] When this is coupled with the sale of rights to televise and broadcast games, the sport comes under the "trade or commerce among the several states" language of the Sherman Act.

Perpetual Reserve Clause

Although the reserve clause in basketball was not struck down until the 1975 case *Robertson v. National Basketball Association,*[15] court decisions in the 1960s backed away from the notion that the reserve clause had perpetual application. In the first of these cases, Richard Barnett played the 1960–61 season with the Syracuse Nationals of the NBA. Although Barnett's contract with the Nationals was a uniform contract that enabled the club to renew it for one year, he signed a contract for the 1961–62 season with the Cleveland Pipers of the ABL. Suing to stop Barnett from playing for the Pipers, the Nationals contended that although Barnett did not sign a contract with them for 1961–62, an oral agreement was reached.[16] The court found strong support for this contention because Barnett admitted requesting a salary advance from the club. Barnett alleged, however, that the contract with the Nationals was a restraint of trade in violation of the law.

The Court of Common Pleas of Ohio, finding for the Nationals, noted that professional basketball requires regulations for the protection of the business, public, and players. So long as these regulations are reasonable, as they were determined to be in this case, there is no violation of the law on restraint of trade. Interestingly, the court applied a test of reasonableness rather than automatically binding Barnett to the Nationals because of the reserve clause.

In a similar case, Louis Hudson, a player who tried to jump from the NBA's St. Louis Hawks to the ABA's Minnesota team, was held to be bound by his contract with the Hawks.[17] Again, the court found a special circumstance, in this case the fact that the Minnesota team did not have clean hands in its dealings with Hudson. As in *Barnett,* however, the result was that the player was not allowed to jump leagues.

In the *Barry* case, which presents some unique twists and turns, the player who tried to jump leagues eventually made it from the NBA to the ABA. The controversy concerned whether Rick Barry would play basketball for the Washington Capitols of the ABA or the San Francisco Warriors of the NBA.[18] In 1966 Barry signed a one-year contract with the Warriors that contained a reserve clause. The Warriors chose to exercise their option to get Barry to play for the 1967–68 season. Meanwhile, in 1967 Barry signed a three-year contract with the Oakland Oaks of the ABA. This prompted the Warriors to sue Barry to enforce their contract rights to his services. The California Court of Appeals held that the Warriors could stop Barry from playing for anyone else until September 30, 1968.[19] Even though Barry had not signed for the Warriors in 1967–68, the club had the option of renewing the contract for one year. As a result of this litigation, Barry did not play for anyone in 1967–68.

Barry began his ABA career in the 1968–69 season, playing for the Oakland Oaks. In 1969 the Oaks were sold and became the Washington Capitols. Because Barry had a three-year contract with the Oaks, he was part of the assets the new owners acquired. Immediately after the sale of the Oaks, however, Barry signed a five-year contract to play for the Warriors again. The U.S. Court of Appeals, affirming the district court, found that Barry was obligated to fulfill his contract with the Capitols. Barry had sought to invoke the clean-hands doctrine against the Capitols, contending that since he was not really free to play for the Oaks back in 1968, the Capitols, as the Oaks' transferee, lacked clean hands. Barry was thus trying to have it both ways, with the degree of his freedom depending on his own convenience. The court dismissed this unheroic argument by noting that it is difficult to imagine that someone who signed as many conflicting contracts as Barry would not be aware that the franchise might fail or be transferred to another city. So Barry was obligated to play for the Capitols, which he did until the ABA merged with the NBA. Then he returned to the Warriors.

Draft Eligibility

Basketball was the first sport in which judicial mandate required modification of a rule prohibiting the signing of college players until four years after high school graduation. A similar rule in football was struck down by the courts in 1984. The controversy in basketball began in 1969 when Spencer Haywood signed a contract to play for the Denver Rockets of the ABA.[20] At the time, Haywood was too young to play in the ABA, but the league made an exception to the rule for him by waiving its application on hardship grounds. Early in the 1970–71 season, a dispute arose between Haywood and the Rockets about his contract. He stopped playing for that team and signed a contract with the Seattle Supersonics of the NBA. The NBA commissioner disapproved this contract because it violated section 2.05 of the NBA's bylaws, which stated,

> A person who has not completed high school or who has completed high school but has not yet entered college, shall not be eligible to be drafted as a Player until four years after his original high school class has been graduated. . . . Similarly, a person who has entered college but is no longer enrolled, shall not be eligible to be drafted or to be a Player until the time when he would have first become eligible had he remained enrolled in college.[21]

The U.S. District Court ruled that the NBA did not provide "procedural safe-guards" for an individual to contest his exclusion under section 2.05. It there-fore determined that the NBA's rule was a violation of the Sherman Act. After the court decision, the NBA settled the suit by fining the Supersonics $200,000, and, because of the settlement, the decision of the district court was not ap-pealed. A further result of the litigation was that the NBA modified its rule to permit hardship cases among college players to be signed by its teams: players had to prove hardship based on financial condition, family, academic record or lack of it, and ability to obtain employment in another field. As a practical mat-ter, proving hardship was not difficult for college underclassmen who wanted to sign with the NBA. The NBA therefore changed its draft rule again to the cur-rent one, which states that any player whose high school class has graduated and who gives the league forty-five days' notice is eligible for the draft.

The liberal stance taken by the NBA in providing little restriction on players who want to be included in the draft pool seems commendable in a way. It is not tainted with hypocrisy, as some have charged in connection with the NFL's rule, which tried to encourage players to stay in college while preventing them from capitalizing on their real value in the labor market. Several highly suc-cessful NBA players have left college early to play in the league, e.g., Isiah Thomas, Michael Jordan, Akeem Olajuwon, Dominique Wilkins, Karl Malone and Shaquille O'Neal. For these players, turning pro was the right decision. Yet, there are many more players who did not make it in the NBA or who played only briefly who would have been better off staying in college. One study found that of 131 underclassmen who declared themselves eligible for the NBA draft since 1971, only 27 "bettered themselves" by entering the league early.[22] Another study shows that of the twenty-eight players who came out early in 1991 and 1992, only nine were in the league in the 1993–94 season; and of the nineteen players who applied for early entry in the 1993 draft, only seven remained.[23] If a player is really good, the big money will be there after he completes his college eligibility. In 1993 the National Collegiate Athletic Association (NCAA) passed a "testing the waters" rule, allowing undergraduates to enter the NBA draft and still choose to return to college with their athletic eligibility intact if they decide within thirty days not to become a professional.

Screening of Owners

Although one might assume that transfer of ownership of a professional sports team is exclusively in the hands of the buyer and seller, transfer of fran-chise ownership requires approval by vote of the other owners. This authorization requirement allows owners to screen potential buyers in order to keep undesirable persons such as known criminals from becoming owners.

But whether a league can arbitrarily keep out any potential owner presents an interesting antitrust issue. In *Levin v. National Basketball Association*, the plaintiffs were two businessmen who had an agreement to buy the Boston Celtics of the NBA.[24] Action by the NBA board of governors was needed for transfer of ownership, with an affirmative vote of three-quarters of the owners. When the plaintiffs applied for approval of the transfer, they were turned down because they were friendly with Sam Schulman, owner of the Seattle Supersonics, who had given other NBA owners problems in the past. It was feared that the plaintiffs, if they gained ownership rights, would side with Schulman on future matters and cause trouble. When they were turned down for ownership, they brought suit charging violation of the antitrust laws. A U.S. District Court dismissed the charge, noting that antitrust laws protect competition, not individual competitors. Exclusion of the plaintiffs by the board of governors was found to have no anticompetitive intent or effect and to cause no public injury.

A related matter arose in 1994 when the Minnesota Timberwolves were sold for $152.5 million to a group including Top Rank of Louisiana, headed by boxing promoter Bob Arum. The intention of the buyers was to move the franchise to New Orleans. An NBA committee, however, turned down the proposed sale, and the league filed a preemptive action in federal district court in Minneapolis asserting its right to set criteria for prospective buyers. Commissioner Stern indicated that Top Rank of Louisiana failed to provide sufficient data concerning the offer to buy the team, so it would stay in Minneapolis for the 1994–95 season. Meanwhile, a group of Minneapolis investors came forth to try to buy the team. A round of lawsuits is anticipated on these developments, testing the NBA's authority to screen owners.

Robertson Case

The most significant litigation in basketball is the *Robertson* case.[25] This case was filed in 1970 as a class action on behalf of all players by several former and current NBA players who had been team player representatives when the suit began. Leading the litigants was Oscar Robertson, who was perhaps the best guard to play the game during his career with the Cincinnati Royals and Milwaukee Bucks. The players charged that the reserve clause, uniform player contract, and college draft all violated the antitrust laws. They also sought to prevent the NBA from merging with the ABA. According to the players, the control of players through the draft and uniform contract was a conspiracy in restraint of trade that violated the Sherman Act. If a player refused to sign another uniform contract and sought to negotiate with another NBA club, he would be subject to a boycott or blacklisting. If such a negotiation occurred, the offending team was subject to a penalty by the NBA. All of this, argued the players, allowed the NBA to enforce their combination to monopolize and restrain trade. They charged that a merger between the NBA and ABA would eliminate what little competition existed for players' services.

In a threshold challenge, the NBA charged that the U.S. District Court lacked jurisdiction to decide the case, arguing that the NLRB had primary jurisdiction since matters within the scope of the National Labor Relations Act were involved. The court rejected this argument, finding that the antitrust issues involved in the case were not within the "special competence" of the NLRB and that therefore the federal court should appropriately decide the case.

Next, the NBA argued that it was protected from the antitrust laws by the so-called labor exemption: that is, that federal labor law encourages collective bargaining for resolving labor disputes, and as a result of this process, the interests of the individual employee must be subordinate to the collective interests of all. The court also rejected this argument, noting that the labor exemption applies only to labor or union activities, not to the activities of employers. It found that the threat employer restraints posed to the ideals of free competition outweighed the need to maintain the labor-management relationship. Moreover, reasoned the court, since the restraints were nonmandatory subjects of bargaining and were imposed unilaterally by the NBA, the labor exemption could not be used to achieve immunity from the antitrust laws. Even if the subjects were mandatory, the court would still not allow immunity, because there had been no bona fide, arm's-length bargaining on the subjects.

Finding no acceptable defense by the NBA, the court determined that the draft, uniform contract, and reserve clause were a per se violation of the Sherman Act and thus illegal. The court also found that the NBA-ABA merger would have the effect of restraining trade by eliminating competition between the two leagues for college players and preventing players from jumping leagues. Despite the decision in *Robertson,* the question of damages for the players as well as the practical effect of the decision on future labor relations arrangements remained open.

In 1976 a settlement was reached on the remaining *Robertson* case issues when the NBA and NBPA negotiated a new collective bargaining agreement. The owners agreed to pay $4.5 million in damages to about five hundred players, plus an additional $1 million for the players' legal fees. Apart from the monetary settlement, the 1976 agreement had four key features: (1) beginning with the 1976–77 season, the option clause would be eliminated from all nonrookie player contracts; (2) beginning in 1980 and continuing through the 1986–87 season, a right-of-first-refusal system was established, under which a player whose contract has expired and who receives an offer from another team can be retained by his original team if that team matches the offer; (3) the old compensation arrangement, i.e., teams that sign free agents must give up players, draft choices, cash, or some combination as compensation, as determined by the commissioner, remained in effect until the end of the 1980–81 season; and (4) the college draft remained in effect, except that if a player chose not to sign with the club that drafted him, he was eligible to be selected by any team in the following year's draft.

The 1976 agreement was approved by the courts.[26] This settlement agreement, reached through collective bargaining, had essentially the same effect on the players as it would have if it had been negotiated in the absence of litigation;[27] however, it was not enforced in the same way as a labor contract usually is. Negotiated agreements are interpreted and applied through the grievance procedure with arbitration available for impartial decision if necessary. In the *Robertson* settlement, the U.S. District Court retained jurisdiction to enforce the terms of the settlement by giving enforcement powers to a special master, whose decisions were subject to review by the court. Thus the judiciary became involved in what is normally carried out by the parties themselves through the grievance procedure and arbitration. The parties' choice of litigation rather than internal dispute resolution mechanisms is indicative of the poorly developed state of labor relations between the NBA and NBPA.

As might be expected, the complex and atypical arrangement for court review resulted in further litigation. This litigation arose over application of the old compensation rule, which the parties had agreed would remain in effect until the end of the 1980–81 season. Under this rule, when a free agent signed with a new team, the two teams in question tried to reach agreement on compensation to the team that lost the player. If they were unable to agree, the commissioner was authorized to decide on compensation. The purpose of compensation was to make whole the old team rather than to punish the team that signed a free agent. Marvin Webster played out his option with the Seattle Supersonics and became a free agent for the 1978–79 season. He signed a five-year contract with the New York Knickerbockers for $600,000 a year. When Seattle and New York were unable to agree on compensation, Commissioner O'Brien took over and ruled that New York would have to give up to Seattle a player, Lonnie Shelton, as well as a first-round draft pick, and $450,000 cash. The special master, Columbia Law School professor Telford Taylor, reviewed this award. When the special master affirmed O'Brien's award, the matter was appealed to federal court by the NBPA. The union opposed O'Brien's award, because of the chilling effect it would have on the market for free agents.

The U.S. District Court found that the special master misinterpreted his authority and should have ruled that the commissioner's award was a penalty in violation of the agreement.[28] This decision was modified in part by the U.S. Court of Appeals, which held that the special master must set aside a compensation award by the commissioner if it is "substantially above" the value of the newly signed free agent so as to constitute a penalty.[29] After these decisions, the Webster compensation matter went back to Special Master Taylor, who overturned the commissioner's award. Later, Commissioner O'Brien modified his award to make it less punitive.

After the 1980–81 season, the compensation rule was eliminated. This left the teams with players who became free agents with only a right of first refusal for matching the player's contract offer from a new team. Since the right of first refusal remained in effect until the end of the 1986–87 season, the special master and federal courts continued to have a role in enforcing terms agreed to by the parties under the 1976 agreement. For example, in 1982 a dispute arose when Bernard King of the Golden State Warriors became a free agent and received an offer from the New York Knickerbockers for a five-year contract for $750,000 a year. Also included in the Knicks' "offer sheet" were a $620,000 signing bonus and a clause that would require a third team to pay King an additional $90,000 a year if the Warriors matched the offer and traded him to another club. The Warriors objected to the signing bonus provision and the trade clause, and the matter went before Special Master Kingman Brewster, former president of Yale University, who upheld the Knicks' offer sheet. After further wrangling between the parties, the Warriors matched the offer, but then traded King to the Knicks for Michael Ray Richardson.

The lack of finality associated with the Brewster award and the early awards by Special Master Taylor illustrate the tenuous nature of enforcement decisions under the 1976 agreement. Although the special masters function like arbitrators, their decisions are not necessarily final or binding because the federal courts retain jurisdiction to review decisions. What are really matters of contract interpretation rather than law have been dragged into the courts, where they do not belong. Nevertheless, the courts and special masters were properly involved under the settlement agreements reached by the parties themselves. Until the 1976 agreement resulting from the *Robertson* case finally expired, this unconventional, cumbersome, and expensive system of decision-making Ping-Pong continued to hinder effective labor relations.

Franchise Movement

Decisions on franchise locations are vital to league interests. All professional team sports require approval for relocation of franchises. With the court decision in the Oakland Raiders, move to Los Angeles, as discussed in Chapter 3, the ability of leagues to prevent teams from moving is uncertain. The NBA's woes over this issue began in 1982 when Donald Sterling, owner of the San Diego Clippers, sought to move his team to Los Angeles because of operating losses. His unsuccessful attempt to secure permission resulted in a tangle of lawsuits and countersuits that caused the team to remain temporarily in San Diego. Then, in 1984, Sterling, still without having obtained approval, moved the team to Los Angeles anyway. This prompted the NBA to initiate a $25 million suit against the Clippers, which sought to enforce the league's rights to approve franchise relocations. In 1984 the NBA changed the rule to require only a majority of owners for approval, but it was questionable whether the rule applied to the Clippers, because approval was not sought for the most recent move before the rule modification. Pending determination of the NBA's suit against the Clippers, the club began play for the 1984–85 season in Los Angeles. Following several rounds of litigation the courts allowed the Clippers to remain in Los Angeles.

The old Kansas City Kings franchise began play in its new home of Sacramento in the 1985–86 season. This move was approved by the NBA, with the proviso that the team might be relocated unless Sacramento built a suitable arena by the 1987–88 season. A new sixteen-thousand-seat arena was completed on time.

1983 Agreement

In 1983, with losses averaging $700,000 per club, the players and owners worked out an agreement to moderate NBA salaries. When negotiations for a new collective bargaining agreement began, the owners took the initiative. They hoped to get financial relief through a salary cap on each team. The owners' other principal demands were to reduce roster size from twelve to ten, eliminate first-class air travel, eliminate guaranteed player contracts, and establish a drug control program. The players showed little willingness to give up rights achieved under previous negotiated agreements. Their contract demands included a share in the percentage of future cable television revenues, guarantees on all contracts, and increases in pensions and severance pay.

Negotiations

Talks began in July 1982. The NBA's negotiating team was led by Commissioner Larry O'Brien and his eventual successor, David Stern, who was chief spokesman. Leading the union's bargaining group was general counsel Larry

Fleisher, as chief negotiator, and NBPA president Bob Lanier of the Milwaukee Bucks. Stern and Fleisher had earlier confronted each other on numerous occasions at the bargaining table. Each had respect for the other, unlike the recent antagonists in baseball and football. When little was accomplished in the early bargaining sessions, the league filed a charge with the NLRB contending that the union had refused to negotiate over mandatory subjects of collective bargaining, particularly the salary moderation plan. It also threatened to put certain of its demands into effect if negotiations reached impasse.

After three months of negotiations, the parties reached tentative agreement on the concept that salary costs would be tied to team revenues, but no specific formula was developed. A gag rule was imposed on owners by the league, which indicated it would levy fines of up to $250,000 for making public statements about the negotiations. Strike talk was in the air, but it was not taken very seriously. Baseball and football had both recently suffered long strikes, and the NBA's financial situation was too precarious to allow it to become another victim. The opening of the regular season without incident was a reassuring sign that there would be no strike. Actually there was a strike, but it was by NBA referees, who walked out for two months of the season, holding out for higher pay.

In February 1983, all twenty-three player representatives voted that the deadline for reaching agreement was April 1. This date was chosen because the regular season ended on April 17, and pressure for settlement would build before the playoffs, which NBA owners count on heavily as a source of income. The focus in negotiations was the salary cap issue: the owners sought to place a $4 million limit on each team's payrolls, and teams with salaries above this limit would be prevented from signing free agents. As a quid pro quo, the owners offered to create a fund, in addition to salaries, that would share NBA revenues with the players. Although the players agreed in principle to a salary cap, they were uncertain as to how much it should be or when it should begin to take effect. The players indicated that if the negotiations were not completed by the deadline, a strike was one of the options they would consider. As a result of media pressure, strike talk began to escalate. Owner Sam Schulman stated publicly that he dared the players to strike. Despite what would seem to be a clear violation of the NBA's gag rule on owners, there is no evidence that a fine was imposed for this statement. Perhaps irritated by the taunt, Fleisher announced shortly thereafter that the players would surely strike if the contract could not be reached on time.

As talks continued, the owners' proposal was revised to pay players' salaries based on 40 percent of the league's gross revenues. Given that several individual players already had salaries close to what salary caps would allow for an entire team, it is not surprising that the NBPA did not accept the offer; however, there was an inducement for players to agree to some percentage of league revenues because of an anticipated bonanza from cable television in future years. The union's other principal objection to the salary cap scheme was that it might violate antitrust law and therefore should begin only after the 1986–87 season when the *Robertson* settlement expired. Moreover, the parties disagreed as to how much the salary cap would be. It was clear that the cap would affect clubs differently, since the current NBA payrolls ranged from $1.1 million for the Indiana Pacers to $5 million for the Philadelphia 76ers.

About a week before the strike deadline, the owners raised their salary offer from 40 percent to 50 percent of league revenues over the next four years. The union countered with a demand of 53 percent. This narrowing in the parties' position renewed hopes for averting a strike.

On March 31, 1983, an agreement was reached between the parties in which the NBA came up to the NBPA's demand for a 53 percent guarantee of gross revenues. The salary cap provision was arranged to start with the 1984–85 season for most teams. Only the five teams with the highest payrolls—Los Angeles, New Jersey, New York, Philadelphia, and Seattle—were frozen at their current salary levels, because they were already paying more than $3.6 million. The cap was scheduled to rise to $3.8 million in 1985–86, and to $4 million in 1986–87. These figures were a minimum cap, since the maximum cap was 53 percent of revenues. Only if the stated cap figures were less than 53 percent did they apply. For the 1985–86 season, the actual salary cap was set by the NBA at $4,233,000 per team. The amount of the salary cap for later years is shown in Table 4.3.

The agreement was designed to provide greater parity between teams. Those in smaller markets, which offer salaries well below the cap, were able to sign

Table 4.3. NBA Salary Cap, 1984–96

Season	Salary Cap
1984–85	$ 3,600,000
1985–86	4,233,000
1986–87	4,945,000
1987–88	6,164,000
1988–89	7,232,000
1989–90	9,802,000
1990–91	11,871,000
1991–92	12,500,000
1992–93	14,000,000
1993–94	15,175,000
1994–95	15,964,000
1995–96	23,000,000

Source: National Basketball Association.

more outstanding players. Rich teams active in the free agency market were still able to sign outstanding players, but they had to reduce their payrolls below the salary cap in order to make room for them. Each team could still match free agent offers made to their players by other clubs without affecting the salary cap.

The agreement is akin to profit-sharing plans in industry, but different in that the guarantees provided were so large. Also, if the cable television bonanza materializes, players get the lion's share. Since the amounts available to players rise with increases in gross revenue, they have an incentive to try to attract fans and spur interest in larger television contracts. At the same time, players do not suffer much on the downside. There are minimum payrolls, determined by a complex formula, that worked out to about 90 percent of the salary ceiling. Cash-poor teams were helped to meet the minimum payroll by league subsidies. The players also won a guarantee of 253 jobs, only slightly fewer than the 276 jobs currently available. This protected salaries in the event of a rash of bankruptcies in the NBA.

Salaries increased to $340,000 when the cap went into effect in 1984–85. The growth rate of salaries did not moderate as expected because of a large increase in television revenues. The overall effect of the agreement was to restrict the movement of star players and allow clubs a better opportunity to keep developing players who might otherwise take advantage of free agency.

Operation of the Salary Cap

The complexity of the salary cap provisions under the 1983 agreement resulted in confusion and uncertainty over club policies in signing players. The cap has generally limited the ability of rich teams to acquire free agents and restricted salaries of many first-year players, but there are loopholes that enable teams and players to evade the restrictions. These loopholes have to some extent undercut the purpose of the salary cap. For instance, teams were allowed to retain at any price one player who became a free agent, without his salary affecting the salary cap, and then re-sign its own free agent regardless of the cost. Some teams have thus delayed signing their free agents until they have signed other free agents. In 1984 the Los Angeles Clippers traded Terry Cummings to the Milwaukee Bucks for three players with combined salaries of over $1.5 million. Two days after this trade, the Clippers signed their own free agent, Bill Walton, for about $1.4 million. The Clippers probably could not have made the trade under the salary cap if they had signed Walton first, because they would have been over the salary cap. This loophole was closed by the 1988 agreement.

The salaries of first-year players also caused controversy. The 1983 agreement provided that any team with a salary level at or over the salary cap could sign a rookie to a one-year contract at the minimum salary of $75,000 for first-round picks ($65,000 for picks in later rounds of the draft). This caused inequities for rookies. Akeem Olajuwon was signed by the Houston Rockets for an estimated $6.3 million over six years, and Michael Jordan by the Chicago Bulls for about $750,000 a year. Leon Wood and Charles Barkley, on the other hand, were signed by the Philadelphia 76ers for only $75,000 apiece, because that team was at the limit of the salary cap. Although a first-year player who signed a one-year contract at the minimum salary level had no restriction on how much he could be paid in subsequent years because later contracts did not count against the team's salary cap, some rookies were at a disadvantage compared to others. This inequity caused Leon Wood to file suit in federal district court challenging the salary cap on antitrust grounds, but the suit was dismissed by the court because the rules had been established by the owners and players' association in collective bargaining.

1988 Agreement

The 1983 agreement expired on June 15, 1987. Although the parties began negotiating a replacement contract several months earlier, little progress was made. Three major issues were being considered: the college draft, the salary cap, and the right of first refusal. The league owners wanted to retain these features, while the union wanted to eliminate them. In an attempt to hasten negotiations, the parties agreed to put a temporary moratorium on signing free agents or rookies. When the moratorium ended in October 1987, the union decided to take the disputed issues to court rather than continue to bargain. It filed a class action antitrust suit in federal district court challenging the draft, salary cap, and right of first refusal.

Like other players' unions, the NBPA has been more successful in achieving its objectives through the courts than at the bargaining table. This time, however, the union's legal position did not appear as strong as it had been in previous cases. This was because the union had previously agreed to the draft, salary cap, and right of first refusal. As such, the league could argue that the labor exemption from the antitrust law was applicable. In other words, because the union had previously agreed on these issues, it could not now argue that the issues were in restraint of trade. The union's rationale, however, was that the agreement had expired and that the league could not undertake the draft, for instance, without restricting player movement.

Despite the clarity of the union's intentions—to remove owner controls over players in the labor market—one had to wonder whether this was really what the union wanted. Elimination of the draft and unrestricted free agency could destroy the stability and continuity that allowed fans to differentiate one team from another and take pride in their own team. An open market would presumably enable wealthy owners to buy up the best players. As a practical matter, these undesirable consequences might not ensue, but this would not be known until it was tried. Experimentation with an open labor market in sports would be risky business.

Both sides pushed for a quick conclusion from Dickinson Debevoise, federal court judge in Newark, New Jersey. Wisely, Judge Debevoise declined this option. His preliminary ruling that the expiration of the collective bargaining agreement did not automatically make the draft and so on subject to the antitrust laws indicated that the legal battle could be a lengthy one and that in the meantime the league apparently could continue to do business under the old rules. Boxed in, the union needed to do something to put pressure on the league. It therefore suggested the possibility of a strike of the all-star game, although most players were not enthusiastic about the idea of disrupting what was a successful season. A milder pressure tactic was chosen instead. That was to have the players vote to decertify the union. The rationale of this maneuver, incongruous as it seemed, was to convince the court to rule in favor of the players. Without a union to represent the players, the NBA would no longer be able to claim that the labor exemption protected it from the antitrust laws, i.e., there could be no agreement if there was no union.

The threat of decertification was a clever ploy, but, in addition to the end of the union, it would also mean the end of a party for the NBA to negotiate with. As a result, when the NBA renewed its interest in bargaining, the union put its decertification plans on ice.

To the surprise of many observers, who were awaiting the outcome of the antitrust litigation, the NBA and NBPA reached a new six-year agreement in April 1988. The agreement provided additional evidence that the parties in basketball can work out their differences without a strike. It was also a tribute to the patience, temperament, and negotiating skills of Larry Fleisher and David Stern. Because of the agreement, the antitrust suit was dropped by the union.

The new contract addressed the three issues that were the focus of attention in collective bargaining and court. The college draft was reduced from seven rounds to three in 1988 and to just two rounds for the remainder of the contract. With league expansion to twenty-seven teams in the 1989–90 season, only fifty-four players were drafted. The rest of the new players were free agents, able to negotiate the best deal they could with any of the clubs in the league. The impact was not great, however, since nearly 80 percent of the current NBA players were drafted in the first two rounds.

The modification of the right of first refusal is the most complex aspect of the agreement. This right allows a team with a player who plays out his option to match the salary offered by another team. Under the new agreement, this right did not apply to a veteran player who has played out his second contract. In other words, a veteran who becomes a free agent could sign a contract with any team, and his old team would not be able to match the offer. From the 1989–90 season through the 1992–93 season, a "veteran" player was one with five years' service. In the last year of the contract, 1993–94, a veteran player was one with four years' service. These significant modifications in the right of first refusal moved the NBA closer to true free agency. Yet the salary cap prevented teams in big cities from dominating the market by buying up all the high-quality free agents.

The salary cap was continued, based on the players receiving a 53 percent guarantee of gross revenues. Under the agreement, however, teams were routinely able to exceed the salary cap because of the opportunity to re-sign their own free agents. Suppose, for instance, that Player A on Team X was a restricted free agent and his team was capped. Team Y, which is under the cap, signs Player A at $3 million a year. Team X now has fifteen days to match the offer or give up Player A. If Team X matches the offer and re-signs Player A, the $3 million does not count toward the cap. Thus, teams could regularly reach or exceed the salary cap.

What blew the lid, however, was the Chris Dudley case. A Yale alumnus and star center for the New Jersey Nets, Dudley became a restricted free agent. Despite receiving offers of about $3 million a year from the Nets and other teams, he signed a seven-year $11 million contract with the Portland Trail Blazers which paid him only about $790,000 in the first year. The kicker was that Dudley could become a free agent after this first year, when he would be able to renegotiate a much bigger contract with the team. The league saw through this "one-year-out" ruse to circumvent the salary cap, and Commissioner Stern brought suit in federal court to invalidate the agreement. But the court ruled in 1993 against the league. Then, as expected, the Trail Blazers tore up Dudley's old contract and signed him to a new multiyear deal for $4 million a year, with no impact on the cap because it re-signed one of its own free agents.

1995 Agreement

The 1988 collective bargaining agreement expired on June 23, 1994. In negotiations for a new contract the NBPA sought the elimination of three provisions from the prior contract; the salary cap, college draft, and right of first refusal. Unable to make progress in negotiations, the union agreed to play the 1994–95 season without a replacement contract. Meanwhile, it sought to invalidate the salary cap, draft, and right of first refusal through an antitrust suit filed in federal district court.

The lawsuit was actually initiated by the league, which sought two rulings. One was that the continued imposition of the 1988 agreement would not violate the antitrust laws, and the other was that the salary cap, draft, and right of first refusal were valid even if the antitrust laws apply. The players counterclaimed that these provisions violated antitrust law because the collective bargaining agreement had expired. In July 1994 U.S. District Court Judge Kevin Duffy granted the NBA's request and dismissed the players' counterclaim. The court relied on the labor exemption which provides immunity from antitrust law as long as a collective bargaining relationship exists. Judge Duffy's decision, consistent with that reached in the *Powell* case in football, was affirmed by the U.S. Court of Appeals.

Negotiations were further interrupted by the abrupt resignation of Charles Grantham as the union's executive director. The resignation was prompted by divisiveness among union members, a problem that would later become a major roadblock to settlement. Simon Gourdine, who replaced Grantham, pushed for a conclusion of the long-stalled negotiations, and a tentative agreement was reached. At this juncture, however, several players, led by Michael Jordan and Patrick Ewing, filed a petition with the National Labor Relations Board to decertify the union. This is a tactic previously used by the football players' union to remove the obstacle of the labor exemption and clear the way for its successful antitrust suit in the *McNeil* case (see Chapter 3). Standing behind the dissident basketball players was a group of attorney/agents led by Jeffrey Kessler and Marc Fleisher, son of the former union leader. The group seeking decertification contended that Gourdine and union president Buck Williams had withheld information on negotiations from the players and that the tentative agreement was not in the players' interests.

In order for a union to be decertified by the NLRB, at least 30 percent of the members of the bargaining unit must give initial approval before an election can be held. Then, a 50 percent plus vote is required for decertification. The initial 30 percent hurdle was cleared easily, and the decertification election was scheduled for September 1995. While the battle was between the NBPA on the one hand and dissident players and their agents on the other, the league had a keen interest in the outcome. If the union was decertified, the tentative agreement between the NBA and NBPA would be invalidated. This would in turn lead to lengthy antitrust litigation. The league's strategy thus became twofold: (1) it declared a lockout on June 30, freezing all dealings with players and putting pressure on them in the form of possible postponement of the season, and (2) it sought to restructure the tentative collective bargaining agreement in such a way as to satisfy the dissident players. Meanwhile, the union was also trying to save its skin by pursuing an aggressive communication campaign to convince players that decertification was a bad idea.

As time ticked away, a growing number of players became concerned that Commissioner Stern would make good on his vow to continue the lockout if no collective bargaining agreement was reached, which posed a real threat to starting the NBA season on time. Also, the league and union revised the tentative agreement, sweetening it in favor of the players. These factors shifted momentum away from continuing the fight, and the players decisively voted 226-134 against decertification. At this point everything fell into place—the owners and players both ratified the agreement, the lockout was lifted, and the 1995–96 season started on time.

The civil war between the NBA players and union was more severe than that witnessed to date in other sports. But basketball contracted only a mild case of the negotiation malady that has afflicted other professional sports, with their simmering labor disputes. Basketball's record remains unblemished in that not a single game has yet been canceled because of a work stoppage.

There was virtually no chance that the union would achieve its major objectives in negotiations—elimination of free agency, the draft, and right of first refusal. More realistically, the union wanted an expansion of the economic pie, not just an increase of the 53 percent guarantee but also a broadening of the revenues on which the percentage is applied. The union wanted to augment the share it received from ticket sales and broadcast revenues by adding revenues from luxury boxes, arena advertising, and sponsorship. The owners too had a busy agenda, seeking to turn the salary cap from soft to hard by not allowing exemption from it when a team signs its own free agents, and capping rookie salaries to avoid big contracts such as those signed before the 1994–95 season by rookies Chris Webber at Golden State ($74 million for fifteen years) and Anfernee Hardaway at Orlando ($45 million for thirteen years).

The final six-year agreement addresses the concerns of both sides. The players' share of NBA revenues rises to 57.5 percent from 53 percent. Players also get some new revenue added to the pie from luxury box rentals. Players are guaranteed $200 million in league licensing revenue over eight years, compared with the $3.8 million they received over the past nine years. The salary cap rises sharply to $23 million in the first year of the contract (up from $15.9 million) and goes up in increments to about $32 million in the final year. Also, the cap remains soft, with various exceptions such as a permitted $1 million over the cap for teams to sign free agents, and the right to sign a replacement for an injured player at up to 50 percent of the injured player's salary. The owners gained a cap on rookie salaries based on the average salaries received by the picks at each draft position over the previous seven years plus an increase of up to 20 percent. Also, the owners won a smaller annual increase in the contribution to player benefits of $3 million, down from the previous $5 million.

Aberrant Behavior

The NBA has an interest in presenting an image that reflects high morals and ethics. Because players are in the public eye, the league scrutinizes their actions both on and off the court to ensure proper behavior. Regulation has focused primarily on gambling, violence, and drugs.

Gambling

League officials have had two concerns about gambling. One is the problem of arrangements between players and gamblers to have players shave points to influence the outcome of games. It is not necessary that they throw the games by deliberately attempting to lose. All that is usually required is that players shave points by making mistakes or playing lethargically so that the final point spread beats the result anticipated by odds makers. It is difficult to determine the extent of such arrangements between players and gamblers because violators are rarely caught. Those cases that have come to light have been in the college ranks more than with professional leagues. Either the pros shave points less or are too clever to get caught.

The other gambling problem among players is direct betting on games. Player betting of any kind on the outcome of basketball games is prohibited by the NBA. Players who bet on the games they are not involved in are in a less reprehensible position than those who bet on their own games. The reason for this is that the presumption is that a player has deliberately taken steps to influence the fate of his team so as to win bets.

The first known case involving gambling and an NBA player resulted from incidents that occurred during the player's college days. Alex Groza was the star center on the University of Kentucky basketball team, which won NCAA championships in 1948 and 1949 and was one of the most celebrated college basketball teams of all time. Groza went on to play for the Indianapolis Olympians, and in his two years in the league, he finished second in scoring to George Mikan. In 1952 Groza admitted guilt in a conspiracy to fix games while playing at Kentucky. Despite his cooperation with the investigation and receipt of a suspended sentence, Groza was banned for life from the NBA by league president Maurice Podoloff.

In 1953 police in Fort Wayne, Indiana, conducted an investigation of the local NBA team known as the Pistons. As a result of the investigation, player Jack Molinas admitted making bets on Pistons' games with bookies on several occasions, although he was not paid to throw games. The NBA constitution provided that players betting on the outcome of league games would be expelled by the league after due notice and hearing. League president Podoloff suspended Molinas indefinitely, without conducting a hearing. Molinas brought suit against the league to set aside the suspension and get back wages because no hearing had been held. The New York Supreme Court for New York County found that to hold a hearing would have been an empty gesture, since the player had already admitted gambling. Dismissing the complaint, the court further noted that to get relief in an equity court required "clean hands," and that the plaintiff's hands in this instance were not judged to be clean.[30] Molinas, who went to law school during his playing career, later became an attorney. In 1975 Molinas was killed, gangster fashion, at his home in Los Angeles. At the time he was under indictment for interstate shipment of pornographic films.

Other lawsuits have arisen when players have been denied admission to the NBA because of charges of gambling involvement during their college careers. One such player was Connie Hawkins, who was barred from the NBA for allegedly introducing a gambler to a fellow player and for association with gamblers in 1961 while at the University of Iowa. Hawkins sued the NBA for $6 million and in 1969 won a $1.5 million settlement. While the suit was in litigation Hawkins played for the Minnesota club in the ABA, and when the suit was settled he joined the Phoenix Suns of the NBA.

A similar court action was taken under the antitrust laws by a player who alleged that he was denied a chance to prove his eligibility for membership in the NBA.[31] Alphra Saunders played basketball at Bradley University between 1957 and 1961. He was not a regular starting player in his senior year and was expelled from school for failing to report receipt of money from men who tried to induce him to shave points in Bradley games. Saunders was not drafted by the NBA, and until 1969 when he filed suit he never communicated to any team that he had an interest in being an NBA player. The U.S. District Court found that the Clayton Act's four-year statute of limitations barred the suit because Saunder's alleged cause of action began in 1961 when he was not drafted by the NBA, but the suit was not filed until 1969. In any event, it seems doubtful that Saunders would have been able to collect damages from the NBA because he was not a player likely to have been drafted by the NBA even if he had not had the gambling incident.

In 1982 the NBA became the first professional sports league to introduce an education program to make players aware of the threats of bribery in sports and the implications of wagering on sports contests. Presentations are made by specially trained FBI agents and former players. This education program also includes instruction on drug abuse.

In recent years the NBA has continued its vigilant opposition to gambling. The state of Oregon was one such target. Because of the success of its NFL lottery, the Oregon State Lottery established betting on the NBA. The league filed a lawsuit contending, in effect, that because it marketed the game and made it popular, it was illegal for Oregon to profit from the NBA's investment. While the NBA's suit was of questionable merit, especially in light of its failure to object to gambling on NBA games in Nevada casinos, Oregon caved in to the pressure of the lawsuit and its high costs of defense. In 1990 the NBA agreed to drop its suit in return for the lottery's promise not to resume NBA betting for at least five years. In another 1990 incident, Commissioner Stern fined Charles Barkley of the Philadelphia 76ers and Mark Jackson of the New York Knicks $5,000 apiece for making bets with each other. Barkley and Jackson had a running wager linked to their play in 76er-Knicks games, so that if either player made a winning play the other would owe him $500. Jackson won one bet and Barkley another, but neither player paid up. Stern imposed the fine when he read about the bets in the newspaper.

In 1993 the NBA's premier player, guard Michael Jordan of the Chicago Bulls, came under league investigation for gambling. Jordan bet on his personal golf matches with his friend Richard Esquinas. Esquinas claimed in a book that Jordan owed him $1.252 million in golf gambling debts, but Commissioner Stern cleared Jordan of any wrongdoing. A few months later Jordan announced his retirement from the Bulls to play baseball for the Chicago White Sox organization. Having achieved his ambitions in basketball, Jordan wanted to try a new career, and his decision to do so apparently had nothing to do with the gambling incident. Jordan returned to the Bulls in 1995, an event that was greeted by fans like the Second Coming. Jordan missed basketball, and, ironically, it was his baseball teammates who were instrumental in getting him back to basketball, because in playing pickup hoops with them he found his passion for basketball rekindled.

Violence

Fighting by players has long been a problem in the NBA. What makes the problem so acute is that players wear hardly any gear to protect them from physical violence. The most publicized fighting incident in the NBA occurred in 1977 in a game between the Los Angeles Lakers and Houston Rockets. When Kermit Washington of the Lakers began to fight with Kevin Kunnert of the

Rockets, Kunnert's teammate Rudy Tomjanovich ran to try to mediate the confrontation. Washington hit Tomjanovich a terrible blow in the face, causing fractures of the face and skull, a broken nose, a separated upper jaw, and a cerebral concussion.[32] Washington was fined $10,000 by Commissioner O'Brien and suspended from further play. He was reinstated after a suspension of twenty-six games and lost a total of $60,000 from the fine and forfeited salary.

Tomjanovich sued the Lakers, and a jury in the Southern District of Texas awarded him $3.2 million in damages. The case was later settled, however, with Tomjanovich getting about a half million dollars.[33] That the Lakers knew of Washington's reputation as a fighter and should have been able to prevent the incident weighed against their escaping liability. Tomjanovich suffered permanent injury, but later returned to play in the NBA.

A few months after the Tomjanovich incident, NBA owners gave Commissioner O'Brien sweeping powers to levy fines and suspend players in order to curb violence during games. A fine of up to $10,000 was authorized even if the fighting player was not ejected from the game. Several players have been fined for fighting since then, usually for $1,500, and fighting in the NBA, which had become almost epidemic in 1977, was reduced. Another step taken by the league was to establish a joint committee on violence with the NBPA. But after about a year of meetings, the player representatives on the committee withdrew because of a disagreement over the NBPA's proposal for a third referee to try to limit violence and provide better-officiated games. The owners' representatives viewed this addition as too expensive to implement.

Incidents of fighting rose significantly during the 1986–87 and 1987–88 seasons, and some celebrated donnybrooks involved several players. In particularly flagrant cases the fines were increased from the usual $1,500 to $5,000, and some players were also given one-game suspensions, which caused significant salary loss. The increase in violence prompted Commissioner Stern to recommend to the owners that the league add a third referee, which the owners accepted for the 1988–89 season.

Fighting has significantly abated in the NBA in recent years, but two incidents are noteworthy. In 1990 an ugly bench-clearing brawl in a game between the Detroit Pistons and Philadelphia 76ers resulted in $162,000 in fines, the highest total ever in professional sports. The principal combatants were Isiah Thomas, Bill Laimbeer, and Scott Hastings of the Pistons and Charles Barkley and Rick Mahorn of the 76ers, but several other players were involved in the ten-minute slugfest. Included in the total fines were $50,000 to each team for failing to control players. In the other incident, Vernon Maxwell of the Houston Rockets was suspended in 1995 for ten games and fined $20,000 for walking into the stands and punching a heckler during a game in Portland. Maxwell's fine was the highest for an individual in league history, and his suspension was the second longest after the one imposed on Kermit Washington for punching Rudy Tomjanovich. Ironically, Tomjanovich was the Houston coach at the time of the Maxwell incident.

Drugs

Drug abuse by NBA players began to surface in 1980. Various reports indicated that anywhere from 40 to 75 percent of the players were using cocaine. Before this time, for about ten years, the NBA had hired a medical consultant and team doctors to inform players regularly about the evils of drug abuse. But the problem was not widespread then, except for the use of pep pills to get up for games. In 1980 the NBA created a Drug Education and Prevention Committee, including owners, coaches, trainers, and team doctors, but no players, to increase drug education programs. A twenty-four-hour counseling service was established in 1981 by the NBA and NBPA. Counselors from the Life Extension Institute, with clinics in New York, Baltimore, Los Angeles, and Minneapolis, were made available to players or members of their families for a variety of problems, including drugs. Participation in this program is confidential, with no disclosure to team or league.

In the 1982–83 collective bargaining the NBA proposed urinalysis for all players. But the players rejected drug testing, and the issue was dropped from negotiations. After agreement was reached on other issues, the parties began to reconsider the need for an elaborate drug control program that included testing. In September 1983, these negotiations produced the most extensive program yet developed in professional sports. Agreement was reached because the players decided to act as a moving force in bringing it about. They had earlier won a 53 percent share of all revenues in the league and reasoned that a strong program would improve their media and fan image. Higher revenues from television and attendance would increase the players' monetary rewards.

The basic program is simple and tough. A player who comes forth voluntarily with a drug (cocaine or heroin) problem is provided treatment with no penalty. If a player comes forth a second time he receives treatment, but his pay is suspended. If this occurs a third time, the player is banned from the game. Three strikes and out. A player who does not come forth voluntarily and gets caught using drugs is immediately banned from further play. Players who are asked to take a drug test and refuse are also banned. So are players involved in the distribution of drugs, without actually using them. Players who are banished can apply for reinstatement after two years. If they are clean then, reinstatement is likely.

An independent expert on drug detection was hired by the league to authorize drug testing for players believed by the NBA or NBPA to be using drugs, based on information given to the NBA or NBPA. This expert can order tests on a player four times during a six-week period, without notice to the player. Instead of requesting testing, the league or players' association can seek a hearing on the player's alleged use of drugs before an impartial arbitrator. If the arbitrator determines that the player has used drugs illegally, the player is expelled from the league.

Shortly after the program was announced, a few players came forward for treatment. An amnesty period was established until December 31, 1983, so that no players would be suspended until after this time. The program was expanded by the NBA board of governors to include owners, general managers, coaches, trainers, and all league employees. The first incident under the new procedure occurred when the New Jersey Nets placed player Michael Ray Richardson on waivers after he refused drug treatment. Richardson had been treated twice previously for cocaine abuse. He filed a grievance to gain reinstatement with the club and entered a drug treatment center for a third time. Richardson was reinstated, but agreed to forfeit pay for games missed, drop his grievance, and take drug tests. Complicating the Richardson matter was the fact that he was waived and reinstated by the Nets during the amnesty period.

In the 1984–85 season, two players who were released by their clubs were found in drug tests to have used cocaine. John Drew of the Utah Jazz and John Lucas of the Houston Rockets were both second-time offenders under the NBA's program. In 1986 Michael Ray Richardson became a third-time offender and thus the first player to be banned under the drug program. The following year two additional players were banished, Lewis Lloyd and Mitchell Wiggins of the Houston Rockets. Unlike Richardson, who was banned for coming forth voluntarily a third time, the two Rockets did not come forward at all. Instead, league officials obtained evidence that Lloyd and Wiggins were using cocaine, and when the players were given a test it showed positive results. Because the players did not disclose their problem and were caught, they were subject to immediate banishment. Both Lloyd and Wiggins returned to the league after two years.

These incidents point up a problem with getting players to come forth voluntarily. It is often difficult to discern a reduction in the quality of play of a basketball player who uses cocaine. From the player's viewpoint, the continued high level of play causes denial that he has a drug problem. Consequently, the player does not come forth for help. Evidence that some players are not willing to acknowledge their problem and seek assistance is the 1987 indictment on drug charges of several current and former players with the Phoenix Suns. An even more bizarre example occurred in 1988 when New Jersey Nets officials acknowledged that they knew player Orlando Woolridge was using cocaine, yet did nothing about it. The Nets were fined $25,000 by the league for failure to report the information.

John Drew was eventually let go by the league for his third offense, and in 1988 Duane Washington of the New Jersey Nets was banned. In 1990 Chris Washburn of the Atlanta Hawks was banned for his third violation. He had received initial treatment in 1987 and then tested positive in 1988, causing him to be suspended for the entire season. Dallas Mavericks forward Roy Tarpley in 1991 was the seventh player to be banned from the league when he refused to take a required drug test. Tarpley became the third player to achieve reinstatement when he returned to the Mavericks in 1994.

To avoid bringing players into the league with existing drug problems, the NBA and NBPA agreed in 1988 to mandatory testing for rookies during training camp. On an unannounced basis, each rookie is required to submit to urinalysis. If a rookie tests positive for cocaine or heroin or refuses to take the test, he is suspended for a year without pay. The expense of drug rehabilitation is paid by the NBA. The goal of the program is to identify and treat players with drug problems before they play in the NBA and to send a message to college players that a professional career is in jeopardy if they use drugs. In 1989 the program was expanded to three additional random drug tests during the regular season, for a total of four tests altogether for rookies.

The NBA's drug control program has been criticized as being too punitive. Some observers feel that threat of punishment will not deter drug abuse. The program, however, is far harder on players who get caught without voluntarily disclosing their problems. It encourages players to acknowledge their illness and obtain treatment. Their pay even continues during the first treatment period. No drug control program is going to work perfectly, but the NBA's approach appears to be the kind of program that should serve as a model for other professional team sports.

Hockey 5

The sport of ice hockey is relatively unfamiliar to persons living in the temperate zones of the United States. But it is fast gaining recognition, especially as a result of the recent location of major league franchises in California, Florida, and Texas. Hockey has long had a wide following in the northern part of the country and is an extremely popular sport in Canada, Europe, and Russia. The game provides a combination between the sports of soccer and field hockey, with five skaters and a goaltender on each side.

Although the exact origins of hockey are obscure, it is thought to have evolved from folk games played on fields with sticks and balls of wood or cork in Britain and France. In France the game was known as hocquet, in England as bandy, in Ireland as hurley, and in Scotland as shinny. Ice hockey, roughly as we know it today, began in Canada in the last half of the nineteenth century. Early rules were laid down by students at Montreal's McGill University in 1875. At that time, organized hockey was played exclusively at the amateur level, and the first national hockey association was formed in 1885 with teams from Montreal, Quebec, and Ottawa.[1] In 1893 the governor general of Canada, Lord Stanley, donated a cup to be presented to the Canadian amateur hockey champions.

Professional hockey became prominent in 1909, when the National Hockey Association (NHA) was organized for teams in eastern Canada, and in 1911 when the Pacific Coast Hockey League was formed among teams in western Canada and the United States. When these two leagues held a championship playoff in 1912, the Stanley Cup presented to the victor became the symbol of professional, rather than amateur, supremacy. When the NHA disbanded in 1917, the National Hockey League (NHL) was formed and today remains the sport's major league. By 1942 the NHL included six teams: Boston, Chicago,

Montreal, New York Rangers, and Toronto. In 1967 the league expanded to twelve teams, and in 1974 to eighteen teams. This expansion was followed by several franchise shifts and realignment of the league, such as the addition of teams from the rival World Hockey Association in 1979. While the NHL had three teams in the Sunbelt in the early 1970s, the franchises in Oakland (called California) and Atlanta were unsuccessful and had to relocate. Only the Los Angeles franchise stayed put. But in 1991 the league made a new, and so far very successful, foray into the Sunbelt with a franchise in San Jose, followed by new teams in Tampa Bay, Anaheim, and Miami (called Florida). In 1993 the Minnesota franchise relocated to Dallas. By 1995 the NHL had 26 teams in the United States and Canada. The evolution of the league since 1942 is shown in Figure 5.1.

Major league hockey is the least economically important of the four sports making up the professional sports industry today. It has not been able to capitalize on television revenues as much as the other sports, and its arenas have limited seating capacities compared to baseball and football. As to its future growth, however, hockey has great potential and could turn out to be the rising star of the 1990s. It is ironic that this potential was dampened by the long and bitter lockout in 1994–95. For many years hockey was a model of cooperation between labor and management in sports. Along with the increased popularity of the game, however, has come a growing intensity among players for a bigger share of the proceeds. The numerous industrial issues in hockey, some similar to those in other sports and some unique, make for interesting comparison.

1942–67 Boston Bruins, Chicago Blackhawks, Detroit Red Wings, Montreal Canadiens, New York Rangers, Toronto Maple Leafs.

1967–68 season (six teams) California Seals (became Cleveland Barons, then merged with Minnesota North Stars, which became Dallas Stars). Los Angeles Kings, Minnesota North Stars, Philadelphia Flyers, Pittsburgh Penguins, St. Louis Blues.

1970–71 (two teams) Buffalo Sabres, Vancouver Canucks.

1972–73 (two teams) Atlanta Flames (since moved to Calgary), New York Islanders.

1974–75 (two teams) Kansas City Scouts (became Colorado Rockies, then New Jersey Devils), Washington Capitals.

1979–80 (four teams from World Hockey Assn.) Edmonton Oilers, Hartford Whalers, Quebec Nordiques (became Colorado Avalanche), Winnipeg Jets.

1991–92 (one team) San Jose Sharks.

1992–93 (two teams) Ottawa Senators, Tampa Bay Lightning.

1993–94 (two teams) Anaheim Mighty Ducks, Florida Panthers

Figure 5.1. NHL Expansion and Relocation, 1942–95

Economics of Hockey

The overall financial health of the NHL has been improving in recent years, after a precarious state in the early 1980s. Hockey is played in relativity small arenas, with typical seating capacities of about seventeen thousand. Similar to basketball, NHL teams play a relatively large number of games per season, so if the arenas are nearly filled, gate receipts can be an attractive source of revenue. The average ticket cost is the league in 1995–96 was a pricey $34.79. NHL arenas are filled to about 85 percent of capacity during the regular season. The proportion of total league revenue derived from ticket sales, about 65 percent, is higher than in any other sport. Home teams keep 100 percent of gate receipts, not having to share these revenues with visiting clubs. The league has an advantage in that roster sizes (twenty per team) are smaller than in football (forty-six) and baseball (twenty-five), albeit somewhat greater than in basketball (twelve).

With comparatively limited television revenues, however, NHL teams do not derive the high income from that source that other professional team sports do. Also, the league has a substantial disparity between big-market and small-market teams. Small-market teams in Canadian cities such as Calgary, Edmonton, and Winnipeg, and American cities such as Buffalo and Hartford, have to struggle to compete with their big-market brethren. They are typically at a disadvantage in terms of stadium capacity, ticket prices, and local television revenues. As player salaries more than doubled between 1990 and 1994, small-market teams were caught in a revenue-cost squeeze. Exacerbating the problem for the Canadian teams has been the depressed Canadian dollar, worth only about two-thirds as much as the U.S. dollar, which makes it difficult to compete for top players.[2] The 1994–95 lockout, discussed later in the chapter, was largely caused by the league's attempt to impose a graduated tax on teams with higher than average payrolls, so as to protect the small-market teams.

Despite the disadvantage of small-market teams, there are signs of a more robust financial future for the league. Since World War II, only one team has gone bankrupt, the Pittsburgh Penguins in 1975. New arenas have been recently built in several cities, increasing seating capacities and raising more revenue from higher ticket prices and luxury boxes. Sale of NHL apparel and novelty items has been growing at a rapid rate, with licensed merchandise sales going from $150 million in 1990 to $1 billion in 1994. In 1992 and 1993 the hottest selling logo in sports licensing belonged to the San Jose Sharks. Indicative of the financial state of the league is the sale of franchises. In 1988 the Hartford Whalers sold for a record $31 million, and in 1990 and 1991 the Minnesota and

Pittsburgh franchises were also sold for $31 million. But the four expansion teams that came in the league in 1992 and 1993—Ottawa, Tampa Bay, Anaheim, and Florida—each paid $50 million. In 1995 the Quebec Nordiques were sold for $75 million (and relocated to Denver as the Colorado Avalanche), and the Los Angeles Kings sold for $114 million. Still, the recent hockey franchise prices are only about half of what a typical team would sell for in other sports.

Attendance

Because television revenues are not so bountiful in hockey as in other sports, the success of individual clubs is closely linked to gate receipts. Although seating capacities are limited, each team plays an eighty-four-game regular season, and there are numerous playoff games for many clubs. Sixteen out the twenty-six teams in the league make the playoffs, which draw to 95 percent of stadium capacity. NHL clubs have also begun to play a larger number of preseason exhibition games in recent years. Revenue from attendance accounts for about 65 percent of total revenue. Attendance at NHL games for the past decade is shown in Table 5.1. Apart from a decline that began in the mid-1970s and continued for several years, attendance has grown steadily, if unspectacularly, in the recent past.

There appears to be a negative correlation between the extent of violence at NHL games and attendance levels. While some fans react favorably to fighting, most are turned off by violence because it detracts from the artistry of the game. Hockey was meant to be played by swift skaters, deft passers, and hard shooters, not by goons and muggers. When played cleanly, hockey is a wonderfully excit-

Table 5.1. NHL Attendance, 1984–94

Year	Total Games	Total Attendance	Average Attendance
1984–85	840	12,307,913	14,640
1985–86	840	12,232,586	14,563
1986–87	840	12,430,794	14,799
1987–88	840	12,750,426	15,179
1988–89	840	12,417,969	14,783
1989–90	840	12,579,651	14,976
1990–91	840	12,343,897	14,695
1991–92	880	12,769,676	14,511
1992–93	1,008	14,158,177	14,046
1993–94	1,092	16,105,604	14,749
1994–95	624	9,233,884	14,798

Source: National Hockey League.

ing sport for live viewing. The skills of great players such as Wayne Gretzky of the Los Angeles Kings and Mario Lemieux of the Pittsburgh Penguins require unspoiled play to develop to their fullest extent, and the NHL's efforts at curbing violence have succeeded in attracting more fans to arenas. The players themselves have control over their salary potential by curbing excessive violence to attract spectator interest.

Television

From 1956 to 1975 two major American television networks, CBS and NBC, had an on-again, off-again contractual arrangement with the NHL for presenting games. After 1975, however, the networks disdained the NHL because of poor ratings. Lacking network exposure, the league shifted its television strategy to cable outlets, in a manner similar to the NBA, catering to local markets rather than a large national audience. Local and network cable and pay television direct hockey to the attention of viewers who have a keener interest in the sport.

In 1985 the NHL agreed to a three-year contract for $20 million with the ESPN cable network for exclusive rights to televise thirty-three regular-season games, the all-star game, and all the Stanley Cup playoffs. These games were presented in the United States but not in Canada. At the time, ESPN had access to about forty-two million homes, providing a large potential audience. The ratings, however, were low. As a result, the NHL revised its approach when the ESPN contract expired. The new idea was to provide even narrower television marketing. Because it is more profitable for the television industry to present selected packages to viewers, it was thought that the revenue base for the league could be increased.

Accordingly, in 1988 the NHL entered into a three-year agreement for $51 million with SportsChannel America, a regional cable company 50 percent owned by NBC. Although this television deal significantly increased revenues to the league, the potential market that SportsChannel covered was only about one-ninth the size of ESPN's. But the NHL was banking on the promise that SportsChannel's coverage would grow at a faster rate than ESPN's. Also, the league liked the idea that SportsChannel's market—which then included the areas of New York, Philadelphia, New England, Chicago, and Florida—would target on an area more likely to watch hockey.

The SportsChannel contract did not work out as expected. One problem was that shortly after the deal was reached, Wayne Gretzky was traded from the Edmonton Oilers to the Los Angeles Kings. Gretzky is the greatest hockey player ever and possibly the best ever in any sport. His relocation sparked viewer interest in the United States, especially on the West Coast. But SportsChannel was not well positioned to capitalize on this heightened national attention because viewers in many parts of the country could not receive SportsChannel on their television sets. SportsChannel eventually expanded its availability to more homes, but it often was an expensive add-on to basic cable coverage. Another problem was that the NHL was mistaken in its notion that hockey would be made available to local cable operators on a "stand-alone" basis. Instead, Sports-Channel required cable stations to carry a package that included events such as boxing and auto racing, which caused some stations to reject participation.

Consequently, SportsChannel lost about $10 million in each year of the three-year agreement. By 1991 when the contract expired, the first signs of a collapse in the sports-television marketplace appeared after several years of soaring television deals. The NHL looked again to ESPN for a new contract, but negotiations were unproductive because ESPN wanted exclusive rights to games it covered and a lifting of local television blackouts in league cities. Unable to overcome these obstacles, the NHL signed a one-year contract in 1991 with SportsChannel for $5.5 million, less than one-third the annual revenue from the previous contract.

By 1992 the NHL had expanded to San Jose and Tampa Bay and was scheduled to add new franchises the following year in Anaheim and Miami. The league was now truly a coast-to-coast operation and looked to extend the scope of its television coverage. At this time ESPN had expanded to reach about sixty million homes, while SportsChannel had grown to cover only about twenty million. In 1991 the league and ESPN agreed to a five-year television deal for $80 million. The contract provided for twenty-five regular-season games a year plus a substantial number of playoff games and the entire Stanley Cup finals. Also provided was that a few games could be shown on ESPN's parent network, ABC. In 1994 the NHL-ESPN agreement was extended for two years, through the 1998–99 season. Under the extension ESPN was given exclusive rights to certain games it telecasts and a lifting of local blackouts during the last two rounds of the playoffs.

Although the 1990 NHL all-star game was shown on NBC, league games had not appeared on U.S. network television since 1975, except for the 1980 Stanley Cup sixth and final game between the New York Islanders and the Philadelphia Flyers. In 1995, however, the NHL finally recaptured this prize as a result of a contract reached the prior year with the Fox network. Under a five-year $155 million deal, Fox acquired the right to televise sixteen games in the first three seasons and twenty in the last two seasons.

The Fox network got off to a rocky start. The network's first game was to be the 1995 all-star game in San Jose, but this game was canceled as a result of the lockout. Still, hockey has again reached the promised land. This time—with national franchise coverage, improved use of cameras to track the elusive puck, and the decrease in player fighting—the NHL just might be on U.S. television to stay. While television may not produce income of the same magnitude for the NHL as it does in football and baseball, it could become just as large a proportion of the smaller-scale revenues of the NHL.

Three other sources of television revenue for NHL teams should be mentioned. One is the arrangements between individual teams and television companies, usually cable, to service local areas. In some areas, hockey coverage is sold to viewers together with NBA basketball games in a single television package, a good example of horizontal integration in marketing. A second source of revenue is the game each week presented on "Hockey Night in Canada" by the Canadian Broadcasting Company. These games receive exceptionally high ratings. Third, the Canadian Sports Network presents games for cable television viewers in Canada, in an arrangement similar to that provided by ESPN in the United States.

Salaries

Until recently hockey has been unable to support the large increases in player salaries that have occurred in other sports. With the growth in league revenues from television, licensing arrangements, and franchise expansion, however, salaries have turned sharply upward. Although average salaries in hockey still trail those in other sports, the gap has narrowed. The principal determinant of salaries at all positions is skill, and there is no evidence of salary discrimination against minority groups such as French Canadians or blacks.[3] Table 5.2 shows the average salaries in the NHL since 1984.

Also shown in Table 5.2 is the annual salary of the highest paid player. Until recently the salaries of top NHL stars did not come close to the levels paid in other sports, and most salaries were tightly bunched around the median. That began to change in 1989 when Wayne Gretzky signed an eight-year contract for $20 million and Mario Lemieux signed a five-year deal for $12 million. Following these contracts several other star players reached multimillion dollar deals, including Mark Messier of the New York Rangers, Eric Lindros of the Philadelphia Flyers, Sergei Fedorov of the Detroit Red Wings, and Pavel Bure of the Vancouver Canucks. Gretzky's contract was renegotiated in 1993, for $25.5 million over three years, making him the highest paid player in hockey and one of the highest paid in all of sports. Lemieux's contract was replaced by a new

Table 5.2. Average Salaries in the NHL

Season	Average Salary	Highest Salary	Highest Paid Player
1984–85	$149,000	$ 725,000	Dave Taylor
1985–86	159,000	775,000	Dave Taylor
1986–87	173,000	825,000	Dave Taylor
1987–88	184,000	900,000	Dave Taylor
1988–89	201,000	1,620,000	Mario Lemieux
1989–90	232,000	2,284,000	Mario Lemieux
1990–91	263,000	2,342,000	Wayne Gretzky
1991–92	369,000	2,786,000	Mark Messier
1992–93	463,000	3,342,000	Wayne Gretzky
1993–94	558,000	7,353,000	Wayne Gretzky
1994–95	600,000	6,545,000	Wayne Gretzky

Source: National Hockey League.

seven-year, $42 million contract in 1992. These new contracts not only raised the league average but continued to make it possible for other outstanding players to get big increases. Consequently, the salary differential between low-paid and high-paid players has widened.

The contracts signed by the number-one draft choices in hockey are another indication of salary trends. Like their counterparts in the NFL and NBA, these players go directly from the amateur ranks to the major leagues, but the top draft choices are similar to those in baseball in that they are usually signed at a younger age. Top draft choices in baseball do not typically go directly to the major leagues since they require seasoning in the minors. Compared with the salaries of football and basketball number-one draft choices in recent years, hockey players are getting only about one-third to one-half as much pay.

The NHL's pension plan was initiated in 1947 with the approval of the players. They agreed to contribute $900 a year from individual salaries, and the league agreed to contribute two-thirds of the proceeds from the annual all-star game plus 25 percent of the ticket sales from playoff games. Eligibility for benefits was established at age forty-five. For the 1985–86 season, the age for eligibility remained at forty-five, but the pension plan no longer required direct out-of-pocket contributions by the players.[4] They received $1,000 (Canadian dollars) annually for each full year of credited service (seventy games), and credit was given even if a player was temporarily assigned to a minor league club. As a result of the 1986 collective bargaining agreement, the pension fund contribution system was changed. Based on a full eighty-game season, contributions of $5,000 (Canadian dollars) were placed in each player's pension account. This change, which was effective for each year through the 1990–91 season, resulted in approximately a doubling of pension benefits. The owners also agreed to a lump sum payment of $250,000 at age fifty-five to players with at least four hundred fifty games of NHL service. As a result of the collective bargaining agreement reached in 1992, annual pension contributions were increased to $8,000 (Canadian dollars) for players who played under four hundred games and $12,500 for those who played over four hundred.

Three-fourths of the funding for pensions is provided by the NHL; one-fourth is an obligation of the NHLPA, which is expected to fund its share out of proceeds from "international" hockey games, including the Canada Cup matches involving amateur and NHL players from countries such as Canada, the United States, Sweden, the Czech Republic, Russia, and Finland. Before 1986 the parties each contributed half of the pension fund. If a player is forced to retire prematurely because of an injury, he is awarded a pension credit for each year of disability until ten years of pension credit have accrued.

Although hockey is not as important from an overall economic standpoint as other professional team sports, its pension plan is relatively generous. A sound pension fund is crucial to hockey, because most players are very young and relatively uneducated when they begin serious competition in preparation for the professional ranks. Many are unable to derive significant incomes from talents apart from their playing skills and professional reputations. Unlike other professional athletes, who are, on the whole, better educated from their college days, hockey players' potential for postretirement income is thus more constricted.

A controversy over pensions began in 1991 when a lawsuit was filed in Toronto by seven former NHL players, including Gordie Howe, Bobby Hull, Carl Brewer, and Eddie Shack. In the original players' pension fund, annuities were purchased under the conservative assumption of a 3 percent annual interest rate for surplus. As a result of the high interest rates of the late 1970s and early 1980s, however, the surplus grew far beyond what was imagined. Therefore, between 1982 and 1985 the owners removed surplus monies from the pension fund in order to finance the pension plan for current players. The suit by the former players sought recovery of $25 million in surplus pension funds for players who retired before 1982. In 1992 the Ontario Court of Justice ruled in favor of the retirees. The court rebuked the owners for plundering the pension fund and cited former NHLPA director Alan Eagleson for "moral shortcomings" in not protesting the owners' raid. In 1994 the Supreme Court of Canada upheld the decision. With accumulated interest and award of attorneys' fees, the ultimate award was nearly $50 million, which tripled the pensions of several hundred former players to about $30,000 a year.

Structure of Employment

Government

The overall influence of government on industrial relations in hockey has not been as significant as in other sports. This is ironic, since the governments of two countries—Canada and the United States—might become involved through the actions of legislatures, courts, and administrative agencies. Perhaps because of the distinctive, international setting for hockey, neither government seems inclined to intrude on developments in the sport. A more likely reason for the relative noninvolvement is that labor and management have not looked to government as a source of dispute resolution so much as in other sports. The parties have chosen to work out their problems at the bargaining table and through informal discussions more often than they resort to outside assistance. This is not to say that government action has been totally absent from hockey, only that labor and management have not typically felt a need to rely on this source.

The American courts were active in helping NHL players jump leagues to play with teams in the World Hockey Association. Nevertheless, government's role in such intraleague matters as free agency, draft rules, collective bargaining conduct, and drug abuse has been limited. In Canada, Parliament has threatened to take a strong position on violence in hockey, but leaders within the sport have succeeded in heading off regulation by trying to clean up their own house.

Apart from the traditional areas of government influence on sports, which are addressed in detail later in the chapter, two interesting applications of government participation have affected the industry. One involves the divergent application of tax laws and currency exchange between Canada and the United States. Canada's tax structure imposes a heavy burden on clubs and players operating in that country. Incomes are taxed at higher rates, and depreciation of players is not allowed. There are also differences stemming from the disparity in value of the Canadian and American dollars, with the latter worth about one-third more in recent years. Canadian teams pay their players in Canadian dollars. Although most of the players in the NHL are Canadian citizens, most of the clubs are situated in the United States. When Canadian athletes play for American teams, they are paid in U.S. currency and gain a substantial advantage on the dollar exchange. Other things being equal, a given player would be more inclined to play for an American rather than a Canadian team.

Determining amateur status for purposes of competing in the Olympic games is a second important area of government involvement that potentially affects all major professional team sports. In many cases, the rules for determining amateur status are left up to the appropriate sports governing bodies. Eligibility rules are stricter in some sports than in others, which causes inconsistencies and inequities. Hockey is governed by the rules of the International Olympic Committee (IOC), but the International Ice Hockey Federation and Olympic committees in the individual countries also influence individual player participation. At the time of the 1984 Winter Olympics in Sarajevo, Yugoslavia, the IOC had not approved the rules for participation set down by the international hockey federation. There was, however, unanimous agreement amoung participating countries that any player not currently under a professional contract would be eligible to compete in the games. A dispute arose when the Canadians tried to use players who were under professional contract. They interpreted the rules to allow this if an athlete had played in fewer than ten NHL games. Their attempt caused a protest to be filed by the United States, which led to heated recriminations between representatives of the two countries. R. Alan Eagleson, a Canadian and executive director of the NHL players' union, objected that certain members of the 1980 United States team had been ineligible to play in Lake Placid. Those players, however, had offers outstanding from NHL clubs that had not yet been accepted, which is different from being under contract and having actually played in NHL games. The dispute was resolved when the IOC ruled that five players—two Canadians, two Italians, and one Austrian—were ineligible for competition at Sarajevo.

NHL players were allowed to compete in the 1988 winter games in Calgary, but few were of top caliber because the regular NHL season was in progress and players under contract to NHL teams stood to lose money by taking time off for the Olympics. It was the same story for the 1992 winter games in Albertville, France. Spurred by the success of the "Dream Team" of NBA athletes who won the basketball gold medal for the United States in the 1992 Barcelona summer games, Commissioner Bettman tried to work out an arrangement for extensive participation by NHL players in the 1994 games at Lillehammer, Norway. But there were to many obstacles to overcome, including too little time for planning, risk of injury to players, and extending the already lengthy NHL season.

The league, however, set its sights on the 1998 winter games in Nagano, Japan. Commissioner Bettman proposed that the NHL shut down for sixteen days to allow about one hundred players to join their countries' teams. The proposal was approved in 1995 by the NHL, the players' union, and the International Ice Hockey Federation. Thus there are six "Dream Teams," with NHL players suiting up for the national teams of their own countries, the United States, Canada, Russia, Sweden, Finland, and the Czech Republic. The hockey tournament changes from twelve teams to a two-tiered fourteen-team affair, with the two survivors of a preliminary tournament playing the six NHL-stocked teams in the final round.

Management

Outspoken owners who meddle with the performance of their teams on the field have always existed in sports. They are probably more conspicuous today because of the high risk of operating teams with rapidly escalating payrolls. Hockey owners have been relatively aloof in the past, but a new breed of owners—flamboyant entrepreneurs and large corporations—is taking a more businesslike approach to running the franchises, which often includes entertainment hype to stir interest among fans and the media. Players are more openly criticized, coaches are fired more often, and team strategy is dictated from the front office—all in the interest of keeping the club in the headlines. The owners reason that since they pay the bills, they have the right to operate the team as they see fit. Sports ownership has never been a totally benign business, but modern owners are far more cutthroat and egotistic. They figure they have to be tougher because competition is keener.

Table 5.3 shows the ownership of teams in the NHL. Like their counterparts in other sports, the new owners are more apt to be individuals or corporations with interests that relate to the entertainment industry and to businesses that derive significant portions of their incomes from sports. Also, a large share of the owners in the NHL have made substantial monies in real estate transactions. Some own sports arenas and teams in other professional leagues. Many are self-made men, throwbacks to the early captains of industry in America and Canada.

Despite an increase in public visibility as individuals, hockey owners as a group hold together more on league policy issues than is the general rule. Each owner has representation on the NHL's board of governors, which, along with the league commissioner, (formerly called the president), determines overall policies. Intraorganizational league strength is in part due to the relative stability of leadership as vested in the office of the NHL commissioner. Enlightened leadership in the office of the president was demonstrated by Clarence Campbell, who headed the league from 1946 to 1977. A former Rhodes scholar, NHL referee (1929–40), and prosecutor at the Nuremberg trials, Campbell oversaw league expansion from six to eighteen teams during his presidency. This kindly but tough Scot was succeeded as NHL president by John A. Ziegler, Jr., the first American to serve in this position. A lawyer, who graduated from the University of Michigan, Ziegler was formerly an executive with the Detroit Red Wings and served as chair of the NHL board of governors.

Table 5.3. Ownership of NHL Franchises

Team	Division	Principal Owner	Other Interests
Anaheim Mighty Ducks	Pacific	Walt Disney Co.	Entertainment
Boston Bruins	Northeast	Jeremy Jacobs	Delaware North Co.
Buffalo Sabres	Northeast	Knox brothers	Real estate, insurance
Calgary Flames	Pacific	Six individuals	Oil, real estate
Chicago Blackhawks	Central	William Wirtz	Diversified interests
Colorado Avalanche	Pacific	COMSAT Video Enterprises	Entertainment, Denver Nuggets
Dallas Stars	Central	Norman Green	Real estate
Detroit Red Wings	Central	Michael Ilitch	Pizza parlors
Edmonton Oilers	Pacific	Peter Pocklington	Meatpacking, real estate
Florida Panthers	Atlantic	Wayne Huizenga	Video stores, Florida Marlins, Miami Dolphins
Hartford Whalers	Northeast	Peter Karmanos	CompuWare Co.
Los Angeles Kings	Pacific	Phillip F. Anschultz Edward P. Roski, Jr.	Railroad magnate and real estate developer
Montreal Canadiens	Northeast	Molson Breweries	Beer
New Jersey Devils	Atlantic	John McMullen	Shipbuilding
New York Islanders	Atlantic	John D. Pickett	Diversified interests
New York Rangers	Atlantic	ITT Corp.	Cablevision, Madison Square Garden
Ottawa Senators	Northeast	Rod Bryden	Terrace Investments
Philadelphia Flyers	Atlantic	Ed Snider	Philadelphia Spectrum (arena), insurance
Pittsburgh Penguins	Northeast	Howard Baldwin Morris Belzberg	Investments
St. Louis Blues	Central	Group headed by Michael Shanahan	Diversified interests
San Jose Sharks	Pacific	Gund brothers	Cleveland Colisium, Cleveland Cavaliers, real estate
Tampa Bay Lightning	Atlantic	Takashi Okubo and others	Lightning Partners, Inc.
Toronto Maple Leafs	Central	Steve Stavro	Maple Leaf Gardens
Vancouver Canucks	Pacific	John McCaw	Cellular telephones
Washington Capitals	Atlantic	Abe Pollin	Capital Centre (arena), Washington Bullets
Winnipeg Jets	Central	Richard Burke Steven Gluckstern	Healthcare facilities, Reinsurance

After fifteen years as president of the NHL, Ziegler formally resigned in 1992. In reality he was bought out with four years remaining on his contract. To Ziegler's credit he had some successes. In 1977 when he replaced Clarence Campbell, the NHL was trying to find a way out of the dilemma posed by money-losing competition with the World Hockey Association (WHA). Ziegler got the league out of that tangle through merger with successful WHA teams. He was also adept at labor relations and smoothly negotiated agreements with the union. But Ziegler's failures may have outweighed his contributions. He was unable to get a U.S. television agreement, and his choice of SportsChannel as a provider of cable television worked out poorly. He lacked marketing and public relations skills and was often indecisive and sometimes invisible regarding problems that called for strong leadership, such as curbing violence by players. Even his collective bargaining skills seemed to desert him when the players struck in 1992.

When the NHL chose a successor to Ziegler, it was with the new title of commissioner rather than president, so as to be consistent with the three other major sports. The NHL chose Gary Bettman. A graduate of Cornell University and New York University's law school, Bettman was an inspired choice, seemingly perfect for the rather stodgy league. He had done an outstanding job as general counsel for the NBA, where he was third in command to David Stern, and devised and implemented basketball's salary cap. Like Stern, Bettman is outgoing, energetic, marketing oriented, innovative, and solidly prepared to deal with the business and legal ends of the game.

Therefore, it is not surprising that Bettman has performed brilliantly on many facets of hockey. He oversaw league expansion, realigned teams in new divisions, and revised the playoff system. He acted decisively on violence and appointed Brian Burke, a former player and general manager, to handle league disciplinary problems. Bettman dealt with the seventeen-day strike by league referees in 1993 by hiring replacement officials and then negotiating a four-year agreement that provided little more than the league had initially offered. Perhaps most important, he negotiated a U.S. network television agreement and cranked the NHL's marketing operation into high gear. But the lengthy 1994–95 players' lockout and the way it was handled tarnished Bettman's image and cost the league dearly. Perhaps because of his success with the salary cap in the NBA he was too insistent on directly limiting NHL salaries, an idea that had to be abandoned. Still, even the negotiations failure could have a silver lining if the 1995 agreement helps small-market teams compete more favorably. Bettman has clearly done the job the owners hired him to do.

Teams in the NHL have working agreements with clubs in the Junior A amateur leagues of Canada (the Ontario Hockey League, Quebec Hockey League, and Western Hockey League)[5], as well as with the professional teams in the American Hockey League and International Hockey League. The United States Hockey League, an amateur association for players under twenty years of age, is a minor league feeder system for NHL teams. Like other major professional team sports, hockey drafts amateur players through a system based on an inverse relationship of final team standings. This is done to achieve parity, but some of the less successful teams have traded away top amateur draft choices for veteran players, which has not usually proved to be a wise strategy.

Labor

At one time nearly all the players in the NHL were from Canada. In recent years this has changed in two important ways. One is the influx of Americans into the league. This is the result of better coaching of U.S. youngsters, increased participation in youth leagues, and improved college programs at schools such as Minnesota, Wisconsin, North Dakota, Cornell, Maine, Boston College, and Providence. The other is the increased signing of players from the burgeoning amateur and professional ranks in Europe.

In the 1993–94 season the percentage of Canadian-born players in the NHL dropped to an all-time low of 64 percent (compared to 96 percent in 1966–67). Nearly all the Canadian players are drafted from the Junior A leagues. The percentage of U.S.-born players in 1993–94 reached an all-time high of 17 percent (up from 12 percent in 1985–86), with most of these players from the states of Minnesota, Massachusetts, Michigan, and New York. In 1983–84 the number-one pick in the amateur draft was for the first time an American, Brian Lawton from Providence, Rhode Island, who was selected by the Minnesota North Stars. About a fifth of the NHL players are now from Europe—mostly Russia, Sweden, Finland, and the Czech Republic—which is the highest proportion ever.

The players from the countries of the former Soviet Union have had a big impact on the NHL. The Soviet Union was for many years the dominant power in international hockey, but it was not until 1989 that the first Soviet player, Sergi Priakin, was allowed by his country to play in the NHL, for the Calgary Flames. Shortly afterward, one of the Soviets' great young players, Alexander Mogilny, defected and became a star for the Buffalo Sabres. Other defections followed, and when the Soviet Union collapsed, many of the very best Russian, Latvian, and Ukrainian players were signed by NHL teams. The reaction to this influx of foreign-born players has not always been positive, especially because of jobs lost by Canadian players. But the dazzling talent of newcomers such as Mogilny, Pavel Bure, and Sergei Fedorov has captured the hearts of fans. Fedorov won the league's most valuable player award in 1993–94.

The average age of players in the NHL is twenty-six, and careers there last an average of five years. Professional hockey players are relatively young because they are eligible to be drafted if they reach at least eighteen years of age by January 1 of the following season.

In 1957 league players established a union, the National Hockey League Players Association (NHLPA), with Ted Lindsay of the Detroit Red Wings as president. The players organized to fill a perceived power vacuum in their relations with management, as well as to provide a means of helping promote the popularity of the sport. The players were generally contented, receiving a minimum salary of $6,500, which was $500 more than that for baseball players. A generous player pension plan had been established a decade earlier. It was not long, however, before the union sought to flex its muscle through its legal counsel, J. Norman Lewis, who also represented major league baseball players. The hockey players were miffed over a 1956 television contract with CBS that provided no share for them. Lewis therefore threatened an antitrust suit against the league, but the dispute was resolved when the owners agreed to contribute monies from television to enhance player pensions.

Other than this confrontation, NHL players did not accomplish much through their union in the next decade or so. Then in 1967 Alan Eagleson, a Toronto lawyer and players' agent in salary negotiations with owners, became head of the reconstituted NHLPA. Eagleson quickly grasped the reins of power and achieved formal recognition of the union by the league. His influence over the years was remarkable. Not only did he help the players attain unimagined salaries, but he took a large measure of control over international hockey, bringing it from a game dominated by amateur play to multimillion dollar professional competition in the Canada Cup. Eagleson came to wear many hats. He headed the union, to which virtually all players now belong; was chief negotiator for Hockey Canada, the nonprofit corporation that administers Canada's involvement in international events; and represented about 10 percent of the NHL players in their salary negotiations with owners. Many observers perceived Eagleson as by far the most powerful individual force in hockey.

Although Eagleson has many admirers, especially among the players, owners, and international hockey officials, he also has numerous critics. Some have charged that he took too soft a line in collective bargaining. Detractors claimed that hockey salaries did not rise as sharply as in other sports and that the free agency system in hockey did not work to the advantage of the players. They also cited the potential conflict of interest that arose when he represented players as a whole, some individual players, and management itself when he negotiated international agreements that brought revenues to owners.

One of Eagleson's most prominent critics, Bobby Orr, a famous defenseman, charged that Eagleson mishandled his financial affairs. In 1976, when Orr became a free agent, he left the Boston Bruins and signed with the Chicago Blackhawks for $3 million over five years. But Orr's damaged knees did not hold up, so he retired in 1978. Orr charged that his Chicago deal, which Eagleson nego- tiated, guaranteed him $1.5 million, but only after lengthy litigation was he able to collect less than $1 million.

A challenge to Eagleson's position as head of the union came in 1989. A group led by Ed Garvey, former director of the NFLPA, and player agents Rich Winter and Ron Salcer got more than two hundred NHL players to contribute $100 apiece to fund a study of Eagleson's performance. As a result of the study, the NHLPA's executive board informed Eagleson that in order to keep his job he would have to take a leave of absence from his law firm, stop representing play- ers as an agent, and personally guarantee loans of about $2 million that he had made with union funds to friends and associates. Although Eagleson agreed to accept the conditions and was able to retain his position, he decided to step down in 1992 with a year remaining on his contract. In 1994 Eagleson was in- dicted in Boston on thirty-two counts of racketeering, embezzlement, and fraud, following a two-year FBI investigation of his activities as union director. Among other things, he was charged with misappropriating thousands of dol- lars in union funds and receiving kickbacks from insurance brokers on league and union disability coverage.

In 1990 Bob Goodenow was hired as Eagleson's deputy at the NHLPA, and in 1992 he became executive director. Goodenow earned a degree in economics and government at Harvard University, where he was captain of the hockey team. He also has a law degree from the University of Detroit. Goodenow tried out unsuccessfully for the Washington Capitals and wound up playing briefly in the International Hockey League. He then became a labor lawyer in Detroit, where he served as an agent for twenty-eight players, including Brett Hull of the St. Louis Blues.

A strong communicator and hard worker, Goodenow spent a great deal of time educating players in seminars about perceived inequities in the collective bargaining agreement and the need for change. In sharp contrast to the clubby gentlemen's contracts negotiated between Ziegler and Eagleson, Goodenow served notice of his acquisitiveness and tenacity when he led the ten-day strike in 1992, the first in NHL history. This was also a warmup for the confrontation that led to the big 1994–95 lockout. Work stoppages are not uncommon among newly appointed heads of unions, who may feel a need to prove their mettle in a crisis. Goodenow demonstrated his talents as well as some shortcomings during the lockout. He will be a formidable adversary for the league in the future. But Goodenow has also showed a conciliatory side in agreeing to play the 1993–94 season without a labor agreement. People who care about the game and its uninterrupted progress can only hope that Goodenow and Bettman learn to work together in the future for reasoned agreement in the absence of open conflict.

Negotiation and Agreements

Hockey has an unusual system of collective bargaining in that negotiation is more apt to be undertaken spontaneously in response to newly emerging issues. Reopening of contractual provisions is not uncommon in American and Canadian industries as a whole, but subsequent negotiations during the life of a contract are usually limited to a specified issue, such as wages. The "evergreen" concept, under which existing contracts are changed or added to in material part, was particularly common in early negotiations in hockey. From 1967, when the NHLPA was formally recognized, until 1975, understandings reached in annual negotiations were recorded in formal minutes that collectively formed the parties' contractual arrangement. In 1975, 1982, and 1986, five-year conventional agreements were negotiated, but these agreements were subject to frequent modification. Responsibility for collective bargaining is vested in the Owner-Player Council, which meets in February and June each year to review contractual arrangements. Continuous bargaining has the advantage of adapting to dynamic conditions affecting the sport.

1992 Strike

When Bob Goodenow took over as head of the NHLPA in 1992, the cooperative relationship with the league ended and an adversarial relationship began. Goodenow's style is confrontational, akin so that of Marvin Miller, Donald Fehr, and Ed Garvey. The five-year agreement negotiated in 1986 expired on September 15, 1991. At that time the NHLPA was in transition from Eagleson to Goodenow, and the league dragged its feet on a replacement contract. The players began the season, but by March 1992, with no bargaining progress and the playoffs approaching, Goodenow got strike authorization. In all team sports the playoffs provide an outsized share of revenues to owners, because television ratings and payments are geared to the crowning of a champion. While player salaries are equalized over the season, owners are especially vulnerable to a strike affecting the playoffs.

Two important issues in the 1991–92 negotiations were also common to all sports. Of keen interest to the NHLPA was a reduction in the number of rounds in the draft, from twelve to six. If fewer players are drafted, more of them can sign as free agents, which drives salaries upward. A second issue was free agency for veteran players, always a sore spot with hockey players, who envy the opportunities allowed by more liberal free agency in other sports. The union wanted to reduce the compensation awards that had to be paid teams that lost free agents. As in football before 1993, free agency in hockey is restricted by relatively stiff compensation penalties. A notable example occurred at the start of the 1991–92 season when forward Brandon Shanahan left the New Jersey Devils to sign with the St. Louis Blues. As compensation for the loss of Shanahan, New Jersey was awarded all-star Blues defensemen Scott Stevens, a player of considerable talent perhaps exceeding that of Shanahan.

On April 1, 1992, the players struck after voting 560 to 4 to do so. The first strike in league history lasted ten days. Postponed games were made up, and the start of the playoffs was delayed. When the dust cleared, both sides claimed victory on some issues, but the players won overall. The league formally recognized the players' rights to use their likenesses on trading cards, although the players' share of card revenues remained at 68 percent. On salary arbitration the union won input into choice of arbitrators plus the understanding that arbitration hearings be completed by the start of the season. The age for unrestricted free agency dropped from thiry-one to thirty. Free agency compensation was modified slightly in the players' favor. The players' playoff fund was increased $3.2 million to $7.5 million in 1991–92 and to $9 million in 1992–93. The owners prevailed in limiting the duration of the agreement to only two years and got the season expanded from eighty to eighty-four games, with players sharing revenues from the final two games. The draft was reduced, but only from twelve to eleven rounds.

1994–95 Lockout

Although the collective bargaining agreement expired on September 15, 1993, the players agreed to play the 1993–94 season uninterrupted. When negotiations proved fruitless, a confrontation erupted. The owners took the preemptive action of a lockout, similar to baseball owners' attempt to forestall a damaging strike by baseball players at the end of the 1990 season. The hockey lockout lasted far longer, however, as 468 games were lost during 103 days. The lockout seriously harmed both sides and came at a time when hockey's prospects never looked brighter. Surveying the wreckage of the 1994–95 season, one can easily conclude that incredible blundering occurred. Out of a depressing season, however, some humor emerged when Nick Kypreos of the New York Rangers, returning from Canada after the lockout, was asked by customs officials if he had anything to declare. "No," he said, "the owners took it all."[6]

As serious negotiations finally commenced during the lockout, things went badly, then turned ugly, and finally became almost hopeless. The sides initially agreed not to talk to the public about the negotiations. This was a fine idea, because much of the difficulty in sports bargaining comes from the fishbowl atmosphere in which it is conducted. The rationale was to cut out the intrusiveness of the media and make progress at the bargaining table. Practically, however, it is hard to sustain a news blackout. After all, the fans are a big part of the game and they want to know what is going on. In any event, the union broke silence by telling the media that it rejected the owners' salary cap proposal. Not surprisingly, this incensed the owners and chilled negotiations. For good measure the owners rescinded several player benefits.

The situation turned ugly when Chicago Blackhawks defenseman Chris Chelios said: "If I was Gary Bettman, I'd be worried about my family, about my well-being right now. Some crazed fan or even a player, who knows, might take it into his own hands and figure that if they get him out of the way this might get settled."[7] Though Chelios later apologized for his remarks, they caused hard feelings.

The big bargaining issue was the so-called salary cap. Apart from its application to the owners' demand on rookie salaries, however, the term was inapt. The league's proposal did not actually cap spending by a team or even the league as a whole. It was designed to limit salaries by requiring high-spending teams to contribute to revenue sharing through a "payroll tax" system. The idea was to reduce the rate of salary escalation and help small-market teams have a greater opportunity to sign and retain top quality players. The league provided data, undisputed by the union, that it lost $67.6 million in the last two seasons, and that player salaries had grown as a proportion of league revenues from 42 percent in 1989–90 to 61 percent in 1993–94.

The union countered with a proposal to impose a 7 percent (its original proposal was 5.5 percent) payroll tax on the four highest spending teams, 5 percent on the next four teams, 3 percent on the next four, and 1 percent on the next four. Thus, sixteen teams would be taxed at varying rates, with the revenues used to help small-market teams. Both sides also proposed a flat tax of 3 percent on all gate receipts of the top sixteen teams in revenue, to be credited against the payroll tax.

The lockout ended in mid-January 1995, just in time to save the season, which had to be cut from eighty-four to forty-eight regular-season games. In the end the owners dropped the payroll tax proposal, which gained some face for the union. While both sides lost heavily from the lockout, however, the owners clearly won the overall war. The agreement is for six years, until September 15, 2000. Initially, either party was able to reopen the agreement at the end of the

1997–98 season, but in late 1995 the union and league agreed to eliminate the reopener provision, thus avoiding a possible work stoppage in 1998.

Several provisions of the new agreement protect the owners from a salary spiral. Rookie salaries for players under age twenty-five are capped at $850,000 in 1995, with the cap rising annually to $1,075,000 in 2000. Before the agreement rookie Paul Kariya of the Anaheim Mighty Ducks signed a three-year contract for $6.5 million, a level of compensation that young first-year players will not get in the future. Also, eligibility for salary arbitration and free agency were severely restricted, as discussed later in the chapter. The players gained slightly from a reduction in the draft from eleven to nine rounds.

Salary and Grievance Arbitration

Salary arbitration was initiated in 1969. The method of arbitration has evolved over the years from the use of two arbitrators, who if unable to reach agreement would be supplemented by a third arbitrator who would decide, to the current practice of having single permanent umpires arbitrate disputes. The jurisdiction of arbitration, however, was limited to salary disputes that arise during the option year in the standard players' contract. This application of arbitration is similar to the practice in baseball; that is, for players not eligible for free agency who wish to sign a new contract with their existing club but are unable to agree on salary terms, either the player or club can instigate arbitration to resolve the dispute. Unlike arbitration in baseball, which uses a variety of arbitrators to resolve disputes, the hockey umpire is not limited to choice from the final offers of the participants. Criteria established in the collective bargaining agreement for making the arbitration decision are similar to those set forth under the baseball agreement, and they include such factors as overall performance by the player, physical defects, length of service, and special qualities of leadership.

In the past two decades about 2 percent of the players have used salary arbitration annually. It appears that salaries reached through arbitration are not significantly different from those arrived at through negotiations. This has meant that there is little incentive for players to use salary arbitration. In the 1990–91 season, for example, 41 players filed for arbitration but only nine of these cases came to hearing. In 1991–92 the number of players filing for arbitration rose to 107 and in 1992–93 the number was 105, but only 14 players in each year had their salaries arbitrated. The other players settled on salary offers from their clubs before the arbitration hearing.

Before the 1992–93 season, salary arbitrators were appointed from a panel of three arbitrators who were usually sitting members of the Ontario Provincial

Court. The players objected to the system because it was perceived that most of the time the arbitrators sided with the owners. For the 1992–93 season an important change was achieved by the union in negotiations. Under the revised arrangement a precondition to being appointed a salary arbitrator is membership in the National Academy of Arbitrators. The newly formed National Hockey League Salary Arbitration Panel consists of eight members. The three Americans on the panel are Tim Bornstein, Richard Bloch, and Rolf Valtin, and the five Canadian members are Howard Brown, Richard McLaren, Michel Picher, Claude Foisy, and Alan Beattie. As a result of the 1995 collective bargaining agreement the system of salary arbitration was modified in favor of the owners by restricting player access. Players who enter the league at ages eighteen to twenty must wait until they reach age twenty-seven before becoming eligible for arbitration, and players who enter the league at ages twenty-one to twenty-five become eligible at age twenty-six.

Following the precedent in other sports, final decisions on grievances resulting from the interpretation or application of negotiated agreements in hockey were initially in the hands of the league president. If the parties were unable to resolve grievances, management had the last word. This practice was changed in hockey through collective bargaining in 1975, and the revised grievance procedure remains operative. Grievances over the interpretation or application of the negotiated agreement, club rules, and propriety of discipline are subject to arbitration. Enforcement of contracts through grievance arbitration is as protective of union interests as in any sport. But as in other sports, the hockey commissioner retains some control on matters of discipline. The commissioner continues to have the final word on issues concerning the severity of discipline meted out to players. Thus, whether a player should have been disciplined in the first place—say, for game violence—is subject to grievance and arbitration, but the reasonableness of the fine or suspension given the player is for the commissioner to determine. The commissioner also retains final jurisdiction for disputes stemming from the interpretation or application of provisions in the standard players' contract negotiated individually between the player and club.

Free Agency

Hockey players were not allowed to become free agents before the World Hockey Association began play in 1972. Legal challenges to NHL control of players resulted in several players moving to teams in the WHA by achieving free agency status. As a result of the law cases, the NHL unilaterally adopted a policy of seeking to retain players for only one year beyond the expiration of their standard players' contracts. In 1975 this policy was incorporated into the

NHL's negotiated agreement with the NHLPA. Under this agreement, a system for compensating clubs that lost free agents was established. In this system, known as "equalization," the club that signed a free agent was required to reach agreement with the player's former team. If the clubs were unable to agree on compensation, the dispute was submitted to final-offer arbitration, under which the arbitrator selects one of the parties' positions without amendment.

The equalization system did not work to the advantage of players. Clubs were reluctant to sign free agents because of the uncertainty of penalties imposed through compensation. Hockey's system was not as onerous as the old Rozelle Rule in football, because final compensation decisions were assigned to an arbitrator rather than to the top league official. Until 1982, when the procedure was changed, just three arbitration cases on equalization were decided. In the most celebrated of these cases, Rogatien Vachon, goaltender for the Los Angeles Kings, became a free agent and signed with the Detroit Red Wings. As compensation, the arbitrator ruled that the Red Wings would have to give up its leading scorer, a young forward named Dale McCourt. This led to McCourt's filing suit to challenge the arbitration procedure on antitrust grounds. The federal court of appeals denied relief to the player, holding that the equalization procedure and subsequent decision of the arbitrator were valid.[8] The court's rationale was that the equalization procedure had been arrived at through collective bargaining between the NHL and NHLPA; and the decision to award McCourt to the Kings as compensation for the loss of free agent Vachon was made by a neutral arbitrator rather than by a league president or commissioner.

In the face of the *McCourt* decision and the inability of players to achieve economic gains through free agency, the NHLPA sought to alter the system of equalization in its favor. During several months of bargaining in 1981–82, the parties remained far apart on the issue. Although the players began talking about a possible strike to enhance their position in negotiations, at no point was a strike imminent, because neither side wanted one and each believed that compromise could be worked out. In August 1982 agreement was finally reached.

The centerpiece of the modified equalization system was a procedure for determining free agency compensation based on the salary of the player involved. No compensation was required if the player made under $85,000. For players with salaries above that amount, a graduated scale allowed choices in the amateur draft or players from the roster of the team that signed the free agent:

$85,000-$99,000: third-round choice.
$100,000-$124,999: second- and third-round choice.
$125,000-$149,999: first-round choice *or* player from new club, with new club having protected eight players, including player signed.

$150,000-$199,999: first- and second-round choices *or* player from new club with six players protected, including player signed.

$200,000 and over: two first-round choices *or* player from new club with four players protected, including player signed.

A right of first refusal was also established to allow an existing club to retain a free agent by matching the offer of a new team. Free agent players thirty-three years of age or over could change teams without compensation required. If a free agent was under age twenty-four or had less than five years' professional experience, the old system of equalization applied, with clubs submitting to final-offer arbitration if they were unable to agree on compensation.

The 1982 agreement, designed to liberalize free agency, had a mixed effect. Judging from the numbers of players who became free agents under the agreement, one might conclude that a great deal of liberalization occurred. Before the 1983–84 and 1984–85 seasons, for example, about 180 free agents were available for signing by new clubs. These figures, however, are misleading for three reasons. Many of these players were given termination contracts by their teams that forced them to become free agents, and, of the total free agents, only about 15 percent (twenty to twenty-five players a year) had salaries that were high enough to justify equalization payments if they were signed by other clubs. Perhaps most important, most of the free agents subject to equalization were players in the lower range of the graduated scale: that is, the team that signed them was not required to give up much, because their salaries were under $150,000. Before the 1984–85 season there were only two players in the maximum compensation category ($200,00 and over), Glenn Anderson and Paul Coffey, both from the Edmonton Oilers. Rather than signing with other teams, these free agents elected to remain with Edmonton, which had won the Stanley Cup championship the year before.

During the life of the 1982 agreement, no free agents changed clubs in situations in which they were subject to significant compensation from the signing club. This lack of movement of high-quality players made free agency the leading topic during talks about a new collective bargaining agreement in 1986. As is customary during negotiations in the NHL, there was talk by the players of a strike. But, as in the past, there was no serious strike threat, and the parties reached agreement in July 1986.

The new five-year agreement revised the rules on free agency compensation. Again, compensation was based on the salary of the free agent player. Under the new system, no compensation was required for players making under $110,000. For higher salary ranges, compensation under the scale was adjusted upward to reflect the rising pay levels since 1982. For instance, if one of the highest paid players (over $400,000 in salary) was signed, compensation was set at two first-round draft choices, both in the top seven players in the draft, plus $100,000.

At the top compensation levels, if a club lacked a qualified draft choice, it had to pay a cash penalty instead. Other features of the previous free agency system remained in effect, e.g., the right of first refusal and rules for players under age twenty-four or with less than five years as a professional. The age at which no compensation for free agents is required was lowered from thirty-three to thirty-one.

In the 1992 collective bargaining agreement the rules on free agency were again liberalized, notably by reducing the bite of the compensation penalties somewhat and lowering the age for achieving unrestricted free agency status from thirty-one to thirty. But player movement continued to be restricted by the need for relatively generous compensation to teams that lost free agents aged twenty-five to twenty-nine. In situations where the clubs were unable to agree on compensation for players under age twenty-five, the practice of final-offer arbitration continued to be used. It became more possible for marginal players to change clubs and enhance their salaries, but top players remained boxed in until they reached age thirty.

While the players inched forward on free agency under the 1982, 1986, and 1992 agreements, they were set back in the 1995 contract. Even under the relatively limited free agency system that had prevailed, salaries had risen so much that owners imposed the draconian measure of a lockout in 1994–95 to get their costs under control. As discussed earlier in the chapter, the owners' primary goal in cost containment was the payroll tax to limit expenditures. The demand was ultimately dropped by the owners in negotiations when they were able to get concessions on free agency.

One significant restriction on free agency under the 1995 agreement is that players who have finished their first contract are no longer eligible for free agency. Players aged twenty-five to thirty-one can still become free agents, but their movement is sharply restricted by draft choice compensation that must be paid by teams that sign them, based on the following schedule:

Below $400,000: none
$401,000–550,000: third-round pick
$551,000–$650,000: second-round pick
$651,000–800,000: first-round pick
$801,000–1,000,000: first- and third-round picks
$1,000,000–$1,200,000: first- and second-round picks
$1,200,000–$1,400,000: two first-round picks
$1,400,000–1,700,000: two first-round picks, one second-round pick
Above $1,700,000: three first-round picks
Each additional $1,000,000: additional first-round pick, up to five

Another key limitation is that players must wait until reaching age thirty-two before achieving unrestricted free agency status (up from age thirty under the old contract) for the 1994–95 through 1996–97 seasons. For the 1997–98 through 1999–2000 seasons, unrestricted free agency can occur at age thirty-one. In effect, the new rules on free agency allow clubs to control players for up to their first twelve seasons in the league. This is by far the most restrictive free agency system in sports.

Antitrust Issues

Significant lawsuits over restraint of trade in hockey have challenged the drafting of players, the signing of NHL players by WHA teams, and attempted relocation of the St. Louis Blues' franchise.

Player Draft

The player draft case is similar to and arose after the federal district court decision involving basketball player Spencer Haywood (see Chapter 4). In 1976 a nineteen-year-old hockey player, Ken Linseman, signed a contract to play professionally with a team in the WHA. At the time, both the WHA and the NHL had a rule requiring that players be at least twenty years old to play in their leagues. When the WHA president voided the deal with Linseman, the player filed suit contending that he was the victim of an illegal restraint of trade under the Sherman Antitrust Act of 1890.[9] The court determined that the age rule harmed Linseman's career potential and constituted a concerted refusal to deal with him. Because the court struck down the age rule, the WHA and NHL lowered the age requirements to eighteen, and no further litigation has been brought challenging the new rule.

WHA

The World Hockey Association was established in 1971 by lawyer Gary Davidson, who had earlier formed the American Basketball Association as a rival to the NBA. Not since its birth in 1917 had the NHL confronted competition for players. At first, the NHL did not take the rival league seriously. But as players began to defect to the new league and it drafted talented players from the amateur ranks, the old league was forced to acknowledge that the battle lines had been drawn. Its first line of defense was to bring suit against the players who jumped to the WHA.

The opening and decisive round in the litigation skirmish was fought when two valuable players for the Boston Bruins, Gary Cheevers and Derek Sanderson, signed contracts with WHA clubs. In favor of the NHL was a reserve clause, similar to that found at the time in other sports, which enabled the club to renew a player's contract into perpetuity. The Boston club sought use of the clause to restrain the two players from joining teams in the new league.[10] The players countered with the charge that the reserve clause violated the Sherman Act. Since the players' contracts with the Bruins were found to have expired at the time they were to play for their WHA teams, and because the reserve clause had not been reached through negotiations with the NHLPA, the federal district court denied the injunction request. Thus Cheevers and Sanderson were not restrained from joining their new WHA clubs. There were several other players who jumped leagues and became embroiled in litigation with the NHL. Although there was some variation in the issues involved, the antitrust laws were relied on to allow nearly all players who wanted to join WHA teams to do so if their contracts with NHL clubs had expired.[11]

By 1979, the NHL owners had suffered enough from the bidding war for players and the rapidly escalating salaries that it caused. In preceding years, the WHA had sent out feelers for a merger, but the NHL was not then ready to come to terms. When finally the NHL board of governors and its WHA counterpart indicated their desire to merge, the players were not so willing. They saw further salary increases in a continuation of competition. NHL players threatened to sue the league as NBA players had done at the time of the NBA-ABA merger. At a crucial meeting between NHL owners and players, Alan Eagleson privately consulted with NHLPA president Phil Esposito, urging him to avoid costly litigation that might imperil weak teams and lose jobs for players. When Eagleson later reported to Esposito that the owners agreed to increase fringe benefits and allow the players to continue to enjoy the fruits of international hockey arrangements, Esposito recommended to the players that they accept the merger.

Thus in March 1979, the seven-year war between the rival leagues ended when the NHL agreed to absorb four WHA teams: the New England (now Hartford) Whalers, the Edmonton Oilers, the Winnipeg Jets, and the Quebec Nordiques. These teams paid $6 million each to join the NHL, and these funds were distributed to the old NHL clubs. The new NHL clubs were allowed to protect only two skaters and two goaltenders. The remainder of the players were made available to the old NHL clubs, with priorities established in cases in which NHL clubs had previously established rights to certain WHA players. To stock the new teams an expansion draft was held, with each of the old NHL clubs allowed to protect fifteen skaters and two goaltenders. In order to ward off future antitrust litigation with the NHLPA, the league described the agreement as an "expansion" rather than a "merger."

Franchise Movement

In April 1983 the St. Louis Blues were sold by the Ralston Purina Company to Coliseum Holdings Ltd. of Saskatoon, Saskatchewan, for $11.5 million. A local consortium had tried to buy the team, but was able to offer only $8 million. The Blues had lost an estimated $20 million in its six years of ownership by Ralston Purina. At the time of the sale, questions were raised about whether the franchise would stay in St. Louis or move to Saskatoon, a city of only 165,000 people without a large hockey arena. As in other professional sports, franchise sales and movements are overseen by the NHL board of governors, which requires three-fourths approval of the owners represented on that board. The board voted to reject Ralston Purina's sale, which prompted the company to file a $20 million lawsuit in U.S. District Court in St. Louis against the NHL for restraint of trade in violation of the antitrust laws. Because awards in antitrust cases are trebled, the suit could effectively cost the NHL $60 million. If the federal courts were inclined to disallow a franchise move, this might well have been an appropriate situation in which to do it, because of the small population and lack of big league stadium facilities in Saskatoon.

In response to the legal action by Ralston Purina, the NHL filed a countersuit in June 1983, alleging that the company must operate the franchise for two more years before it could withdraw its ownership. The two years' notice is required by the NHL constitution. In its suit, the NHL sought $3 million in damages plus punitive damages of $75 million or 5 percent of the assets of Ralston Purina, whichever is greater. About two weeks after the suit was filed the NHL board of governors took over the Blues franchise from Ralston Purina, assuming control of all assets, in order to keep the club in St. Louis. This was another attempt to encourage the company to drop its antitrust action, because by taking over the club the NHL would assume responsibility for paying the company for its team. Subsequently, however, a sale of the team was arranged with California real estate entrepreneur Harry Ornest. Meanwhile, the Canadian government's antitrust division began investigating the possibility of taking legal action on behalf of the province of Saskatchewan against the NHL for discrimination and conspiracy within a monopoly. Toward this end, the Supreme Court of Canada ordered the NHL owners to turn over their financial records to the Canadian antitrust division. After several days of hearings in U.S. District Court in St. Louis, the parties reached an out-of-court settlement in 1985. The terms of the settlement were generally favorable to the NHL, which got the antitrust monkey off its back. Ralston Purina received $12 million, the same amount Ornest paid for the Blues.

Unlike the St. Louis situation, litigation was avoided when owner Norman Green moved his Minnesota Stars to Dallas for the 1993–94 season. Green, a Calgary real estate developer, had acquired the franchise in 1990 and promised to keep it in the Twin Cities. Although attendance rose during Green's tenure, he claimed to be losing money and wanted out. The NHL approved the franchise relocation. Also approved was the move of the Quebec Nordiques to Colorado for the 1995–96 season.

Aberrant Behavior

Violence has always been a problem in the NHL. With players skating at speeds of up to thirty miles per hour, with sticks that can serve as weapons, and with a code of honor that condones roughhouse tactics, it is little wonder that players are susceptible to violence. Although many hockey players are beer drinkers and some players have had problems with excessive consumption, the problems of alcoholism do not appear to be significantly greater for them than for the general population of males their age. Drugs are a relatively new thing to hockey players. Like their counterparts in other sports, many have smoked marijuana. But serious drug abuse—substances like cocaine and heroin—has not been nearly as widespread in the NHL as in other major leagues.

Violence

In other team sports, most players lose respect for teammates who consistently pick fights or engage in other behavior aimed at injuring players on opposing teams. Violence in hockey is different in that it is often regarded as good strategy. Hockey players learn at a young age that they must face up to violence, that intimidation can be used to good effect.[12] For many years, officials in the NHL accepted fighting as part of the game, a kind of boys-will-be-boys approach. Fighting was penalized, but winked at as a problem. It was thought that the fans liked violence and that subduing the "enforcers" on teams would keep fans away from arenas.

Two developments have changed the conventional wisdom in recent years. One is the increased reliance on finesse that has come from awareness of the creativity, crisp passing, and quick transitions of the game as it is played in Europe. Victories by the smooth-skating foreigners in the Olympic games and Canada Cup events and an infusion of European hockey players into the NHL have led to a realization that the forceful brand of North American hockey is clumsy by comparison. The other development has been that players have been seriously injured because of excessive violence in the NHL. Even though most players to-day wear protective headgear, they are vulnerable to debilitating injuries that can end careers.

One of the worst incidents ever took place in 1933 during a game between the Boston Bruins and the Toronto Maple Leafs. From the outset play was very rough, and several skirmishes broke out. After King Clancy of the Maple Leafs knocked Eddie Shore of the Bruins hard to the ice, Shore got up and checked another Maple Leaf player, Ace Bailey, hitting him from behind. Bailey flew through the air and landed on his head. He nearly died over the next few weeks from serious injuries. Although Bailey recovered, his hockey career was over. Shore was suspended for sixteen games.

Under hockey's honor code, players who wish to fight drop their sticks and gloves and slug it out with bare fists. In the 1950s, for example, Gordie Howe of the Detroit Red Wings broke the nose of Lou Fontinato of the New York Rangers in a celebrated slugfest. During this era, there was rugged checking against the boards, clean contact in motion, and the occasional brawl between players. Malicious incidents increased during the 1960s and 1970s, especially as the Philadelphia Flyers, the most penalized team in hockey, rose to prominence with their bully-boy tactics. The game moved away from emphasis on skills to emphasis on intimidation, wrestling in the corners, and more acts of malicious intent to injure that resembled rugby or roller derby as much as hockey. With only three officials on hand to regulate this mayhem on ice, games frequently got out of hand. Sophisticated fans began to stay away.

Some remarkably ugly incidents occurred. In 1969 Wayne Maki of the St. Louis Blues struck Ted Green of the Boston Bruins on the head with his stick. This injury necessitated brain operations from which Green never fully recovered. In 1975 the Bruins' Dave Forbes launched a vicious attack on Henry Boucha of the Minnesota North Stars that included poking his stick into Boucha's eye. In 1978 Wilf Paiement of the Colorado Rockies swung his stick like a baseball bat against the head of Red Wings player Dennis Polonich. In each of these cases the offending players were fined and suspended by the NHL— Maki for eleven games, Forbes for ten, and Paiement for fifteen. Polonich achieved an $850,000 verdict in court for his injuries. But, given the seriousness of these actions, the penalties imposed by the NHL were relatively light. Perhaps most symptomatic of the state that hockey was in is the case of Paul Mulvey of the Los Angeles Kings. When he was told by his coach to leave the bench to par-ticipate in a fight in 1982, Mulvey refused. As a result he was sent packing to the minor leagues. Reacting to this action against Mulvey, league president John Ziegler fined the Kings $5,000 and suspended coach Don Perry for fifteen days.

In the early 1980s there were some signs that violence was finally beginning to decrease in the NHL. Average penalty minutes declined somewhat, and the league tightened up its rules on fighting. For the 1982–83 season, a tough new rule provided that all players not involved in a fight must keep away, and stiffer fines were assessed to clubs and players who joined a fight. Rules were also established for punishing players who abused officials. In 1983, for example, Tom Lysiak of the Chicago Blackhawks was given a twenty-game suspension for intentionally tripping a referee. In contrast, a few years earlier Paul Holmgren of the Flyers was given only a five-game suspension for a similar offense.

For the past few years, violence has become the leading topic of concern in professional hockey. Despite considerable discussion and several changes in league rules, progress has been slow. Table 5.4 shows that while the average team penalty minutes declined in the late 1980s, there is still significant mayhem on the ice. This is reflected not only in penalties but in individual incidents of violence and public reaction to them. Complicating the search for solutions is the disagreement over the extent of the problem. Some fans like violence and attend games to see it. They are disappointed if they do not see at least one good brawl during a game. Evidence suggests, however, that these fans are in a minority. Two polls taken in 1986 indicate that 63 percent and 67 percent of the hockey fans in the United States and Canada felt that hockey was too violent.[13]

Hockey players are a unique group of hard-nosed, macho swashbucklers who have a fierce feeling of camaraderie. They are very protective of each other. Consider, for example, the situation that arose in 1987 when Dave Brown of the Philadelphia Flyers blindsided Tomas Sandstrom of the New York Rangers with a vicious cross-check to the neck and jaw. Brown's justification for his action was that Sandstrom had first speared Flyer Mark Howe in the protective cup. This "eye-for-an-eye" retaliation is behind much of the violence. Fortunately, Sandstrom was not seriously injured. Brown was suspended for fifteen games. Although this was a stiff suspension by NHL standards, it was probably not enough to deter similar acts in the future.

Table 5.4. Average Team Penalty Minutes in the NHL

1984–85	1985–86	1986–87	1987–88	1988–89	
37.4	43.3	45.2	52.8	50.4	
1989–90	1990–91	1991–92	1992–93	1993–94	1994–95
48.0	47.8	49.8	45.3	41.8	39.3

Source: National Hockey League

The NHL continues to deal with violence by imposing stricter rules. In 1987, for instance, the league's board of governors made a distinction between one-on-one fights and bench-clearing brawls, which had been particularly troublesome. The first player from each team to leave the bench to join a fight is suspended for ten games, and subsequent players are suspended for five games. Coaches are subject to suspensions of three to five games under such circumstances, and both coaches and players are subject to fines. As a result there have been virtually no bench-clearing brawls in recent years. In 1992 new rules provided that any player who starts a premeditated fight will be thrown out of the game, instead of getting only a five-minute penalty, and high-sticking was redefined from a blow above the shoulders to one that is waist high or above. These rules have reduced fighting by about half.

The league has also continued to impose harsh penalties on flagrant miscreants. In 1993 Dale Hunter of the Washington Capitals blindsided New York Islander Pierre Turgeon with a vicious check that separated his shoulder. Commissioner Bettman suspended Hunter for twenty-one games and fined the club $150,000, the most severe penalty in league history. In 1994 Tony Granato of the Los Angeles Kings was suspended for fifteen days and fined $500 for smashing his stick with both hands over the helmet of Neil Wilkinson of the Chicago Blackhawks. Mitigating the penalty was the fact the Granato, who previously had a clean record, had routinely collided with Wilkinson along the boards, receiving what was later diagnosed as a concussion. Miraculously, Wilkinson was not seriously injured.

Drugs

Drug abuse has not been extensive in the NHL. The league does not have a program for handling cases as the other three sports do, but it has taken a hard line against offenders. In 1979 Don Murdoch of the New York Rangers was suspended for forty games after he tried to carry marijuana through Canadian customs. Montreal Canadiens player Rick Nattrass was arrested in 1981 for possession of two grams of hashish and one gram of marijuana. He was later fined $150 by a court in Canada. After the fine, which was usual in cases of this type, President Ziegler suspended Nattrass for a year, but he later reduced the suspension to thirty games. Another incident involved a former NHL player, Steve Durbano, who was convicted in Canada for cocaine smuggling in 1984 and sentenced to seven years in prison. Durbano admitted using cocaine regularly when he played in the NHL and estimated that 20 to 25 percent of the players are "doing drugs."[14] Based on the number of incidents reported among the five hundred players in the NHL, Durbano's estimate seemed too high. The estimate could be reasonably accurate, however, because it includes use of marijuana and speed as well as cocaine. Although hockey players are relatively uneducated as professional athletes go, they appear to recognize the dangers of using hard drugs. But, despite what seems to be a lower incidence of hard drug usage by hockey players, labor and management in the sport might do well to establish a drug control program along the lines of the ones in basketball and baseball.

It appeared that the NHL was going to take action when President Ziegler and the NHLPA's Eagleson recommended that the league institute a mandatory drug-testing program for the 1986–87 season. Their recommendation was based on three incidents alleging that NHL players were using drugs.[15] One was that law enforcement officials from Edmonton and the Royal Canadian Mounted Police confirmed that there were drug users on the Edmonton Oilers. Second, several members of the New York Rangers were said to have used cocaine, although this was based on information from the late 1970s. Third, in response to an admission in 1986 by Borje Salming of the Toronto Maple Leafs that he has used cocaine five years before, he was suspended by President Ziegler for the first eight games of the 1986–87 season.

No action was taken by the league and union, however, nor was a formal drug control program instituted despite more recent incidents. In 1986 Bob Probert, forward for the Detroit Red Wings, was caught trying to smuggle a half-ounce of cocaine into Detroit from Windsor, Ontario. Customs officials had first found a cocaine mill, a device used to grind cocaine into powder, in Probert's coat pocket. This prompted a strip search that found the cocaine concealed in his underpants. Probert pleaded guilty and spent three months in federal prison and another three months in a halfway house. Shortly after his arrest Probert was suspended by President Ziegler, presumably permanently. But he was allowed to play again in 1990 after an eighty-game suspension, longest in league history. Probert then faced the odd dilemma of being unable to travel to Canada to play games, because as a Canadian citizen he faced deportation and would have been denied permission to reenter the United States.

Another drug suspension involved Grant Fuhr, goalie for the Edmonton Oilers. In 1990 Fuhr acknowledged that for the past seven years he had used cocaine and had recently gone through drug rehabilitation. This revelation prompted President Ziegler to suspend Fuhr indefinitely. He was allowed, however, to apply for reinstatement and returned to the league in 1991, after serving a suspension of sixty days. One other drug-related incident is the strange case of John Kordic, forward for the Quebec Nordiques. Like Probert, Kordic was an enforcer who was frequently in the penalty box. He drank heavily and used drugs. In 1992 it took nine police officers to subdue Kordic during a disturbance at a motel. He died in an ambulance on the way to the hospital. At first it was believed that his death might be linked to steroid abuse. A report by a Quebec pathologist, however, found that Kordic died from ingestion of an enormous amount of cocaine.

These incidents suggest that the NHL's drug problem may be worse than thought to be. The league provides drug education to players by a Toronto physician, but overall policy is reactive and punitive. Because all the NHL teams play often in both the United States and Canada, players are subject to customs checks when they travel between countries. As illustrated in the Probert case, this provides a form of drug surveillance not found as much in other sports.

Alcohol

There is a history of alcohol-related problems in the NHL, yet the league has no policy for either assistance or punishment. In 1985 all-star goalie Pelle Lindbergh of the Philadelphia Flyers died in an alcohol-related accident. Probert had been in several alcohol rehabilitation centers before his drug bust. Kordic was a heavy drinker. So are many others, perhaps 20 percent of league players. At the minimum the league should step up its educational efforts on alcohol abuse. The involvement in such education of former players who have suffered from alcoholism would seem to be a good idea.

Gambling

There have been no revealed incidents of gambling by NHL players in recent years, although this was a problem in the past. Babe Pratt of the Toronto Maple Leafs was expelled in the 1945–46 season for gambling but was reinstated after nine games. In 1949 two players were banned from the league by President Clarence Campbell. In the face of evidence from telephone wire taps, Billy Taylor and Don Gallinger of the Boston Bruins admitted gambling on NHL games, including bets against their own team. Neither player challenged the ban at the time, and it was not until 1970, long after they were able to perform, that they were reinstated by the league.

Past as Prologue 6

The sports business and its labor relations are in the midst of a transition period, the outcome of which will have a significant impact on the future viability of professional sports in America. In making predictions it is helpful to assess the significance of past events and the likelihood of their continuance in the future. For example, given the important effects that law and economics have had thus far, these variables can be expected to have still farther reaching influences on professional sports, especially the rulemaking process. Because of the newness and rapidly changing nature of industrial relations in sports, however, it is hazardous simply to extrapolate past developments to assess the future. Caution is necessary because the environment itself is unstable. This is evidenced by shifting social and public policies on sports, by the changes in the technological context of sports broadcasting, and by market constraints on team budgets and player incomes. The struggle for economic power between owners and players will doubtless continue. But whether it will involve increased hostility or greater cooperation between the parties is difficult to say for certain.

The games themselves are played in a relatively stable context. Rules of play are changed from time to time, but the sports retain a pattern that appeals to the audience's sense of continuity. The objective will always be putting points on the scoreboard. People like tradition and simplicity of outcomes. The intriguing nature and public appeal of sports are decisive to the overall success of the industry. Nevertheless, it is possible that the public's infatuation with spectator sports in general will wane, and as for the individual sports, popularity is even more variable. It depends to some extent on television exposure. Spectators can be fickle, shifting their enthusiasm from one sport to another. A sport may be "in" for a time, but then lose its allure.

Baseball has the advantage of a rich tradition, as the national pastime that fits nicely with the rhythms of summer. Although the game is too slow for some, its measured pace and infinite variability are attractive to many. Football, the upstart sport that has challenged baseball by winning the hearts of countless fans, is unusually well suited to television. It provides the vicarious experience of controlled violence that appeals to one's baser instincts. Basketball is also well adapted to television, displaying the subtle and artistic graces of exceptionally talented athletes. Hockey has the violence element for thrill seekers, yet if cleanly played has a marvelous cadence that excites the mind with visions of crisp execution. Yet, hockey is the least suitable of the sports for television.

With the rise in leisure time and discretionary incomes, it appears certain that professional sports will remain an important segment of the larger entertainment industry. As particular sports move into and out of mass popularity they prosper or decline economically. We think of the four major sports as continuing their dominance, but it may be that an emerging sport, such as indoor soccer, arena football, or indoor lacrosse, will capture the loyalty of a widespread audience in the future. Or perhaps an entirely new sport will be discovered by fans.

Commonality and Uniqueness

Each of the major professional team sports has characteristics common to the industry. At the same time, the individual sports face different constraints that affect economic health, making each sport to some extent unique economically. In terms of collective bargaining, certain structural features, strategies and tactics, and methods of dispute settlement are found in all sports. But each sport has developed variations on the basic collective bargaining model that are uniquely adapted to the needs of the actors.

Commonality of Sports Models

In each sport, the actors in the industrial relations system can be clearly identified in terms of the labor-management-government model (Figure 1.1). Players in all sports are organized into unions. The principal rationale for creating employee organizations is economic. Careers of players are short, and they recognize the importance of banding together to increase power vis-à-vis management. About three to four years is the average major league career of players in the NFL and NBA, and five years in the NHL. Although the average major league baseball player has slightly longer career, players have a short time in which to maximize their incomes from sport. They realize that they are the ones providing entertainment, and the games cannot go on without them. This fact of economic life means that players can generate significant bargaining power through the threat or use of pressure tactics.

Although the early unions in sports were poorly organized and relatively weak, as players became better educated and sought professional help from attorneys, negotiators, and agents, they developed cohesive structures to countervail the power of management. What took the players so long to break through and achieve substantial economic gains was the reserve clause found in the player contracts. These clauses bound the player to the club, thus limiting his bargaining power in the labor market. Baseball was the first sport in which players drove a wedge in the reserve clause and then later broke it entirely. The players gave back to management some control over their labor market mobility through collective bargaining, but baseball players are today more able to change teams voluntarily—and therefore use free agency to achieve higher salaries—than players in any of the professional team sports except basketball.

Management in professional sports consists primarily of individual entrepreneurs who own sports franchises and corporations that own teams. In the latter instance, ownership may be spread among numerous stockholders so the functions of ownership and management are more separate than when a single individual both owns and operates a team. In recent years, more individual owners have incorporated their sports franchises for tax purposes, but control remains in the hands of a single or a few individuals. Because of the importance of cable television, a growing number of sports franchises are being acquired by individuals or corporations that also have interests in the broadcast media. Ted Turner, the Atlanta-based owner of a cable television network, is probably the best example of this new kind of sports entrepreneur.

Although vertical integration may be the wave of the future in sports management and ownership, most franchises are not integrated operations; nor do the owners of teams constitute "big business" as regards their individual operations. Although the sports industry as a whole, especially when considered in terms of its relationship with television and the various satellite industries that derive income from sport, has become an important American industry, it is still dwarfed by industrial gains such as IBM or Exxon. In many respects, sports franchises are Mom-and-Pop businesses, and too frequently they are also operated that way. Professionalism of management in sports has been encouraged by increased television revenues, but for the most part, the labor relations function is professionalized only at the league level where collective bargaining takes place.

Augmenting the management of team sports is the office of the commissioner. The role of the commissioner has been strengthened and broadened over the years. Pete Rozelle became the dominant personality in football, and his successor, Paul Tagliabue, has continued this tradition. David Stern in basketball is a superlative executive with control over nearly every aspect of the game. Hockey commissioner Gary Bettman's influence is far greater than that of his predecessor, John Ziegler, and he exemplifies the modern commissioner, who is more corporate CEO than caretaker. Only in baseball has there been a departure from this model. With the firing of Fay Vincent, baseball owners decided to go without a formal commissioner. Many of the commissioner's duties were assumed by Bud Selig, owner of the Milwaukee Brewers. Vincent was probably too successful for his own good. That baseball's fortunes have diminished since Vincent's departure is due to the lack of an able commissioner.

Vincent was fired for becoming involved in the 1990 baseball lockout. Ironically, he was simply trying to get the games resumed, a sensible idea. Similarly, Bettman learned a hard lesson from his even more extensive involvement in the 1994–95 hockey negotiations and lockout. Just as it is unwise for a corporate president or chief executive officer to be the principal negotiator in collective bargaining, so is it inappropriate for the commissioner to perform this role. The top manager is too vulnerable at the bargaining table and would have no backup authority figure. But he can become involved in various ways by keeping in close contact with the professional negotiator employed by the owners. Collective bargaining has become such an important aspect of professional sports that a commissioner must have expertise in labor relations and the ability to influence negotiation outcomes. He ignores them at his peril. At the same time, however, the commissioner is expected to remain above the fray, aloof from the personal conflicts of negotiations, and to act as a public spokesperson on behalf of the sport, remaining unsullied. This is an exceptionally difficult role to play, and only the most astute executives can successfully walk the tightropes of the commissioner's office.

Government's role in sports industrial relations is varied and at times ambiguous. Despite all the clamor and din of legislative soundings, there have been relatively few important new laws passed regulating the industry. The National Labor Relations Act, as amended, was well in place by the time sports unions got around to utilizing its provisions. Its administrative agency, the National Labor Relations Board, has been active in trying to protect the rights of unions and players, but often its pronouncements have had little real impact on the relationships between labor and management. There has been some tinkering with the tax laws involving depreciation of players, but this too has not resulted in much fundamental change in industrial operation. Numerous bills to regulate professional sports have been defeated in Congress. Thus, on the legislative side, government has encroached little on the freedoms of the parties to carry out the mission of the industry and carve up the rewards through collective bargaining. Perhaps this is just as well, since excessive government regulation does little to promote economic growth and prosperity in any industry.

Government has taken a more activist and regulatory position in the judicial arena. To a large extent, the important battles affecting collective bargaining outcomes in baseball, football, and basketball have been waged in the courts. In all the professional sports, unions have secured protections from the courts in winning greater freedoms for players in the labor market. Even management has gained selectively, as in the case of Al Davis moving the Oakland Raiders to Los Angeles. Why the courts have exempted baseball from the application of the antitrust laws remains something of a mystery. Although there are still many contests to be staged over tissues such as drafting procedure, rights of amateur athletes, and free agency, a good argument can be made that the influence of the judicial system on sports will ultimately diminish. This has been the situation in other industries that have grown to rely less on legal measures as they mature. These industries have developed more sophisticated collective bargaining models and placed greater reliance on third-party neutrals in a private system of industrial jurisprudence. Whether sports can evolve toward such models, with reduced outside judicial influence, remains to be seen.

One aspect of negotiations that may well come under closer scrutiny by government is the role of agents. The importance of agents has increased with player salaries and wealth. With the lowering of the maximum federal tax rate on individual incomes, highly paid athletes are able to keep more of their earnings than before. Players are better educated today, but few are able to cope with the sophisticated world of contract negotiation and money management. During the season their time and energy are devoted to utilizing their playing skills. Thus athletes need help, and agents can provide it. Public disclosures of duplicity by some agents, however, has called into question their role and whether it should be regulated. Unfortunately, as with many ethical issues that come to public attention, a small proportion of unethical agents can tarnish the reputations of the vast majority, who operate at high ethical levels.

Agents, like other people involved in matters of business, are susceptible to shortcomings. Misjudgments can occur, especially in the three main service areas that agents provide: (1) representing the player in individual salary negotiations with his team; (2) soliciting and negotiating product endorsements, speaking engagements, and other uses of the player's name and image for commercial and public purposes; and (3) managing the player's asset portfolio, e.g., making arrangements for the purchase and sale of stocks, bonds, real estate, and other investments; and assisting in tax and estate planning, budgeting, and tax returns. Some players turn over their entire financial affairs to an agent, usually for far better than worse.

As much as athletes need agents and as valuable as agents can be, they do not provide a uniformly high level of service. No one can expect agents to make the right decisions all of the time. Not all investments turn out to be winners, even when the most exacting care is exercised in their selection. Although risk is inherent in any investment, agents can be expected to be reasonably prudent, to avoid conflicts of interest, and not to take unnecessary risks. Existing laws that impose a fiduciary responsibility on those who handle the money of others may be adequate to provide redress to athletes who are victims of financial mismanagement.

Greater protection seems necessary against solicitation of players by agents, especially college athletes who are pressured into signing personal services contracts in exchange for payments that are prohibited by NCAA rules. Players also need protection from agents who simply are not qualified to provide the services they offer, or who charge excessive fees for their services. Screening of agents and oversight of their activities by players' associations should help avoid exploitation and incompetence. Additional regulation and redress will stem from court actions. While much of the recent focus has been on agents, we should not lose sight of the fact that the players themselves have to take some responsibility for their actions. Despite full knowledge of NCAA rules, some players have eagerly sought out agents to induce improper payments. Other players have adopted reckless investment strategies, against the advice of their agents. Thus the principal-agent relationship is two-way street, and players must be expected to bear responsibility for their actions if, through their own fault, they are harmed financially.

The football and basketball players' unions are now screening agents that represent their members. California passed the first state law regulating sports agents operating within a state.[1] Similar laws took effect a few years later in Oklahoma and Texas. Agents in California must file with the state labor commissioner an application along with affidavits of two persons vouching that the agent is of good moral character. Copies of agency contracts and fee schedules must be submitted to the labor commissioner for approval and a $10,000 surety bond posted. Agents must keep certain business records and have them available for inspection. Before contacting a student at a secondary or collegiate school in California, an agent must file a copy of his registration certificate with the school. Recent disclosures of agents tampering with amateur players who are not yet eligible for professional careers and mishandling of player funds by some agents may cause such laws to become more widespread.

In a significant case, sports agents Norby Walters and Lloyd Bloom were convicted by a federal court jury for fraud, conspiracy, and racketeering. The agents had signed forty-three college football and basketball players to personal services contracts while the players had college eligibility remaining. By signing the players prematurely, the agents violated NCAA rules, which the jury found to constitute fraud against the players' universities. Walters was sentenced to five years in prison and Bloom to three years, but both were released on bond pending appeal. In 1990 the U.S. Court of Appeals reversed the convictions on the technical ground that the jurors were not allowed to consider certain testimony about criminal intent. Nonetheless, the case has had a positive effect on cleansing sports agentry.

Uniqueness of Individual Sports

The most dramatic signs of the acrimonious industrial relations in sports are the baseball strikes of 1981 and 1994–95, the football strikes of 1982 and 1987, and hockey lockout of 1994–95. These were all full-scale work stoppages that disrupted the season for lengthy periods. Strikes and strike threats are not unusual in collective bargaining, although the number of strikes nationally has diminished sharply since 1981 and reached all-time lows in recent years. Contrary to the national trend, however, work stoppages in sports are commonplace. Until 1992 hockey had not experienced a work stoppage by players but has had two since then. Basketball is the only sport that has managed to avoid a shutdown. What difference between these sports causes extreme hostility on the one hand and relatively peaceful negotiations on the other?

The difference is not explained by the collective bargaining structure, because all sports are characterized by multiemployer bargaining. Nor is it necessarily related to the stability of the industry itself or the potential for big money. One would expect to see more strikes in unstable segments of the industry, yet basketball and hockey were probably more unstable than baseball and football when the early strikes occurred; and basketball is the quintessential big money game for players. What appears to explain the difference in large part is the attitudes of the chief negotiators (selected by management and union), who have regarded negotiations as a potential bloodbath. High financial stakes from television were probably also part of the problem, but personality conflict between the chief negotiators makes any kind of reasoned outcome short of a strike difficult to achieve.

Successful negotiations require a large measure of trust, respect, and willingness to compromise. These factors, however, have often been absent from sports bargaining. Part of the reason is historical. Because of the early domination by the owners, who operated under reserve clauses that tied players to their teams, aggressively militant union leaders were perceived as necessary in baseball and football to break through the barriers. Yet football seems to have overcome its preoccupation with conflicts. The owners and players in football came to realize that continued fighting was not in their best interests. They compromised on a quid pro quo of liberalized free agency in exchange for a salary cap. While neither side is completely satisfied with this arrangement, it appears to be something they can live with. Hockey, on the other hand, has lurched toward conflict. The NHL was pressured to take draconian measures because of the economic disparity between big-market and small-market teams, which became more evident as a result of rapid salary escalation, and the 1994–95 lockout was devastating to the game.

There is no easy way to reconcile the differences between sports. Yet basketball, with its record of relatively placid labor relations, may provide some answers. The salary cap, even though it has been loosely applied, helps promote league balance and allows teams in smaller markets to thrive. The cap makes it less feasible for some teams to load up on talented players. The other apparently worthwhile feature is revenue sharing between owners and with players, providing stability, a salary guarantee, and a stake in future growth. Some kind of basketball-type revenue sharing is necessary among teams to eliminate a have–have not system in which teams in big cities dominate. All sports share revenues, but getting the right balance is difficult.

Revised Bargaining Methods

Conventional approaches to negotiation, which have been adopted in professional sports, regard it as an adversary proceeding, with each side contending for a greater share of the economic pie.[2] Models explaining the role of collective bargaining in sports have therefore concentrated on this conflict of interests and how best to resolve disputes between labor and management. In the future, the principal emphasis of improvements in sports bargaining will center on rationalizing the adversary model.

Adversary and Cooperative Models

The adversary model is contrasted here with the cooperative model to illustrate their essential differences, and a synthesis of the two is suggested to make the adversary model better suited to the needs of the parties and the long-run prosperity of sports.

The adversary model, geared toward conflict, prescribes the acquisition, preservation, and protection of wage and nonwage objectives through negotiations. The parties' strategies in negotiations are effectuated through offensive tactics calculated to force the adversary to grant concessions and defensive tactics calculated to prevent the adversary from gaining concessions. In contrast, bargaining based on the cooperative model focuses on measures designed to increase the exploration of joint gain and the economic health of the industry. This approach invites the parties to go beyond the usual provisions of the negotiated agreement to establish programs that resolve problems of mutual interest. Instead of conducting negotiations in an atmosphere of crisis confrontation, the parties recognize and accept each other as partners in a cooperative venture. Rather than viewing negotiations as a contest, the parties pool their creative resources to devise new arrangements in which both sides recognize the need for mutual survival and sharing in financial rewards.

Given the traditional exercise of the adversary model throughout American industry, it was perhaps inevitable that the parties in sports would adhere to its precepts. But the results flowing from the application of this model to sports have not been encouraging. In the beginnings of the modern era of sports labor relations, from the late 1960s until the late 1970s, the adversary model was probably needed to make the owners realize that the industrial peonage of players could not continue. But the players have made their point, and further adherence to strong adversary positions is potentially damaging to the public image of sports and the stability of the industry. The sports unions may be able to continue to achieve generous economic gains through adversary tactics, but there is the risk of jeopardizing the ability of owners to operate successfully. Instability of franchises, especially when they not only change hands but move from city to city, destroys the tradition and continuity vital to the economic health of the industry. Over the longer term, both sides can lose if the public rebels against continued manifestations of greed.

A Synthesizing Model

In the past, management has preferred the adversary approach because of its fears that collaboration with players' unions would reduce its authority. These fears were well grounded, because owner power was reduced by liberalized free agency and relinquishment of the lion's share of revenues. Sports unions, too, have viewed the adversary approach as consistent with their role as bargaining organizations and defenders of players' interests. They have been quite successful.

It does not seem likely that sports will be able to adapt to a full-scale cooperation model in the near future. It would be too much to expect that the unions would put aside their weapons and embrace management in widespread accommodation. But mutual survival of the industry depends more on future cooperation than on continuation of armed conflict. There are encouraging signs of a growing realization of joint interests and exploration of ways to enhance economic growth through greater cooperation. Good examples of this emerging recognition are the drug control programs in basketball, football, and baseball, and the salary cap and profit sharing in basketball. Also encouraging is the growing use of third-party neutrals—mediators and arbitrators—to help resolve disputes when the parties are unable to reach agreement.

In the adversary mode the goal is to win. In the cooperative mode the goal is concession. A synthesis of the adversary and cooperative approaches would turn the goal away from simple domination or capitulation, toward achieving a reasoned outcome that serves the parties' mutual needs. This synthesis recognizes the essential competition between labor and management for shares of the economic pie, but maintains a commitment to cooperation in creative programs that increase the overall size of the pie. It makes joint labor-management programs to attract fan interest and promote industrial growth central to negotiations.

Outside neutrals fit into this model in two important ways. One is to help bring the parties together in reasoned agreement over complex bargaining issues. Mediation is a particularly suitable stimulus to negotiations. It has the advantage of allowing the parties to make up their own minds on the issues, yet assisting them with creative ideas, facilitating trade-offs, and drafting contract language. Once the agreements are formulated and converted to documentary form, arbitrators perform a second useful service, the interpretation and application of contract terms if the parties are unable to agree in earlier steps of their grievance procedures. This mechanism provides a private system of industrial jurisprudence that serves as an alternative to lengthy and costly courtroom litigation. It has proven successful for several decades in American industry, and a large body of useful precedent has evolved. More contract interpretation disputes—involving issues such as discipline, injuries, salaries, and enforcement of a variety of agreed-upon rules—are being resolved through arbitration. The scope of grievance arbitration in sports is likely to continue to expand, with positive rather than negative effects.

Economics

The economic health of professional sport is closely linked to television. It will be even more so in the future. Existing leagues will expand, new leagues may form, and entirely new sports could evolve. But the common denominators of success in sports ventures are the extent of their television broadcasts and the ratings that broadcasts receive. Nearly all the other important economic elements of sport—player salaries, pensions and other fringe benefits, profitability of enterprises, profit sharing—depend in large part on television revenues. The United States is in the midst of a radical change in sports television broadcasting, which is occurring as a result of the growth of cable and pay television. The effect of this revolution in video entertainment is only beginning in terms of its impacts on sports. Although the eventual outcomes will remain unclear for some time, there are indications of the direction that they will take. It is likely that the most significant collective bargaining issue in sports will be how labor and management divide future television revenues. There is, however, less certainty about whether the bonanza that some expect will actually materialize.

Network Television

Although professional sports are popular on television, they are not necessarily profitable for the networks. In the past the three major networks paid big money for the rights to broadcast sporting events because they were able to pass the costs along to advertisers. In the mid-1980s, however, advertisers began to redirect their budgets away from sports. Automobile companies, for instance, realized that because cars are increasingly purchased by women, who do not watch sports as much as men, a larger portion of their advertising should appear in nonsports programming.

By the early 1990s there were signs that the golden age of network television and professional team sports was over. Ratings were down significantly, except for basketball, which televised relatively few games. CBS took writeoffs for losses totaling $604 million on its contracts with major league baseball and the NFL.[3] Although the NFL was able to increase its network television revenues somewhat, baseball's revenues were cut in half. Basketball and hockey improved their revenues, especially with hockey regaining a presence on U.S. network television. But, overall, network television was not spending as much on professional team sports in the mid-1990s as it did in the past. Also, in baseball and basketball the networks shifted some of the risk to the leagues by arrangements that tie league revenues to future television revenues from advertising.

The networks have also been affected by the glut of sports on television, which has caused ratings for many individual events to weaken. Moreover, cable television has emerged as a major competitor. The networks commanded about 90 percent of the sports television audience in 1980, but only about 70 percent of the audience in 1990. This restructuring of the television marketplace does not bode well for the networks or the leagues, although the leagues are in a somewhat better position because they can augment their revenues from the networks with revenues from cable and pay television.

Cable and Pay Television

While the 1960s and 1970s were the decades of network television, the 1980s ushered in the era of cable and pay television. The latter may not displace network television as the dominant element of the broadcast media in the near future, but there is little doubt that it is here to stay and will be an increasingly competitive presence.

There is some confusion over the terms *cable* and *pay* television, because these terms are often used synonymously. *Cable* simply means that a coaxial, or special compound, cable is extended through underground channels to a location for sending television impulses. These impulses can be transmitted through the cable by a conventional transmitter or satellite. All cable services are paid for by viewers. *Pay cable* is a premium service offered to basic cable customers on a separate channel at extra cost (there is also a form of pay television that can provide signals to homes that do not have cable).

Pay television is the wave of the future for professional sports franchises. Basketball, baseball, and hockey have been particularly aggressive in arranging for contracts with pay television services. The NBA has chosen to build the league's following in regional markets, where it is strong, rather than placing greatest emphasis on attracting a national network television audience, where exposure is limited and ratings are low.

The New York Yankees became baseball's pioneering regional pay television venture in 1978; however, the concept did not really catch on until 1984, when the San Diego Padres sold the team's broadcasting rights for forty games to Cox Communications for approximately $400,000. In the same year, viewers in fifteen states gained access to Sports Time, one of six new regional pay television services affiliated with eight major league baseball teams.[4] As a result of these new enterprises, for the first time more baseball games were shown on local pay television than on local free television (free television is something of a misnomer, because advertising costs are passed on to consumers). Many major league teams have both free and pay television services available to local viewers, but the trend is clearly in the direction of fewer free games on local stations. As a result, the networks are showing concern over the encroachment on their markets. In 1984, in a move toward horizontal integration of its operation, ABC paid $202 million for the nation's most popular cable service, the Entertainment and Sports Programming Network (ESPN). ABC previously owned 15 percent of ESPN, which has a twenty-four-hour sports channel.

The fastest growing segment of sports television is the regional sports network. These are pay cable companies that establish a package of events for sports viewers in a metropolitan area. Viewers may have to buy theses packages on a subscription basis, in addition to whatever basic cable service they receive. Fans can thus watch their home teams play rather than having to see teams that are chosen arbitrarily by a network. A problem, however, is that teams in the big-market cities get far more lucrative contracts than those in small-market areas. In 1988, for instance, the New York Yankees signed a twelve-year $486 million deal with Madison Square Garden Network. Yet small-market teams such as the Kansas City Royals, Milwaukee Brewers, Minnesota Twins, and Seattle Mariners have deals that pay only about $10 to $20 million each per year.

This market restructuring is already having a significant effect on revenues in the sports industry. But the future may hold even more dramatic changes. Suppose, for example, that the NFL or all four major professional sports leagues put up their own satellite to televise all games on a fee basis, a scenario dreaded by sports fans. If it happened, a segment of the entertainment industry would be created that would rival the film component in size. There are, however, reasons why it may not occur. One is that Congress might not allow pay television, which is relatively unregulated at present, to be used by the leagues for a profit cornucopia at the expense of the viewing public. Another is that there is still some uncertainty over the public's acceptance of pay television. If people have to pay for services that they are now getting free, they may not be willing to continue their sports viewing. There are fans who are so keen on their local teams and sports in general that they will pony up the added expense, as many are doing now. But pay-per-view requires the viewer to make the effort to order an event, and, once it is ordered, the viewer feels compelled to block out about three hours to watch it. Most sports fans are casual viewers who do not take the time to watch an entire game, unless it is a big game. Thus, how far this market extends is an interesting question, one on which the future profitability of pay television and professional sports depends.

It appears likely that whatever the future success of pay television, it has already established something of a track record and this is having an effect on the disparity of team revenues. Teams in small population markets are simply not able to compete with those in large metropolitan areas that garner vast revenues from pay television. This accentuates the have, have-not disparity of teams in the acquisition of exceptionally talented players. With the extension of free agency, players can opt for teams in big-market locations, which can afford to pay higher salaries and load up with superstars. Basketball's collective bargaining agreement addresses this problem to some extent, as does football's corporate socialism of equal sharing of all television revenues by teams. But the vast profit potential from pay television may shatter the revenue-sharing arrangements as owners in population centers seek to grab off a larger piece of the action.

Franchise Worth

As shown in the chapters on the individual sports, franchise values have risen sharply for many years. In 1991 *Financial World* magazine released the first comprehensive study of franchise values in the major team sports. All 102 franchise in existence at that time were appraised. Because most sports teams are privately held and do not release financial information, the magazine had to estimate much of its data. Sources such as estimates of ticket sales, player salaries, television revenues, and stadium rental fees were used in the compilation. Since the original survey, *Financial World* has made its estimates of franchise worth annually. The data for the ten most valuable franchises in baseball, football, basketball, and hockey are shown in Table 6.1.

The study shows that football franchises are worth the most, with the Dallas Cowboys valued at $190 million as the most valuable individual franchise in 1993. In contrast, the initial study by *Financial World* in 1991 found that the New York Yankees was the most valuable franchise at $225 million, far more than its estimated worth of $166 million in 1993. In reality, a franchise is worth what it will fetch in the marketplace, which may be significantly more or less than the estimates shown. Still, the data in Table 6.1 are interesting because they show relationships between sports as well as which franchises in individual sports appear to be of the highest value in a particular year.

International Expansion

Because the bloom is off the rose of the rapid rise in television revenues going to major league sports, both the networks and the leagues are looking for new ventures to maintain profitability. League expansion, pay-per-view, and new stadiums are important aspects of this quest. Another attractive prospect is international marketing of U.S. professional sports.

In recent years both the media corporations and sports leagues have emphasized international investment and exposure. Several of the principal media firms have positioned themselves for increased international programming through arrangements for production and distribution in overseas outlets. Among the companies with sports interests in the global marketplace are NBC,

Table 6.1. Estimated Value of Sports Franchises, 1993

Most Valuable Football Franchises	Total Revenue, 1993 (millions)	Franchise Value (millions)
1. Dallas Cowboys	$92.9	$190
2. New York Giants	65.3	176
3. Philadelphia Eagles	68.9	172
4. San Francisco 49ers	70.4	167
5. Cleveland Browns	65.1	165
6. Buffalo Bills	64.9	164
7. Miami Dolphins	74.4	161
8. Chicago Bears	65.4	160
9. Washington Redskins	60.9	158
10. Houston Oilers	62.0	157

Most Valuable Baseball Franchises	Total Revenue, 1993 (millions)	Franchise Value (millions)
1. New York Yankees	$107.6	$166
2. Toronto Blue Jays	88.4	150
3. New York Mets	80.8	147
4. Boston Red Sox	77.5	141
5. Los Angeles Dodgers	79.7	138
6. Chicago White Sox	78.8	133
7. Texas Rangers	60.3	132
8. Baltimore Orioles	81.3	129
9. Chicago Cubs	82.8	120
10. Oakland Athletics	60.1	114

Most Valuable Basketball Franchises	Total Revenue, 1993 (millions)	Franchise Value (millions)
1. Los Angeles Lakers	$68.7	$168
2. Detroit Pistons	60.6	154
3. Chicago Bulls	50.3	149
4. New York Knicks	61.6	136
5. Portland Trailblazers	39.2	122
6. Cleveland Cavaliers	40.6	118
7. Boston Celtics	41.9	117
8. Phoenix Suns	55.6	108
9. Charlotte Hornets	38.3	104
10. San Antonio Spurs	33.1	100

Most Valuable Hockey Franchises	Total Revenue, 1993 (millions)	Franchise Value (millions)
1. Detroit Red Wings	$47.9	$104
2. Boston Bruins	39.4	88
3. Los Angeles Kings	43.8	85
4. Montreal Canadiens	35.0	82

Table 6.1. *continued*

Most Valuable Hockey Franchises	Total Revenue, 1993 (millions)	Franchise Value (millions)
5. New York Rangers	37.7	81
6. Chicago Blackhawks	42.1	80
7. Toronto Maple Leafs	45.5	77
8. Philadelphia Flyers	35.1	69
9. Vancouver Canucks	32.4	69
10. Pittsburgh Penguins	32.7	62

Sources:*Financial World,* May 10, 1994, with the ten most valuable franchises in each sport cited in Richard L. Worsnop, "The Business of Sports," *CQ Researcher* (Congressional Quarterly, Inc.), 5, no. 6 (February 10, 1995): 134.

CBS, Capital Cities (ABC, ESPN), Fox, and the Turner Broadcasting System. ESPN, for example, has one-third ownership in the recently established Eurosport Consortium, which broadcasts in English, German, and Dutch to forty million homes.[4] Although television is a relatively mature industry in the United States, it is in the midst of a boom period throughout the rest of the world.

Oxford University historian Arnold Toynbee wrote extensively about the idea of "mimesis" in his epic eleven-volume *Study of History.* Mimesis is an imitation of a country by other countries, as Great Britain in the nineteenth century was venerated and copied within its colonial empire and by Anglophiles around the world. In the twentieth century the United States has been emulated worldwide. Mimesis stems from a "charm" exhibited by the nation, its culture, and its people.

Toynbee's concept of mimesis can be applied to the development of American sports around the world. Baseball has taken root in virtually all countries, and it is so popular in Japan (where it is called "besuboru") as to be considered the national sport along with sumo wrestling. American football has not traveled so well because of competition from soccer and rugby, but it is catching on here and there, especially in Europe. Basketball, another distinctly American game, is played around the world and there are numerous professional leagues in Europe. Hockey is played at the amateur and professional levels in all the cold-climate countries.

That American sports are played globally does not, ipso facto, guarantee opportunities for U.S. professional sports leagues. But it is a big foot in the door. Fans with an interest in a particular sport want to see the best players in action and to identify with the best teams. There is no doubt that American professional leagues provide play at the very highest skill levels in the world. Also, the American sports media and marketing systems are well established, with high standards of business operation, and have already geared up for international sales of everything from live and televised games, to equipment and clothing, to memorabilia and trading cards. There are, of course, obstacles to this expansion, such as time zones, nationalism, self-determination, language barriers, and entrenched foreign commercial interests that jealously guard their turf. But it seems likely that big-league U.S. sports will continue to secure a growing share of an ever larger international market. What are the prospects for each sport?

Baseball has a long tradition of postseason barnstorming tours to foreign nations. Babe Ruth was a very popular figure in the many countries he visited. American military personnel have had a fondness for teaching the game to youngsters in the nations they are stationed in. There is a large base of support for the game in Asia and Latin America, and increasingly in Europe and Australia. In 1992 baseball became an Olympic sport. Major league baseball has formed MLB International Partners to promote and market the game abroad. The All-Star game and World Series are already televised to much of the world, and more programming is on the way to educate as well as entertain. Europe is a priority target, as baseball wants to build a strong fan base that will sustain media interest and promote sale of merchandise. But it is doubtful that major league baseball will establish franchises abroad in the near future, except perhaps in Mexico City.

The NFL's international marketing efforts have been gaining momentum. The Super Bowl is shown around the world, and in 1986 the league began a series of two or three annual exhibition games abroad when the Dallas Cowboys played the Chicago Bears in London. The World League of American Football (WLAF) began play in the spring of 1991 with six U.S. teams and teams in Barcelona, Frankfurt, London, and Montreal. The WLAF, sponsored by the NFL, initially offered a salary of only $20,000 to most of its players ($25,000 to quarterbacks), who are minor leaguers hoping to make it in the NFL. Although the European franchises in the WLAF were profitable, the league lost about $20 million in each of its two years of operation. The WLAF suspended play as a result of the squabbling between the NFL and NFLPA, but it resumed operations in 1995 as an all-European league. The NFL has also established an organization called NFL World Partnership to promote football as a participation sport in Europe.

More than any of the leagues the NBA has secured a strong international position and may be the best bet for global franchise operation, perhaps as early as the end of the century. The league has a unit called NBA International, which does market research and other work toward global expansion. NBA playoff games are shown live or on tape in about sixty countries, on every continent except Antarctica. The league is also involved in an international tournament called the McDonald's Basketball Open, in which NBA and European teams compete. NBA merchandise is sold in about fifty countries. In the 1995–96 season the league added franchises in two Canadian cities, Toronto and Vancouver. Increasing the likelihood of NBA international expansion is the global popularity of the sport. Basketball has long been played in the Olympic games, and the U.S. Olympic team now features NBA stars.

The NHL also has a solid chance to go global, although perhaps only in Europe and countries of the former Soviet Union. It already has seven Canadian franchises, and a growing proportion of its players come from Europe. For many years the NHL has participated in international tournaments. The league has television arrangements with Eurosport, Russian state television, and ESPN International. Hockey has a strong Olympic presence, and NHL players participate in the winter Olympic tournament. An NHL European Division would appear to have a good chance of success. Its teams would probably compete mostly within Europe, except for occasional tours across the Atlantic.

Law

Much of the past strife between players and owners in professional sports has involved labor and antitrust issues stemming from long-standing practices such as the reserve clause and drafting of players. Free agency continues to be a source of litigation, as evidenced by the recent suits brought by the players' associations in basketball and football. Legal battles will also arise over who is going to get how much of the revenues generated by television. As cable and pay television allow deeper penetration into lucrative local markets, negotiation and litigation will increasingly focus on breaking old arrangements and forging new ones to exploit these markets. Television rights constitute a permissive rather than a mandatory subject for bargaining. But even though television agreements are regarded as a management prerogative, and thus not an obligatory bargaining topic between labor and management, the sports unions may push for shared authority.

As labor and management mature and power is equalized, there will probably be less emphasis on antitrust litigation and increased attention to working out problems at the bargaining table and through the assistance of neutral third parties. Lawsuits have diminished in other areas of private industry and public employment as the parties develop greater reliance on their own resources for determining outcomes. Respect, trust, and accommodation take time to establish and require seasoned leaders at the helm. There are, however, several antitrust issues from the past that remain open to further litigation. One area of future courtroom conflict concerns new leagues. The USFL was established in large part as a television league, seeking to attract viewers during the spring. The expected television revenues never materialized, at least not in sufficient quantities, because of low ratings and limited exposure. The antitrust suit filed by the USFL against the NFL was at bottom a belated attempt to acquire television revenues forgone from lack of exposure.

Another area of continued antitrust action is franchise movement. The NBA's lawsuit against the San Diego Clippers, who moved to Los Angeles, was similar to the football litigation over the Oakland Raiders' move to Los Angeles. This issue also arose in hockey when the NHL refused to allow the St. Louis Blues to be sold to investors who wanted to move the team to Saskatoon, Saskatchewan. These lawsuits raise questions of the leagues' authority under antitrust law to prevent franchise movement. Although baseball has an exemption from antitrust law, it is possible that this exemption will not extend to relocation of franchises should a challenge arise. The Raiders' litigation would seem to put the question at rest by allowing free movement, but the federal appeals court in that case made reference to certain factors that a league can take into account in permitting a team to move, such as geographical balance, financial viability, population, economic projections, quality of facilities, and fan loyalty. Thus it appears that some franchise relocations may be blocked by the leagues, while others may not.

This point is illustrated by the Los Angeles Rams' move to St. Louis in 1995. Team owner Georgia Frontiere reached agreement with St. Louis to move the team there. The deal for the Rams was the most generous ever offered to lure a team from one city to another. For instance, St. Louis was required to sell at least forty thousand "Personal Seat Licenses" (PSLs). This instrument required fans to pay up to $4,500 in order to obtain the right to buy a season ticket, with the cost of the ticket extra. Amazingly, St. Louis had orders for seventy-four thousand PSLs, which is eleven thousand more fans than the new stadium could accommodate. The Rams were also offered use of a taxpayer-funded $26 million stadium, 100 percent of concession revenues, and 75 percent of advertising.

Commissioner Tagliabue initially indicated that the Rams did not meet the criteria specified in the NFL guidelines for franchise movement. Of the league's eight criteria for evaluating moves, two were particularly applicable to the Rams. Criterion number four indicates that the league can make its decision to approve or disapprove a move partly on the "degree to which the ownership or management of the team has contributed to any circumstance which might otherwise demonstrate the need for such relocation." Criterion number six considers the "degree to which the team has engaged in good-faith negotiations with appropriate persons concerning terms and conditions under which the team would continue to play its games in such community or elsewhere within its current home territory."

As to criterion four, critics of the franchise move contended that Rams management was responsible for its own problems. The team had been in southern California for forty-nine years, but its last five seasons were poor and management did little to market or otherwise help the team to success. Regarding criterion six, the Rams gave short shrift to an attempt by local buyers to keep the team in Anaheim. A group called "Save the Rams," headed by football players' agent Leigh Steinberg, offered a new stadium and guaranteed revenues. Thus, the commissioner and owners who were against the Rams' proposed move to St. Louis thought that mismanagement and greed were the primary factors behind the move, which NFL criteria four and six weighed against. Moreover, there was a television problem created by a move from the second largest market in the nation to the twentieth largest. The Fox Network sought a rebate from the NFL for lost revenues under its television contract. But when the Rams and St. Louis principals threatened a massive lawsuit against the league, the owners recanted and decided to allow the Rams to move after all.

Baseball and basketball have had more team relocations than football and hockey (Table 6.2).[5] Although there has been far more instability in sports franchises since the 1960s, this is due to the rise and fall of rival leagues and the teams in those leagues rather than movement of franchises within the previously established major leagues. Franchise movement is endemic in fledgling leagues such as the old American Basketball Association and United States Football League. It cannot be said that the pace of franchise movement in the established major leagues has quickened in recent years, although there is a danger that this could happen in the future as a result of court decisions restricting league hegemony over where its teams operate. League expansions have headed off team relocation by placing new teams in cities that might otherwise try to lure away an existing franchise.

The principal arguments in favor of allowing unrestricted movement of professional sports franchises begin with the need to uphold the sanctity of the free enterprise system. Although it is well known that leagues prefer to function as cartels that retain power over who is going to enter the business and where franchises are to be located, free markets are fundamental to capitalism, and individual owners should have the right to determine the market area in which they will operate. Unrestricted franchise movement provides an opportunity for population growth areas to get franchises that they might not otherwise get. It also gives owners a greater opportunity to get out of cities that are not supporting their teams because of lack of interest or limited population growth.

Advocates further contend that the threat of departure by a team causes improvements in stadium facilities and may induce league expansion so that greater numbers of fans can enjoy live professional team sports. There is also a

Table 6.2. Franchise Movement since 1953

Year	Baseball	Football (AFL/NFL)	Basketball	Hockey
1953	Boston to Milwaukee			
1954	St. Louis to Baltimore			
1955	Philadelphia to Kansas City			
1956			Milwaukee to St. Louis	
1958	Brooklyn to Los Angeles New York to San Francisco		Fort Wayne to Detroit Rochester to Cincinnati	
1960		Chicago to St. Louis		
1961	Washington to Minneapolis	Los Angeles to San Diego	Minneapolis to Los Angeles	
1963		Dallas to Kansas City	Philadelphia to San Francisco	
1964			Chicago to Baltimore Syracuse to Philadelphia	
1966	Milwaukee to Atlanta			
1968	Kansas City to Oakland			
1969			St. Louis to Atlanta	
1970	Seattle to Milwaukee			
1972	Washington to Arlington, Tex.		San Diego to Houston	
1976				Kansas City to Colorado
1979			Buffalo to San Diego	
1980			New Orleans to Salt Lake City	Atlanta to Calgary
1982		Oakland to Los Angeles		Colorado to New Jersey
1984		Baltimore to Indianapolis	San Diego to Los Angeles	
1985			Kansas City to Sacramento	
1988		St. Louis to Phoenix		
1993				Minnesota to Dallas
1995		Los Angeles to St. Louis Los Angeles to Oakland		Quebec to Colorado

Note: Not included in the table are movements to stadium locations within the same metropolitan area, such as the Los Angeles Rams' move to Anaheim, California, or the New York Giants' move to a football stadium in New Jersey.

Source: Paul D. Staudohar, "Team Relocation in Professional Sports," *Labor Law Journal* 36, no. 9 (September 1985): 729, as updated by author.

possibility that free movement of franchises inject new private capital into sports, i.e., new owners are willing to spend more on their teams if they have an ability to relocate readily.

Opponents of unrestrained franchise movement contend that it introduces a risk factor into expenditure of public funds to finance stadiums. They also express cynicism over the unfairness of relocation, because it deprives loyal fans of their teams. Franchise movement creates a large element of instability to leagues, team recognition, and players who would like to be settled with their families in an area. Cities are deprived of an important part of their economic base when teams leave.

Moreover, critics charge, free franchise movement exposes cities to a form of political blackmail: "Build a new stadium or improve existing facilities or we will move." Cities trying to lure professional franchises resort to enticements that exacerbate franchise hopscotch, and may themselves fall prey the extortion game later on. It is further contended that excessive relocation hurts the overall public image of professional team sports, which is already beset with problems of drug abuse, declining television ratings, and fan resentment of high player salaries.

There are good arguments on both sides of the issue. No obvious solution to the problem seems indicated. It appears that a good case can be made for a compromise solution that gives the leagues some measure of control over franchise movement but which does not require a three-fourths vote by the league owners before a team can relocate. Basketball has reduced the requirement so that only a majority of owners is needed to grant approval. In addition, criteria for determining whether a franchise can move are needed to guide the decisions of owners. Greed is not a valid criterion, yet it was this factor that appears to have motivated Al Davis to move the Raiders out of Oakland, which had long supported the Raiders by sold-out crowds at games. Cities may have too great an emotional and financial stake in their stadiums and teams to be susceptible to losing their franchises simply because of a desire to heap larger profits on what is already a nicely profitable situation. If a team is clearly losing money because of lack of fan support, it should be able to change location.

Several bills have been introduced in Congress that would prevent teams from moving at will. The most sweeping proposals were those introduced by Slade Gorton, senator from the state of Washington, and Senators John Danforth and Thomas Eagleton, both from Missouri. Features of these bills, which were approved by the Senate Commerce Committee in 1984 and 1985, include (1) league approval of franchise movement; (2) consideration by the league of factors such as a team's profitability, playing facilities, fan support, and competition in the cities involved; and (3) that the league decision be approved by a board composed of a league representative, a person from the community threatened with a franchise loss, and a neutral party appointed by the American Arbitration Association. Another bill, introduced in 1986, would require an owner to give six months' notice before moving and provide justification to the league on various grounds, including finances, fan support, and facilities. Teams, cities, and stadium owners could appeal a league franchise ruling to a federal court in a neutral city. All these bills appear to allow a team to move if it can prove financial hardship at the present location.

This legislation is designed to protect cities and fans from greedy owners and mayors who ingratiate themselves with owners they are trying to attract to their cities. Passage of any bill in Congress is now unlikely, but there is pressure to develop rules to curb nomadic franchises. On the other hand, respect for the free enterprise system that allows owners to pursue their economic interests is a difficult obstacle to overcome. It is also questionable whether legislation can be developed that will satisfy the conflicting interests and put an end to further litigation.

It may be that Congress will be able to develop a compromise law that will limit franchise movement and place it on a more rational basis than what we have now. If so, it will require more careful evaluation of proposed franchise shifts to protect fans and cities. But Congress has been traditionally wary of passing laws affecting sports. If it fails to act, and perhaps even if it does pass a law, we have not seen the end of lawsuits over franchise movement. It may well be that the leagues will try to head of litigation by moving up their plans for expansion to additional cities.

What the future may hold is adoption by the courts of the eminent domain concept. This would recognize that sports franchises are too important to cities to allow indiscriminate relocation. Should such a concept be adopted, however, it would raise questions of how cities will come up with sufficient funds to allow them to buy a franchise and how the price of a franchise would be determined in the first place.

What about extension of the Green Bay Packers concept? This professional football team is privately owned by a large number of citizens of that city who support the team and would not be likely to permit it to leave. A variation on this theme would be the creation of a quasi-private corporation, authorized by voters, city ordinance, or both to buy out the existing ownership. Most of the modern baseball stadiums are financed with public funds. Many indoor arenas are already publicly owned. It would thus be one more step in ownership to acquire the team itself. Shares of stock could be offered to the public in a franchise city. It is also possible that the city itself could be the sole or perhaps the majority owner and have the responsibility for overseeing the operation of the franchise. The city of Pittsburgh purchased a large share of the Pirates baseball team in 1985 to prevent franchise movement.

Some cities have owned a minor league baseball franchise. But extension of this concept to the major leagues presents difficulty in that all teams are privately owned, by individuals or corporations. The leagues and owners want to keep their businesses a private affair. So do the unions that represent players. Yet the lamentable incidents in Oakland and Baltimore have aroused public indignation and prompted calls for a stop to franchise shifts motivated by cupidity. Should Congress choose not to set standards for team relocation, it is likely that creative financing through government will become a viable option in some cities.

Public Image

Virtually all productive enterprises depend on consumer markets for their viability and economic growth. Industries that produce goods and those that render services to the public tend to rise and fall in accordance with the consumer image of the attractiveness and reliability of their performance. Public image is especially crucial to the success of sports, because the consumption of this service is based on a derived joy from entertainment rather than biological need to sustain life. Dollars spent to view sports are from discretionary incomes, which can be allocated among various competing sources in the marketplace. Professional sport is a golden goose that feeds from a trough of monies supplied by the viewing public. Sport provides a world of myth and fantasy, but this world is not indestructible.

Illuminated by fantasy, sport is a world of players unspoiled by corruption. Contests staged on green fields, polished hardwood courts, and gleaming ice rinks reflect heroic deeds of forever youthful supermen. The games recall the playful, simpler times of spectators' own childhoods and help keep them young. But the myth is shaken by the rapacity of players and owners, the vitriol of their labor relations, and drug abuse among those so fortunate as to be big league athletes. Has the dream disappeared? How did sports slip from the age of innocence to the era of egoism? Have we seen too many games? These are questions being asked increasingly by sports fans.

The reality of professional sports has always been different from the myth. If cynicism with fallen heroes is on the rise, it is largely because their failures are more visible. The intense light of the media has exposed their humanity. Along with the drug issue, media attention has the greatest influence on the way the public perceives today's athletes. It shows players as little more than wealthy mercenaries with exceptional talents, which do not necessarily include emotional maturity. Still, there remain many true heroes among them. Owners have always been motivated by greed, but the sports business is more competitive and impersonal today. There are great men among the owners, but too often they are motivated by the quick buck and self-aggrandizement. Strikes, lawsuits, and holdouts have spoiled much of the fun.

To the extent that effective collective bargaining can help deal with problems that affect public image—drug abuse, strikes, and excessively high salaries—it can contribute to industrial success. In the past, collective bargaining has been as much a part of the problem as it has the solution. This is why the models of collective bargaining in the sports industry require change.

There are three principal behavior problems in professional sports: violence, gambling, and chemical abuse. Controlled violence is inherent in each of the sports covered in this book. Violence becomes aberrant when it goes beyond the rules of the games and threatens or causes malicious injury. Although violence is most commonly associated with football, the players are so well covered by protective gear that mischief leading to a lawsuit is relatively rare. Fights are endemic to football, but it is difficult to hurt someone wrapped in a shell of plastic. Hockey sticks and baseball bats are another matter, and so is the vulnerability of basketball players to a hard punch or kick. Violence could give rise to a special sports court that would determine fault and award damages. Bills for such a court or federal regulatory commission have been introduced in Congress.[6] Violence is currently handled by player fines and possible suspension or banishment from the game, with additional monetary remedy for players injured by violence sought in the existing civil or criminal courts. The high salaries of players have placed greater importance on forgone income from injuries caused by excessive violence. Accused players are represented in whole or in part by their unions, as they would be if accused of other forms of aberrant behavior. Judging from the relatively light penalties that have been handed out, unions have been effective in protecting players by mitigating punishment and hastening their reinstatement.

Because of the high salaries of players, risk of apprehension, and heavy penalties for violation, gambling has not been a serious problem in professional sports. All sports strictly prohibit betting on league games. Only occasional incidents have occurred. Although gambling by players on their own games has rarely occurred, it cannot be ignored as a potential problem. Many athletes use cocaine, which is an expensive habit, and drug dealers might try to use their powers as suppliers to induce players to throw games.

A national media debate on sports gambling erupted in 1990 as a result of Cincinnati Reds manager Pete Rose's banishment from baseball for betting on games, and New Yankees owner George Steinbrenner's suspension for admitting that he paid $40,000 to a known gambler to keep him from revealing damaging information about former team employees. Some of the participants in the debate argued that all sports gambling should be legalized so that the illegal betting portion of the total of $38 billion bet on sporting events annually could be taxed by the government. This tax revenue would benefit society. Also, claimed proponents of this idea, it would drive the criminal operators out of business and eliminate potential for fixing games. Among the arguments against legalization are that it would induce more people to gamble, illegal bookies would not disappear because they give credit to gamblers which government lotteries could not, and the get-rich-quick notion of gambling would replace the devotion to hard work and saving and would encourage young people to gamble.

There is also the position that all sports gambling should be prohibited. Bills were introduced in Congress in 1991 and 1992 that would have banned gambling on professional and college sports except in the three states in which it was already allowed. League officials from baseball, football, and basketball testified at Senate hearings about the problems that gambling presents and urged that a ban be approved. Though the legislative initiatives were not passed, there has not been an apparent increase in opportunities for gambling legally on sports, and the status quo has prevailed. Perhaps this is a recognition of the adage that "you can't legislate morality."

Chemical abuse is a long-standing problem among athletes. In years past, alcohol took a heavy toll in shortening careers. Contemporary professional athletes have progressed from pill-popping to get up for games to the more serious aberration of cocaine abuse. It was widely estimated that as many as 75 percent of NBA players used cocaine at one time or another. High percentages have also been cited in football and baseball. Although the drug abuse problem has not been as visible in hockey, there have been incidents suggesting that it is not unknown to players of that sport. It is misleading to suggest, as Commissioner Rozelle once did, that drug abuse in sports is no greater than it is in society as a whole. Many athletes live in the fast lane, and all have the financial capability to acquire drugs. Reckless youth coupled with the pressures of achievement make players easy marks for addictive consumption of drugs. Cocaine, generally inaccessible in large quantities to less affluent sports fans, is viewed by the public as a hard drug. Its qualities are notoriously insidious and have arrested or ruined numerous players' careers. The rash of publicity attending drug busts and the revelation of drug habits among players have already done significant damage to the image of basketball, football, and baseball. To the credit of these sports, they are moving out of the dark ages of ignoring the problems toward recognition and assistance and finally to substantial treatment programs. The

public need for vindication for perceived betrayal by sports heroes has been as-
suaged by tough penalties for repeat offenders and those who fail to come forward with problems.

All professional team sports except hockey now have comprehensive drug
control programs that include testing. Observers who emphasize player rights
on drug matters and who argue that what the players do is their own business
miss some basic points. Testing can only help the players, and the public image
of sports is enhanced by removing the cloud of uncertainty over commitment
to facing up to the problem. A societal problem of critical proportions, drug
abuse is magnified in and by sports. If sport wants a good public image, it has
to earn it by presenting an example that is exemplary, not debilitating.

AIDS and Sports

The problem of AIDS in professional and amateur sports has recently become a lively topic, largely as a result of the Magic Johnson case.[7] AIDS is an
acronym for Acquired Immunodeficiency Syndrome, which is associated with
and probably results from infection with the Human Immunodeficiency Virus
(HIV). In the overwhelming majority of cases, the inevitable outcome of HIV
infection is a diagnosis of AIDS, an invariably fatal condition.

What dangers does HIV/AIDS pose to sports? Would it be possible, for instance, for HIV to be transmitted from one player to another during an athletic
contest? Considering the fact that about 1 percent of American men are HIV-
positive, there is a good chance that in any given game there could be a player
who is infected with the virus.

The most intriguing case about HIV transmission during a sporting event
was reported in a letter to the British medical journal *Lancet,* from Donato
Torre, a physician from the Division of Infectious Disease in Varese, Italy. Dr.
Torre wrote that in 1989 a twenty-five-year-old man collided with a drug
abuser who was HIV-positive during a soccer match between drug addicts and
volunteer workers and aides at a rehabilitation center. The collision caused severe head lacerations around the eyebrows and both players bled profusely. According to Dr. Torre, the man who became infected as a result of the collision
had tested negatively for HIV a year earlier. He had had a four-year relationship with a woman, was not homosexual or an intravenous drug user, and had
not had a blood transfusion. This supports Dr. Torre's belief that HIV transmission was caused by the collision. This is only a supposition, however, because the Italian doctors did not compare particles of the blood of the two
men to see if they matched. The HIV virus leaves a distinctive "fingerprint"

that would be identical or nearly so in two cases that were linked by transmission. Thus, the link was never positively established.

The surgeon general of the United States reported that one cannot get AIDS from casual social contact, such as shaking hands, hugging, kissing, crying, or sneezing. HIV is found in body fluids such as blood, semen, and vaginal secretions. It is not typically found in urine, feces, nasal secretions, sweat, sputum, or vomit, unless they contain visible blood. Of the persons diagnosed with AIDS, a small percentage has "no identified risk factor," which means it is not known how they contacted the disease. This suggests an information gap in how the AIDS virus is transmitted. Accordingly, there seems to be some risk of getting the virus through contact sports, especially because bleeding sometimes results from sports injuries. Several health care workers have been infected with HIV by accidental needle pricks or cuts during surgery.

Ironically, it is the behavior of athletes off the field that is far more likely to result in HIV infection. A study of collegiate athletes by Dr. James C. Puffer of UCLA's School of Medicine found them to be (1) one a half times more likely than nonathletes to have greater numbers of sexual partners, (2) less likely to use contraceptive devices, and (3) four times more likely to get sexually transmitted diseases.[8] It is not surprising that athletes are more active sexually. They are often physically attractive, full of energy, and enjoy risk-taking behavior. Well-conditioned and highly skilled, they like to test their limits in the fast lane. Professional athletes are adored by legions of fans and have abundant time between games to indulge themselves sexually.

Earvin "Magic" Johnson is one of the finest basketball players ever. In 1990, at the peak of his career with the Los Angeles Lakers, he became the sixth player in NBA history to win the regular-season Most Valuable Player award three times. He brought many honors to his team and himself during his eleven-year career. On November 7, 1991, Johnson announced his retirement at age thirty-two after testing positive for HIV during a routine medical examination for an insurance policy. Johnson claimed he contracted the virus from a heterosexual experience, but that he did not know who the woman was.

Although Johnson retired from the Lakers, he made a spectacular one-time return to the league by winning the MVP award in the NBA all-star game in February 1992. Encouraged by this performance, he played for the U.S. Olympic basketball team in the 1992 Barcelona games. After these games, in September 1992, Johnson announced that he would rejoin the Lakers for the coming season, which would have made him the first known HIV-positive player in professional sports. His intention was to play fifty to sixty of the eighty-two regular-season games, sitting out games scheduled on consecutive nights.

Over the course of the next month or so there was mixed reaction to Johnson's decision to return to the league. Mostly the fans were delighted. But there were negative rumblings about risk to other players, and rumors began to spread about the way Johnson contracted the virus. In a widely referenced article in the *New York Times* on November 1, 1992, Karl "Mailman" Malone of the Utah Jazz was critical of Johnson's decision to return because of the risk to young players. Also critical was Jerry Colangelo, president of the Phoenix Suns, who verbally underscored the risk factor. The comments of Malone and Colangelo triggered numerous newspaper stories. Adding fuel to the fire was Johnson's cutting his arm a few weeks earlier in an exhibition game for the Lakers, and this had affected him as well as the other players. As the pressure mounted, Johnson decided to retire permanently from the NBA.

While Magic Johnson is the most prominent example of an athlete with HIV, other sports figures have been afflicted more seriously because their virus has escalated into AIDS. The first known professional athlete to die of AIDS, in 1986, was Jerry Smith, who had played tight end for the Washington Redskins. In 1989 stock car driver Tim Richmond died of AIDS. Several figure skaters have died of AIDS, including Olympic gold medalist John Curry of Great Britain. In 1993 Arthur Ashe, U.S. Open and Wimbledon tennis champion, died of AIDS contracted after becoming HIV-positive from a blood transfusion during heart surgery. Greg Lougainis, gold medal Olympic diver, revealed that he had AIDS in 1995.

Whether to test athletes for HIV is controversial. In 1991 a doctor reported that a woman he treated, who later died of AIDS, had had sex with about fifty NHL players. This prompted NHL teams to warn players about the incident and recommend that they be tested. Bill Goldsworthy, former player for the Minnesota North Stars, announced that he had AIDS in 1995, reportedly contracted from heterosexual relations, but there was apparently no link established between him and the woman who earlier died of AIDS. In 1992 the New York Giants became the first professional sports team to include a test for HIV, and the Philadelphia Eagles have followed suit.

HIV testing in sports has not become common because of questionable necessity. No one has become HIV-positive as a result of playing sports. From a public health and humanitarian standpoint, however, testing makes some sense because players are susceptible to HIV in their activities off the playing field. It is quite possible, for instance, that Magic Johnson had HIV long before he discovered it. Also, when teams give multiyear guaranteed contracts to players, they are at risk if a player develops a disease that ends his career. Johnson, for example, walked away with $14.6 million that he was guaranteed for agreeing to return to the Lakers.

As a practical matter, however, HIV testing presents difficulties. One is invasion of privacy, which comes up if mandatory testing is imposed. Insurance companies favor mandatory testing because of the high cost of AIDS-related claims. Such tests have been challenged as unfair discrimination, but federal and state courts have upheld insurers' rights to test for AIDS. Another problem is that it takes three to six months after a person gets HIV for it to show up in a blood test. Thus, effective testing would have to occur fairly frequently, say two or more times a year. Because it is a blood test rather than the usual urine tests given athletes, HIV testing would add substantially to testing costs. Still, it would not place an undue economic burden on sports franchises. But if a player tests positive it would be difficult to ensure confidentiality because some states require reporting positive HIV test results to public health authorities.

There is also a question as to whether mandatory testing can be imposed unilaterally by a club or league. Under the National Labor Relations Act, changes in work rules are considered a mandatory subject for bargaining. No HIV testing cases have been decided yet by the National Labor Relations Board, but that board has determined that mandatory drug testing is negotiable under the law as a term and condition of employment.

AIDS education is a concern at the professional level, and some teams are providing information to players on the disease, as to how it is contracted, and how and where to get tested. Major league baseball and the Major League Baseball Players Association have jointly established the AIDS Education Initiative. This program provides for meetings with players to discuss HIV and AIDS, offers an informational brochure printed in English and Spanish, and urges voluntary HIV testing, which is arranged confidentially by the program's medical advisors. The NBA and NFL also provide seminars and literature to players. For better or worse, professional athletes are role models and leading members of society. It is important that they become knowledgeable about HIV/AIDS, for themselves as well as for the people they influence.

It seems likely that in the future there will be active professional athletes who are HIV-positive, if there are not some already. This is something Americans are going to have to learn more about and adjust to, for the sake of possibly infected persons as well as their own health. AIDS is a preventable disease only insofar as HIV infection is preventable, and HIV infection is preventable.

Thoughts on the Future

Various scenarios are possible for the future of sports. One major theme is that the relations between owners and players will remain rancorous, with strong adherence to adversary bargaining. Another is that the bargaining model will be characterized by cooperation, with joint problem solving rather than a test of wills. It seems probable that the future will see an admixture of these models, with adversary bargaining tempered by a gradual shift in the direction of accommodation on areas of mutual concern. Labor and management in professional sports cannot simply continue to pursue their own ends without concern for the effects of their decisions on the public. Fan support determines the bottom line of successful operation, and arrangements worked out between labor and management will have to recognize the need to preserve the public image. Government regulation may help to rationalize industrial operation in certain areas in which the parties are unable or unwilling to come to grips with problems, but the future health of the industry is going to be influenced in major part by what the parties do to resolve emerging problems.

Success implies a balancing of interests and a recognition of the need for mutual survival. For example, the NBA's sharing of pay television revenues should allow for increased competitive balance among teams, the ultimate result of which should be greater prosperity for owners and players. It is not corporate socialism but a kind of player-induced socialism-for-all that seems likely to emerge. The inherent instability of professional sports operation suggests the need for basing salary structures more on profit sharing than on the ability of individual players to command higher salaries. On the one hand, what may emerge is a narrowing of the dispersion between player salaries, perhaps through establishment of salary scales that reflect seniority, with wages above scale determined by team or league profits. This implies a reduced role for agents, although their complete disappearance is unlikely to occur in the foreseeable future. On the other hand, greed may prevent such arrangements from more widespread adoption, and the sports industry may move toward a free market approach based on survival of the fittest. What argues against this latter course is the destruction of competitive balance that could diminish fan interest and contract the market potential for the leagues as a whole.

There is no doubt that unions have been extraordinarily successful in enhancing the economic status of players. A question arises as to whether this success may sow the seeds of future problems in the growth and stability of the industry. If we look at the automobile, steel, airline, and trucking industries, we see a string of union successes that was later broken by industrial decline and restructuring. Could this happen in sports? Perhaps, but not for the same reasons. The decline of certain heavily unionized American industries has been the result of foreign and domestic competition, with the latter caused by deregulation. American professional team sports do not face foreign competition except in the limited sense of European soccer games on television. Since sports are not now heavily regulated, deregulation would not create domestic competition. But competition does exist from nonindustrial components. For instance, the fitness revolution has caused more active participation in sports, and many persons now do this as an alternative to being spectators. The decline in network television ratings of professional sports suggests that the industry is not immune from competition. There are many other entertainment choices that compete with sports. Some observers have argued that the big strikes in sports have turned off the fans. Although attendance was not much affected in the past, the recent baseball strike reduced attendance by about 20 percent in 1995.

Despite the past success of the professional sports industry in America, a growing number of observers are worried about the future. During the 1970s, the number of sports heroes who were revered as much for their dignity as for their achievements on the playing field declined. Who inspired noble actions in society, especially among young people? Where have you gone, Joe DiMaggio, Stan Musial, Lou Gehrig, Joe Louis, Connie Mack, Red Grange, Elgin Baylor? Today's professional athletes are celebrities who achieve notoriety more for their media images and cupidity than for their playing skills and personal integrity.[9] It is little wonder that many fans have lost their appetite for the seemingly endless parade of superstars that the media-sports complex churns out. To these fans, the whole of sports is becoming increasingly banal. They feel alienated because the games and players seem to be meant less for them and more for promoting the business of sport as a haven for the privileged participants.[10] The boundaries defining professional sports are becoming blurred and seem carelessly mingled into a shadowy kind of "moneyball." This change is part of a general shift in American society, away from a sense of common identity rooted in tradition and toward emphasis on economic achievement based on individualism.

While there are some signs that the industry is leveling off its growth curve, there are no obvious indications that it will not have a reasonably prosperous future. The degree to which this prosperity is realized will depend largely on the growth of television viewing, especially on a pay basis, and the extent to which labor and management can work out problems of mutual concern in collective bargaining. Heated conflicts in negotiations may eventually decline. Drug abuse issues have subsided, although they will continue to surface. The future will not likely be one of unparalleled growth in professional sports. Many problems will persist, and new ones will arise. But sports should remain a vibrant industry that brings much satisfaction to the public.

NOTES

1. Introduction

1. This quotation, perhaps apocryphal, like some other words and gestures attributed to the colorful Babe, is cited in many sources, including Dale Yoder and Paul D. Staudohar, *Personnel Management and Industrial Relations,* 7th ed. (Englewood Cliffs, N.J.: Prentice-Hall, 1982), 332. In addition to this textbook, the reader who is generally unfamiliar with the industrial relations literature should see especially Arthur A. Sloane and Fred Witney, *Labor Relations,* 8th ed. (Englewood Cliffs, N.J.: Prentice-Hall, 1994); Richard E. Walton and Robert B. McKersie, *A Behavioral Theory of Labor Negotiations* (Ithaca: ILR Press, Cornell University, 1991); and Robert L. Sauer and Keith E. Voelker, *Labor Relations: Structure and Process,* 2d ed. (New York: Macmillan, 1993).

2. Marie Hart and Susan Birrell, eds., *Sport and the Sociocultural Process,* 3d ed. (Dubuque, Iowa: Wm. C. Brown 1981), x.

3. A good reference on this subject is Johan Huizinga, *Homo Ludens: A Study of the Play Element in Culture* (Boston: Beacon, 1950).

4. For another view, see Douglas A. Noverr and Lawrence E. Ziewacz, *The Games They Played: Sports in American History, 1865–1980* (Chicago: Nelson-Hall, 1983). An interesting essay on the advantages and disadvantages of competitive sports is Bil Gilbert, "Competition," *Sports Illustrated,* 16 May 1988, 88–100.

5. John T. Dunlop, *Industrial Relations Systems,* 2d ed. (Boston: Harvard Business School Press, 1993).

6. For a separate model based on this idea, see Thomas A. Kochan, Robert B. McKersie, and Peter Cappelli, "Strategic Choice and Industrial Relations Theory," *Industrial Relations* 23, no. 1 (Winter 1984): 16–39.

7. David Tajgman, "A Primer of Labor Relations in the Entertainment Industry," *ILR Report* 21, no. 2 (Spring 1984): 8.

8. This definition is adapted from Jack Barbash, *The Elements of Industrial Relations* (Madison: University of Wisconsin Press, 1984).

9. Portions of this discussion are from Robert C. Berry, William B. Gould IV, and Paul D. Staudohar, *Labor Relations in Professional Sports* (Dover, Mass.: Auburn House, 1986), 31–32, and are reprinted here with the permission of the publisher.

10. Yoder and Staudohar, *Personnel Management and Industrial Relations*, 477.

11. Barbash, *Elements of Industrial Relations*, 6.

2. Baseball

1. Material in this section is drawn from David Q. Voigt, "Serfs versus Magnates: A Century of Labor Strife in Major League Baseball," in *The Business of Professional Sports*, ed. Paul D. Staudohar and James A. Mangan (Urbana: University of Illinois Press, 1991), 95–114. See also Lee Lowenfish and Tony Lupien, *The Imperfect Diamond* (New York: Stein and Day, 1980); Harold Seymour, *Baseball: The Early Years* (New York: Oxford University Press, 1960); Harold Seymour, *Baseball: The Golden Age* (New York: Oxford University Press, 1971); and David Q. Voigt's three-volume study *American Baseball* (University Park: Pennsylvania State University Press, 1983).

2. For a good discussion of the unique characteristics of baseball as an economic enterprise, see Jesse W. Markham and Paul V. Teplitz, *Baseball Economics and Public Policy* (Lexington, Mass.: Lexington Books, 1981), 17–33.

3. Michael J. McCarthy, "Sinking Attendance Leads Baseball Clubs to Come Up with a New Play: Marketing," *Wall Street Journal*, 6 July 1993, B1.

4. Survey published in *Time*, 3 April 1995, 22.

5. Interestingly, the economics literature maintains that a labor market with monopolistic control by owners would lead to the same allocation of players and team strengths as would occur if the labor market were competitive. Only the distribution of wealth between the players and owners would be affected. See Joseph W. Hunt, Jr., and Kenneth A. Lewis, "Dominance, Recontracting, and the Reserve Clause: Major League Baseball," *American Economic Review* 66, no. 5 (December 1976): 936.

6. *American League of Professional Baseball Clubs*, 180 NLRB 189 (1969).

7. *Federal Baseball Club* v. *National League*, 259 U.S. 200 (1922).

8. *Flood* v. *Kuhn*, 407 U.S. 258 (1972). See also *Toolson* v. *New York Yankees*, 346 U.S. 356 (1953).

9. For an interesting account of Kuhn's experiences, see Bowie Kuhn, *Hardball: The Education of a Baseball Commissioner* (New York: Times Books, 1987).

10. Some of the material in this section is from Paul D. Staudohar, "Player Salary Issues in Major League Baseball," *Arbitration Journal* 33, no. 4 (December 1978): 17–18.

11. For a profile of Miller's background, see Robert H. Boyle, "This Miller Admits He's a Grind," *Sports Illustrated*, 11 March 1974, 22–26.

12. E. M. Swift, "The Perfect Square," *Sports Illustrated*, 8 March 1993, 32–35.

13. These factors are analyzed quantitatively in Gerald W. Scully, "Pay and Performance in Major League Baseball," *American Economic Review* 64, no. 6 (December 1974): 915–30.

14. Materials in this section are based on Paul D. Staudohar and Edward M. Smith, "The Impact of Free Agency on Baseball Salaries," *Compensation Review* 13, no. 3 (Third Quarter 1981): 51–52.

15. James Richard Hill and William Spellman, "Professional Baseball: The Reserve Clause and Salary Structure," *Industrial Relations* 22, no. 1 (Winter 1983): 16.

16. Henry J. Raimondo, "Free Agents' Impact on the Labor Market for Baseball Players," *Journal of Labor Research* 4, no. 2 (Spring 1983): 192.

17. Leonard Koppett, "Change," *Sports Illustrated,* 3 May 1992, 13–14.

18. *Basic Agreement between the American League of Professional Baseball Clubs and the National League of Professional Baseball Clubs and Major League Baseball Players Association,* effective 1 January 1980.

19. *In the Matter of Arbitration between Major League Baseball Players Association and the 26 Major League Baseball Clubs,* Grievance No. 86–2, by the Major League Baseball Arbitration Panel, Thomas T. Roberts, Chairman; Barry Rona; and Donald M. Fehr, 21 September 1987.

20. Dale Yoder and Paul D. Staudohar, *Personnel Management and Industrial Relations,* 7th ed. (Englewood Cliffs, N.J.: Prentice-Hall, 1982), 488.

21. James B. Dworkin, *Owners versus Players: Baseball and Collective Bargaining* (Boston: Auburn House, 1981), 153.

22. John L. Fizel, "Play Ball: Baseball Arbitration after 20 Years," *Dispute Settlement Journal* 49, no. 2 (June 1994): 44–45. See also John B. LaRocca, "Reforming Baseball Salary Arbitration," in *Proceedings of the Forty-Seventh Annual Meeting, National Academy of Arbitrators,* ed. Gladys W. Gruenberg (Washington, D.C.: Bureau of National Affairs, 1994), 227.

23. Fizel, "Play Ball," p. 44.

24. This section is from Paul D. Staudohar, "Baseball Labor Relations: The Lockout of 1990," *Monthly Labor Review* 113, no. 10 (October 1990): 32–36; and Paul D. Staudohar, "Locking Out for Number One," *New York Times,* 11 March 1990, 27.

25. *American Ship Building Co. v. National Labor Relations Board,* 380 U.S. 300 (1965).

26. *Time,* 20 April 1987, 63.

27. National Institute on Drug Abuse, *Drug Use in Industry,* Services Research Report, Alcohol, Drug Abuse and Mental Health Administration (Washington, D.C.: U.S. Government Printing Office, 1979), 11. See also Harrison M. Trice and Paul M. Roman, *Spirits and Demons at Work: Alcohol and Other Drugs on the Job,* 2d ed. (Ithaca: New York State School of Industrial and Labor Relations, Cornell University, 1978); and Tia Schneider Denenberg and R. V. Denenberg, *Alcohol and Drugs: Issues in the Workplace* (Washington, D.C.: Bureau of National Affairs, 1983).

28. Players suspended in separate incidents include San Francisco Giants outfielder Rick Leach (1990), Atlanta Braves outfielder Otis Nixon (1991), Montreal Expos catcher Gilberto Reyes (1992), New York Yankees pitchers Pascual Perez and Steve Howe (1992), New York Mets pitcher Dwight Gooden (1994), and San Francisco outfielder Darryl Strawberry (1995).

3. Football

1. Good sources on the origins of professional football are Gene Brown, ed., *The New York Times Encyclopedia of Sports,* vol. 1, *Football,* with introduction by Frank Litsky (New York: Arno, 1979); and Douglas A. Noverr and Lawrence E. Ziewacz, *The Games They Played: Sports in American History, 1865–1980* (Chicago: Nelson-Hall, 1983), 83–87.

2. Portions of this discussion are based on Paul D. Staudohar, "Professional Football and the Great Salary Dispute," *Personnel Journal* 61, no. 9 (September 1982): 673–79.

3. *National Football League Management Council and National Football League Players Association*, 203 NLRB 165 (1973), 83 LRRM 1203 (1973).

4. "NFL Owners Told to Bargain on Rules That Involve Safety," *Wall Street Journal*, 26 July 1976, 25.

5. *NFL Players Association* v. *NLRB*, 503 F. 2d 12 (1974), 87 LRRM 2118 (1974).

6. Collective Bargaining Agreement between National Football League Players Association and National Football League Management Council, 1977, 8.

7. Collective Bargaining Agreement between National Football League Players Association and National Football League Management Council, 1982, 32–33.

8. Ira Miller, "Upshaw's Line Isn't Offensive," *San Francisco Chronicle*, 14 September 1983, 67.

9. Portions of this section are from Paul D. Staudohar, "The Football Strike of 1987: The Question of Free Agency," *Monthly Labor Review* 111, no. 8 (August 1988): 27–31.

10. Discussion of the reserve clause is found in Edward R. Garvey, "From Chattel to Employee: The Athlete's Quest for Freedom and Dignity," *Annals of the American Academy of Political Science*, no. 445 (September 1979): 92–95.

11. *Radovich* v. *NFL*, 352 U.S. 445 (1957).

12. *Kapp* v. *National Football League*, 390 F. Supp. 73 (1974), *aff'd.* 586 F. 2d 644 (9th Cir. 1978), *cert. denied*, 441 U.S. 907 (1979).

13. *Mackey* v. *National Football League*, 543 F. 2d 644 (8th Cir. 1976), *cert. dismissed*, 434 U.S. 801 (1977). For further discussion of the *Kapp* and *Mackey* cases, see Steven M. Strauss, "Sport in Court: The Legality of Professional Football's System of Reserve and Compensation," *UCLA Law Review* 28, no. 2 (December 1980): 252–90.

14. Portions of this section are from Paul D. Staudohar, "McNeil and Football's Antitrust Quagmire," *Journal of Sport and Social Issues* 16, no. 2 (December 1992): 105–6. Copyright © 1992 by the Center for the Study of Sport in Society, Northeastern University, and reprinted by permission of Sage Publications, Inc.

15. Portions of this section are from Paul D. Staudohar, "Free Agency Won't Set Players Free," *New York Times*, 25 November 1990, L+S7.

16. *Smith* v. *Pro Football, Inc.*, 420 F. Supp. 738, 593 F. 2d 1173 (1978).

17. Robert B. Terry, "Application of Antitrust Laws to Professional Sports' Eligibility and Draft Rules," *Missouri Law Review* 46, no. 4 (Fall 1981): 797–828.

18. *NFL et al.* v. *Oakland Raiders et al.; Oakland-Alameda County Coliseum* v. *Oakland Raiders et al.*, 105 S. Ct. 397 (1984).

19. *City of Oakland* v. *Oakland Raiders*, 646 P. 2d. 835 (1982).

20. Jim Byrne, *The $1 League: The Rise and Fall of the USFL* (Englewood Cliffs, N.J.: Prentice-Hall, 1987).

21. *USFL* v. *NFL*, 842 F. 2d 1335 (1988).

22. Leigh Steinberg, "The Role of Sports Agents," in *The Business of Professional Sports*, ed. Paul D. Staudohar and James A. Mangan (Urbana: University of Illinois Press, 1991), 258.

23. Peter King, "Inside the NFL," *Sports Illustrated*, 4 November 1991, 58.

24. "Report NFL Cocaine Use Now 50 Percent," *San Francisco Sunday Examiner and Chronicle*, 14 August 1983, C6.

25. "Four Players Suspended by Rozelle for Drug Use," *Los Angeles Times*, 26 July 1983, pt. 3, 1.

4. Basketball

1. For detailed discussions of the origins of basketball, see Glenn Dickey, *The History of Professional Basketball since 1896* (New York: Stein and Day, 1982), 3–9; Douglas A. Noverr and Lawrence E. Ziewacz, *The Games They Played: Sports in American History, 1865–1980* (Chicago: Nelson-Hall, 1983), 31–32; and *The New York Times Encyclopedia of Sports*, vol. 3, *Basketball*, ed. Gene Brown with introduction by Frank Litsky (New York: Arno, 1979).

2. Roger G. Noll and Benjamin A. Okner, *The Economics of Professional Basketball*, reprint no. 258 (Washington D.C.: Brookings Institution, 1973), 2.

3. Roger Noll, "Professional Basketball: Economic and Business Perspectives," in *The Business of Professional Sports*, ed. Paul D. Staudohar and James A. Mangan (Urbana: University of Illinois Press, 1991), 31–34.

4. *Sporting News*, 9 May 1988, 10.

5. The original ABL teams were located in Cleveland, New York, Kansas City, Pittsburgh, Chicago, Hawaii, and San Francisco.

6. Michael S. Jacobs and Ralph K. Winter, Jr., "Antitrust Principles and Collective Bargaining by Athletes: Of Superstars in Peonage," *Yale Law Journal* 81, no. 1 (November 1971): 5.

7. Gerald W. Scully, "Economic Discrimination in Professional Sports," *Law and Contemporary Problems* 38 (Winter-Spring 1973): 68.

8. *The Modern Encyclopedia of Basketball*, ed. Zander Hollander (New York: Four Winds, 1969), 218.

9. Damon Stetson, "N.B.A. Acts to Bar Racial Incidents," *New York Times*, 23 January 1959, 15.

10. "Cousy to Discuss Union with Labor Executive," *New York Times*, 13 January 1957, sec. 5, 9.

11. Erwin G. Krasnow and Herman M. Levy, "Unionization and Professional Sports," *Georgetown Law Journal* 51, no. 4 (Summer 1963): 764.

12. Ray Kennedy and Nancy Williamson, "Money: The Monster Threatening Sports," *Sports Illustrated*, 17 July 1978, 52.

13. Lawrence M. Kahn and Peter D. Sherer, "Racial Discrimination in the National Basketball Association," in *Business of Professional Sports*, 71–94.

14. 147 F. Supp. 154 (1956).

15. 389 F. Supp. 867 (1975).

16. *Central New York Basketball, Inc. v. Barnett*, 181 N.E.2d 506 (1961).

17. *Minnesota Muskies v. Hudson*, 294 F. Supp. 979 (1969).

18. *Washington Capitols Basketball Club, Inc. v. Barry*, 419 F.2d 472 (9th Cir.), which affirmed 304 F. Supp. 1183 (N.D. Cal. 1969).

19. *Lemat Corporation v. Barry*, 80 Cal. Rptr. 240 (1969).

20. The case that eventually resulted from the chain of events that occurred is *Denver Rockets v. All-Pro Management, Inc.*, 325 F. Supp. 1049 (C.D. Cal. 1971).

21. Ibid., 1055.

22. This study, by the *Houston Chronicle*, is cited in Jeff Lenihan, "Evaluating Early Eligibility," *Sporting News*, 6 July 1987, 41.

23. Jack McCallum, "Draft Daze," *Sports Illustrated*, 16 May 1994, 15.

24. *Levin v. National Basketball Association*, 385 F. Supp. 149 (1974).

25. *Robertson v. National Basketball Association*, 389 F. Supp. 867 (1975). The *Robertson* case is discussed in Leslie Michele Lava, "The Battle of the Superstars: Player Restraints in

Professional Team Sports," *University of Florida Law Review* 32, no. 3 (Spring 1980): 683–86; and Michael S. Hobel, "Application of the Labor Exemption after the Expiration of Collective Bargaining Agreements in Professional Sports," *New York Law Review* 57, no. 1 (April 1982): 164–202.

26. *Robertson* v. *National Basketball Association,* 72 F.R.D. 64, S.D.N.Y. (1976), *aff'd,* 556 F.2d 682 (2d Cir. 1977).

27. John C. Weistart, "Judicial Review of Labor Agreements: Lessons from the Sports Industry," *Law and Contemporary Problems* 44, no. 4 (Autumn 1981): 135.

28. *Matter of Robertson Class Plaintiffs,* 479 F. Supp. 657 (S.D.N.Y. 1979).

29. *Robertson Class Plaintiffs* v. *National Basketball Association,* 625 F.2d 407, 416 (2d Cir. 1980).

30. *Molinas* v. *Podoloff,* 133 N.Y.S.2d 743 (1954).

31. *Saunders* v. *National Basketball Association,* 348 F. Supp. 649 (N.D. Illinois 1972).

32. Curry Kirkpatrick, "Shattered and Shaken," *Sports Illustrated,* 2 January 1978, 46; and John F. Carroll, "Torts in Sports—'I'll See You in Court!' " *Akron Law Review* 16, no. 3 (Winter 1983): 537–53.

33. Barbara Hink, "Compensating Injured Professional Athletes: The Mystique of Sports versus Traditional Sports Principles," *New York University Law Review* 55, no. 5 (November 1980): 973.

5. Hockey

1. Gene Brown, ed., *The New York Times Encyclopedia of Sports,* vol. 8, *Soccer/Professional Hockey* (New York: Arno, 1979), 213. See also Joseph Romain and Dan Diamond, *A Pictorial History of Hockey* (New York: Gallery Books, W. H. Smith, 1987).

2. Regarding the plight of the Canadian teams generally, see Michael Farber, "Giant Sucking Sound," *Sports Illustrated,* 20 March 1995, 105–10.

3. J. C. H. Jones and William D. Walsh, "Salary Determination in the National Hockey League: The Effects of Skills, Franchise Characteristics, and Discrimination," *Industrial and Labor Relations Review* 41, no. 4 (July 1988): 592–604.

4. While player contributions are not required, voluntary payments may be made into the pension fund to increase a player's share.

5. Although Junior A players are considered amateurs for most purposes, the National Collegiate Athletic Association in the United States regards Tier One Junior A players as professionals because they receive money and room and board for their services.

6. *Sports Illustrated,* 23 January 1995, Scorecard section.

7. Helene Elliott, "Players Say No Strike if There's No Lockout," *Los Angeles Times,* 30 December 1994, C7.

8. *McCourt* v. *California Sports, Inc.,* 600 F.2d 1193 (1979). See also Mark S. Miller, "The National Hockey League's Faceoff with Antitrust: McCourt v. California Sports, Inc.," *Ohio State Law Journal,* 42, no. 2 (1981): 603–26.

9. *Linseman* v. *World Hockey Association,* 439 F. Supp. 1315 (1977).

10. *Boston Professional Hockey Ass'n, Inc.* v. *Cheevers,* 348 F. Supp. 261, *remanded,* 472 F.2d 127 (1972).

11. See, for example, *Nassau Sports v. Hampson,* 355 F. Supp. 733 (1972); and *Philadelphia World Hockey Club* v. *Philadelphia Hockey Club,* 351 F. Supp. 462 (1972). In one of these cases, however, a player whose contract had expired was not allowed to change leagues until a one-year option renewal elapsed, *Nassau Sports v. Peters,* 352 F. Supp. 870 (1972).

12. See Edmund W. Vaz, *The Professionalization of Young Hockey Players* (Lincoln: University of Nebraska Press, 1982).

13. The polls, one by *Sporting News* and the other by Angus Reid Associates, are reported in *Sporting News,* 15 September 1986, 60.

14. "Durbano in Prison, Says NHL Has A Drug Problem," *Los Angeles Times,* 19 March 1984, pt. III, 8.

15. These reports are summarized in Armen Keteyian and Donald Ramsay, "The Joyless End of a Joyride," *Sports Illustrated,* 12 May 1986, 32–43.

6. Past as Prologue

1. This law is further discussed in Phillip J. Closius, "Not at the Behest of Nonlabor Groups: A Revised Prognosis for a Maturing Sports Industry," *Boston College Law Review* 24, no. 2 (March 1983): 397–98.

2. For a more detailed discussion of the ideas in this section, see Dale Yoder and Paul D. Staudohar, "Rethinking the Role of Collective Bargaining," *Labor Law Journal* 34, no. 5 (May 1983): 311–16; and Roger Fisher and William Ury, *Getting to Yes: Negotiating Agreement without Giving In* (Boston: Houghton Mifflin, 1981, 1991).

3. Jill Lieber, "Fat and Unhealthy," *Sports Illustrated,* 27 April 1992, 35.

4. Robert V. Ballamy, Jr., "Issues in the Internationalization of the U.S. Sports Media: The Emerging European Marketplace," *Journal of Sport and Social Issues* 17, no. 3 (December 1993): 171.

5. Portions of this section are from Paul D. Staudohar, "Team Relocation in Professional Sports," *Labor Law Journal* 36, no. 9 (September 1985): 728–33.

6. Ronald A. DiNicola and Scott Mendeloff, "Controlling Violence in Professional Sports: Rule Reform and the Federal Professional Sports Violence Commission," *Duquesne Law Review* 21, no. 4 (Summer 1983): 843–916.

7. Portions of this section are from Paul D. Staudohar and Bruce W. Kieler, "The Impact of AIDS on Sports," *Journal of Individual Employment Rights,* 3, no. 4 (1994–95): 1–9, copyright © 1995 by Baywood Publishing Co., Inc. and published by the Baywood Publishing Co., Inc.

8. Michael Knisley and Steve Meyerhoff, "AIDS and Sports," *Sporting News,* 9 November 1992, 15.

9. For further discussion of media impacts on sports personalities, see Benjamin G. Rader, *In Its Own Image: How Television Has Transformed Professional Sports* (New York: Free Press, 1984), 175–95.

10. An interesting description of the sources of fan alienation can be found in John Underwood, *Spoiled Sport: A Fan's Notes on the Troubles of Spectator Sports* (Boston: Little, Brown, 1984), 59–78.

NAME INDEX

SUBJECT INDEX